FREE Study Skills Videos/DVD Offer

Dear Customer,

Thank you for your purchase from Mometrix! We consider it an honor and a privilege that you have purchased our product and we want to ensure your satisfaction.

As part of our ongoing effort to meet the needs of test takers, we have developed a set of Study Skills Videos that we would like to give you for <u>FREE</u>. These videos cover our *best practices* for getting ready for your exam, from how to use our study materials to how to best prepare for the day of the test.

All that we ask is that you email us with feedback that would describe your experience so far with our product. Good, bad, or indifferent, we want to know what you think!

To get your FREE Study Skills Videos, you can use the **QR code** below, or send us an **email** at <u>studyvideos@mometrix.com</u> with *FREE VIDEOS* in the subject line and the following information in the body of the email:

- The name of the product you purchased.
- Your product rating on a scale of 1-5, with 5 being the highest rating.
- Your feedback. It can be long, short, or anything in between. We just want to know your impressions and experience so far with our product. (Good feedback might include how our study material met your needs and ways we might be able to make it even better. You could highlight features that you found helpful or features that you think we should add.)

If you have any questions or concerns, please don't hesitate to contact me directly.

Thanks again!

Sincerely,

Jay Willis
Vice President
<u>jay.willis@mometrix.com</u>
1-800-673-8175

LSAT®

Prep 2025-2026

3 Full-Length Practice Tests

LSAT® Secrets Study Guide and Exam Review Book with Detailed Answer Explanations

9th Edition

Written and edited by Matthew Bowling

Printed in the United States of America

This paper meets the requirements of ANSI/NISO Z39.48-1992 (Permanence of Paper).

Mometrix offers volume discount pricing to institutions. For more information or a price quote, please contact our sales department at sales@mometrix.com or 888-248-1219.

Paperback
ISBN 13: 978-1-5167-2750-6
ISBN 10: 1-5167-2750-9

DEAR FUTURE EXAM SUCCESS STORY

First of all, **THANK YOU** for purchasing Mometrix study materials!

Second, congratulations! You are one of the few determined test-takers who are committed to doing whatever it takes to excel on your exam. **You have come to the right place.** We developed these study materials with one goal in mind: to deliver you the information you need in a format that's concise and easy to use.

In addition to optimizing your guide for the content of the test, we've outlined our recommended steps for breaking down the preparation process into small, attainable goals so you can make sure you stay on track.

We've also analyzed the entire test-taking process, identifying the most common pitfalls and showing how you can overcome them and be ready for any curveball the test throws you.

Standardized testing is one of the biggest obstacles on your road to success, which only increases the importance of doing well in the high-pressure, high-stakes environment of test day. Your results on this test could have a significant impact on your future, and this guide provides the information and practical advice to help you achieve your full potential on test day.

Your success is our success

We would love to hear from you! If you would like to share the story of your exam success or if you have any questions or comments in regard to our products, please contact us at **800-673-8175** or **support@mometrix.com**.

Thanks again for your business and we wish you continued success!

Sincerely,
The Mometrix Test Preparation Team

Need more help? Check out our flashcards at:
https://MometrixFlashcards.com/LSAT

TABLE OF CONTENTS

Introduction

Thank you for purchasing this resource! You have made the choice to prepare yourself for a test that could have a huge impact on your future, and this guide is designed to help you be fully ready for test day. Obviously, it's important to have a solid understanding of the test material, but you also need to be prepared for the unique environment and stressors of the test, so that you can perform to the best of your abilities.

For this purpose, the first section that appears in this guide is the **Secret Keys**. We've devoted countless hours to meticulously researching what works and what doesn't, and we've boiled down our findings to the five most impactful steps you can take to improve your performance on the test. We start at the beginning with study planning and move through the preparation process, all the way to the testing strategies that will help you get the most out of what you know when you're finally sitting in front of the test.

We recommend that you start preparing for your test as far in advance as possible. However, if you've bought this guide as a last-minute study resource and only have a few days before your test, we recommend that you skip over the first two Secret Keys since they address a long-term study plan.

If you struggle with **test anxiety**, we strongly encourage you to check out our recommendations for how you can overcome it. Test anxiety is a formidable foe, but it can be beaten, and we want to make sure you have the tools you need to defeat it.

Secret Key #1 – Plan Big, Study Small

There's a lot riding on your performance. If you want to ace this test, you're going to need to keep your skills sharp and the material fresh in your mind. You need a plan that lets you review everything you need to know while still fitting in your schedule. We'll break this strategy down into three categories.

Information Organization

Start with the information you already have: the official test outline. From this, you can make a complete list of all the concepts you need to cover before the test. Organize these concepts into groups that can be studied together, and create a list of any related vocabulary you need to learn so you can brush up on any difficult terms. You'll want to keep this vocabulary list handy once you actually start studying since you may need to add to it along the way.

Time Management

Once you have your set of study concepts, decide how to spread them out over the time you have left before the test. Break your study plan into small, clear goals so you have a manageable task for each day and know exactly what you're doing. Then just focus on one small step at a time. When you manage your time this way, you don't need to spend hours at a time studying. Studying a small block of content for a short period each day helps you retain information better and avoid stressing over how much you have left to do. You can relax knowing that you have a plan to cover everything in time. In order for this strategy to be effective though, you have to start studying early and stick to your schedule. Avoid the exhaustion and futility that comes from last-minute cramming!

Study Environment

The environment you study in has a big impact on your learning. Studying in a coffee shop, while probably more enjoyable, is not likely to be as fruitful as studying in a quiet room. It's important to keep distractions to a minimum. You're only planning to study for a short block of time, so make the most of it. Don't pause to check your phone or get up to find a snack. It's also important to **avoid multitasking**. Research has consistently shown that multitasking will make your studying dramatically less effective. Your study area should also be comfortable and well-lit so you don't have the distraction of straining your eyes or sitting on an uncomfortable chair.

 The time of day you study is also important. You want to be rested and alert. Don't wait until just before bedtime. Study when you'll be most likely to comprehend and remember. Even better, if you know what time of day your test will be, set that time aside for study. That way your brain will be used to working on that subject at that specific time and you'll have a better chance of recalling information.

Finally, it can be helpful to team up with others who are studying for the same test. Your actual studying should be done in as isolated an environment as possible, but the work of organizing the information and setting up the study plan can be divided up. In between study sessions, you can discuss with your teammates the concepts that you're all studying and quiz each other on the details. Just be sure that your teammates are as serious about the test as you are. If you find that your study time is being replaced with social time, you might need to find a new team.

Secret Key #2 – Make Your Studying Count

You're devoting a lot of time and effort to preparing for this test, so you want to be absolutely certain it will pay off. This means doing more than just reading the content and hoping you can remember it on test day. It's important to make every minute of study count. There are two main areas you can focus on to make your studying count.

Retention

It doesn't matter how much time you study if you can't remember the material. You need to make sure you are retaining the concepts. To check your retention of the information you're learning, try recalling it at later times with minimal prompting. Try carrying around flashcards and glance at one or two from time to time or ask a friend who's also studying for the test to quiz you.

To enhance your retention, look for ways to put the information into practice so that you can apply it rather than simply recalling it. If you're using the information in practical ways, it will be much easier to remember. Similarly, it helps to solidify a concept in your mind if you're not only reading it to yourself but also explaining it to someone else. Ask a friend to let you teach them about a concept you're a little shaky on (or speak aloud to an imaginary audience if necessary). As you try to summarize, define, give examples, and answer your friend's questions, you'll understand the concepts better and they will stay with you longer. Finally, step back for a big picture view and ask yourself how each piece of information fits with the whole subject. When you link the different concepts together and see them working together as a whole, it's easier to remember the individual components.

Finally, practice showing your work on any multi-step problems, even if you're just studying. Writing out each step you take to solve a problem will help solidify the process in your mind, and you'll be more likely to remember it during the test.

Modality

Modality simply refers to the means or method by which you study. Choosing a study modality that fits your own individual learning style is crucial. No two people learn best in exactly the same way, so it's important to know your strengths and use them to your advantage.

For example, if you learn best by visualization, focus on visualizing a concept in your mind and draw an image or a diagram. Try color-coding your notes, illustrating them, or creating symbols that will trigger your mind to recall a learned concept. If you learn best by hearing or discussing information, find a study partner who learns the same way or read aloud to yourself. Think about how to put the information in your own words. Imagine that you are giving a lecture on the topic and record yourself so you can listen to it later.

For any learning style, flashcards can be helpful. Organize the information so you can take advantage of spare moments to review. Underline key words or phrases. Use different colors for different categories. Mnemonic devices (such as creating a short list in which every item starts with the same letter) can also help with retention. Find what works best for you and use it to store the information in your mind most effectively and easily.

Secret Key #3 – Practice the Right Way

Your success on test day depends not only on how many hours you put into preparing, but also on whether you prepared the right way. It's good to check along the way to see if your studying is paying off. One of the most effective ways to do this is by taking practice tests to evaluate your progress. Practice tests are useful because they show exactly where you need to improve. Every time you take a practice test, pay special attention to these three groups of questions:

- The questions you got wrong
- The questions you had to guess on, even if you guessed right
- The questions you found difficult or slow to work through

This will show you exactly what your weak areas are, and where you need to devote more study time. Ask yourself why each of these questions gave you trouble. Was it because you didn't understand the material? Was it because you didn't remember the vocabulary? Do you need more repetitions on this type of question to build speed and confidence? Dig into those questions and figure out how you can strengthen your weak areas as you go back to review the material.

 Additionally, many practice tests have a section explaining the answer choices. It can be tempting to read the explanation and think that you now have a good understanding of the concept. However, an explanation likely only covers part of the question's broader context. Even if the explanation makes perfect sense, **go back and investigate** every concept related to the question until you're positive you have a thorough understanding.

As you go along, keep in mind that the practice test is just that: practice. Memorizing these questions and answers will not be very helpful on the actual test because it is unlikely to have any of the same exact questions. If you only know the right answers to the sample questions, you won't be prepared for the real thing. **Study the concepts** until you understand them fully, and then you'll be able to answer any question that shows up on the test.

It's important to wait on the practice tests until you're ready. If you take a test on your first day of study, you may be overwhelmed by the amount of material covered and how much you need to learn. Work up to it gradually.

On test day, you'll need to be prepared for answering questions, managing your time, and using the test-taking strategies you've learned. It's a lot to balance, like a mental marathon that will have a big impact on your future. Like training for a marathon, you'll need to start slowly and work your way up. When test day arrives, you'll be ready.

Start with the strategies you've read in the first two Secret Keys—plan your course and study in the way that works best for you. If you have time, consider using multiple study resources to get different approaches to the same concepts. It can be helpful to see difficult concepts from more than one angle. Then find a good source for practice tests. Many times, the test website will suggest potential study resources or provide sample tests.

4

Practice Test Strategy

If you're able to find at least three practice tests, we recommend this strategy:

UNTIMED AND OPEN-BOOK PRACTICE

Take the first test with no time constraints and with your notes and study guide handy. Take your time and focus on applying the strategies you've learned.

TIMED AND OPEN-BOOK PRACTICE

Take the second practice test open-book as well, but set a timer and practice pacing yourself to finish in time.

TIMED AND CLOSED-BOOK PRACTICE

Take any other practice tests as if it were test day. Set a timer and put away your study materials. Sit at a table or desk in a quiet room, imagine yourself at the testing center, and answer questions as quickly and accurately as possible.

Keep repeating timed and closed-book tests on a regular basis until you run out of practice tests or it's time for the actual test. Your mind will be ready for the schedule and stress of test day, and you'll be able to focus on recalling the material you've learned.

Secret Key #4 – Pace Yourself

Once you're fully prepared for the material on the test, your biggest challenge on test day will be managing your time. Just knowing that the clock is ticking can make you panic even if you have plenty of time left. Work on pacing yourself so you can build confidence against the time constraints of the exam. Pacing is a difficult skill to master, especially in a high-pressure environment, so **practice is vital**.

Set time expectations for your pace based on how much time is available. For example, if a section has 60 questions and the time limit is 30 minutes, you know you have to average 30 seconds or less per question in order to answer them all. Although 30 seconds is the hard limit, set 25 seconds per question as your goal, so you reserve extra time to spend on harder questions. When you budget extra time for the harder questions, you no longer have any reason to stress when those questions take longer to answer.

Don't let this time expectation distract you from working through the test at a calm, steady pace, but keep it in mind so you don't spend too much time on any one question. Recognize that taking extra time on one question you don't understand may keep you from answering two that you do understand later in the test. If your time limit for a question is up and you're still not sure of the answer, mark it and move on, and come back to it later if the time and the test format allow. If the testing format doesn't allow you to return to earlier questions, just make an educated guess; then put it out of your mind and move on.

On the easier questions, be careful not to rush. It may seem wise to hurry through them so you have more time for the challenging ones, but it's not worth missing one if you know the concept and just didn't take the time to read the question fully. Work efficiently but make sure you understand the question and have looked at all of the answer choices, since more than one may seem right at first.

Even if you're paying attention to the time, you may find yourself a little behind at some point. You should speed up to get back on track, but do so wisely. Don't panic; just take a few seconds less on each question until you're caught up. Don't guess without thinking, but do look through the answer choices and eliminate any you know are wrong. If you can get down to two choices, it is often worthwhile to guess from those. Once you've chosen an answer, move on and don't dwell on any that you skipped or had to hurry through. If a question was taking too long, chances are it was one of the harder ones, so you weren't as likely to get it right anyway.

On the other hand, if you find yourself getting ahead of schedule, it may be beneficial to slow down a little. The more quickly you work, the more likely you are to make a careless mistake that will affect your score. You've budgeted time for each question, so don't be afraid to spend that time. Practice an efficient but careful pace to get the most out of the time you have.

Secret Key #5 – Have a Plan for Guessing

When you're taking the test, you may find yourself stuck on a question. Some of the answer choices seem better than others, but you don't see the one answer choice that is obviously correct. What do you do?

The scenario described above is very common, yet most test takers have not effectively prepared for it. Developing and practicing a plan for guessing may be one of the single most effective uses of your time as you get ready for the exam.

In developing your plan for guessing, there are three questions to address:

- When should you start the guessing process?
- How should you narrow down the choices?
- Which answer should you choose?

When to Start the Guessing Process

Unless your plan for guessing is to select C every time (which, despite its merits, is not what we recommend), you need to leave yourself enough time to apply your answer elimination strategies. Since you have a limited amount of time for each question, that means that if you're going to give yourself the best shot at guessing correctly, you have to decide quickly whether or not you will guess.

Of course, the best-case scenario is that you don't have to guess at all, so first, see if you can answer the question based on your knowledge of the subject and basic reasoning skills. Focus on the key words in the question and try to jog your memory of related topics. Give yourself a chance to bring the knowledge to mind, but once you realize that you don't have (or you can't access) the knowledge you need to answer the question, it's time to start the guessing process.

It's almost always better to start the guessing process too early than too late. It only takes a few seconds to remember something and answer the question from knowledge. Carefully eliminating wrong answer choices takes longer. Plus, going through the process of eliminating answer choices can actually help jog your memory.

Summary: Start the guessing process as soon as you decide that you can't answer the question based on your knowledge.

7

How to Narrow Down the Choices

The next chapter in this book (**Test-Taking Strategies**) includes a wide range of strategies for how to approach questions and how to look for answer choices to eliminate. You will definitely want to read those carefully, practice them, and figure out which ones work best for you. Here though, we're going to address a mindset rather than a particular strategy.

Your odds of guessing an answer correctly depend on how many options you are choosing from.

Number of options left	5	4	3	2	1
Odds of guessing correctly	20%	25%	33%	50%	100%

You can see from this chart just how valuable it is to be able to eliminate incorrect answers and make an educated guess, but there are two things that many test takers do that cause them to miss out on the benefits of guessing:

- Accidentally eliminating the correct answer
- Selecting an answer based on an impression

We'll look at the first one here, and the second one in the next section.

To avoid accidentally eliminating the correct answer, we recommend a thought exercise called **the $5 challenge**. In this challenge, you only eliminate an answer choice from contention if you are willing to bet $5 on it being wrong. Why $5? Five dollars is a small but not insignificant amount of money. It's an amount you could afford to lose but wouldn't want to throw away. And while losing

$5 once might not hurt too much, doing it twenty times will set you back $100. In the same way, each small decision you make—eliminating a choice here, guessing on a question there—won't by itself impact your score very much, but when you put them all together, they can make a big difference. By holding each answer choice elimination decision to a higher standard, you can reduce the risk of accidentally eliminating the correct answer.

The $5 challenge can also be applied in a positive sense: If you are willing to bet $5 that an answer choice *is* correct, go ahead and mark it as correct.

Summary: Only eliminate an answer choice if you are willing to bet $5 that it is wrong.

Which Answer to Choose

You're taking the test. You've run into a hard question and decided you'll have to guess. You've eliminated all the answer choices you're willing to bet $5 on. Now you have to pick an answer. Why do we even need to talk about this? Why can't you just pick whichever one you feel like when the time comes?

The answer to these questions is that if you don't come into the test with a plan, you'll rely on your impression to select an answer choice, and if you do that, you risk falling into a trap. The test writers know that everyone who takes their test will be guessing on some of the questions, so they intentionally write wrong answer choices to seem plausible. You still have to pick an answer though, and if the wrong answer choices are designed to look right, how can you ever be sure that you're not falling for their trap? The best solution we've found to this dilemma is to take the decision out of your hands entirely. Here is the process we recommend:

Once you've eliminated any choices that you are confident (willing to bet $5) are wrong, select the first remaining choice as your answer.

Whether you choose to select the first remaining choice, the second, or the last, the important thing is that you use some preselected standard. Using this approach guarantees that you will not be enticed into selecting an answer choice that looks right, because you are not basing your decision on how the answer choices look.

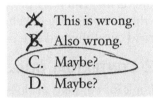

This is not meant to make you question your knowledge. Instead, it is to help you recognize the difference between your knowledge and your impressions. There's a huge difference between thinking an answer is right because of what you know, and thinking an answer is right because it looks or sounds like it should be right.

Summary: To ensure that your selection is appropriately random, make a predetermined selection from among all answer choices you have not eliminated.

Test-Taking Strategies

This section contains a list of test-taking strategies that you may find helpful as you work through the test. By taking what you know and applying logical thought, you can maximize your chances of answering any question correctly!

It is very important to realize that every question is different and every person is different: no single strategy will work on every question, and no single strategy will work for every person. That's why we've included all of them here, so you can try them out and determine which ones work best for different types of questions and which ones work best for you.

Question Strategies

☑ READ CAREFULLY

Read the question and the answer choices carefully. Don't miss the question because you misread the terms. You have plenty of time to read each question thoroughly and make sure you understand what is being asked. Yet a happy medium must be attained, so don't waste too much time. You must read carefully and efficiently.

☑ CONTEXTUAL CLUES

Look for contextual clues. If the question includes a word you are not familiar with, look at the immediate context for some indication of what the word might mean. Contextual clues can often give you all the information you need to decipher the meaning of an unfamiliar word. Even if you can't determine the meaning, you may be able to narrow down the possibilities enough to make a solid guess at the answer to the question.

☑ PREFIXES

If you're having trouble with a word in the question or answer choices, try dissecting it. Take advantage of every clue that the word might include. Prefixes can be a huge help. Usually, they allow you to determine a basic meaning. *Pre-* means before, *post-* means after, *pro-* is positive, *de-* is negative. From prefixes, you can get an idea of the general meaning of the word and try to put it into context.

☑ HEDGE WORDS

Watch out for critical hedge words, such as *likely, may, can, sometimes, often, almost, mostly, usually, generally, rarely,* and *sometimes*. Question writers insert these hedge phrases to cover every possibility. Often an answer choice will be wrong simply because it leaves no room for exception. Be on guard for answer choices that have definitive words such as *exactly* and *always*.

☑ SWITCHBACK WORDS

Stay alert for *switchbacks*. These are the words and phrases frequently used to alert you to shifts in thought. The most common switchback words are *but, although,* and *however*. Others include *nevertheless, on the other hand, even though, while, in spite of, despite,* and *regardless of*. Switchback words are important to catch because they can change the direction of the question or an answer choice.

10

⊘ Face Value

When in doubt, use common sense. Accept the situation in the problem at face value. Don't read too much into it. These problems will not require you to make wild assumptions. If you have to go beyond creativity and warp time or space in order to have an answer choice fit the question, then you should move on and consider the other answer choices. These are normal problems rooted in reality. The applicable relationship or explanation may not be readily apparent, but it is there for you to figure out. Use your common sense to interpret anything that isn't clear.

Answer Choice Strategies

⊘ Answer Selection

The most thorough way to pick an answer choice is to identify and eliminate wrong answers until only one is left, then confirm it is the correct answer. Sometimes an answer choice may immediately seem right, but be careful. The test writers will usually put more than one reasonable answer choice on each question, so take a second to read all of them and make sure that the other choices are not equally obvious. As long as you have time left, it is better to read every answer choice than to pick the first one that looks right without checking the others.

⊘ Answer Choice Families

An answer choice family consists of two (in rare cases, three) answer choices that are very similar in construction and cannot all be true at the same time. If you see two answer choices that are direct opposites or parallels, one of them is usually the correct answer. For instance, if one answer choice says that quantity x increases and another either says that quantity x decreases (opposite) or says that quantity y increases (parallel), then those answer choices would fall into the same family. An answer choice that doesn't match the construction of the answer choice family is more likely to be incorrect. Most questions will not have answer choice families, but when they do appear, you should be prepared to recognize them.

⊘ Eliminate Answers

Eliminate answer choices as soon as you realize they are wrong, but make sure you consider all possibilities. If you are eliminating answer choices and realize that the last one you are left with is also wrong, don't panic. Start over and consider each choice again. There may be something you missed the first time that you will realize on the second pass.

⊘ Avoid Fact Traps

Don't be distracted by an answer choice that is factually true but doesn't answer the question. You are looking for the choice that answers the question. Stay focused on what the question is asking for so you don't accidentally pick an answer that is true but incorrect. Always go back to the question and make sure the answer choice you've selected actually answers the question and is not merely a true statement.

⊘ Extreme Statements

In general, you should avoid answers that put forth extreme actions as standard practice or proclaim controversial ideas as established fact. An answer choice that states the "process should be used in certain situations, if..." is much more likely to be correct than one that states the "process should be discontinued completely." The first is a calm rational statement and doesn't even make a definitive, uncompromising stance, using a hedge word *if* to provide wiggle room, whereas the second choice is far more extreme.

⊘ Benchmark

As you read through the answer choices and you come across one that seems to answer the question well, mentally select that answer choice. This is not your final answer, but it's the one that will help you evaluate the other answer choices. The one that you selected is your benchmark or standard for judging each of the other answer choices. Every other answer choice must be compared to your benchmark. That choice is correct until proven otherwise by another answer choice beating it. If you find a better answer, then that one becomes your new benchmark. Once you've decided that no other choice answers the question as well as your benchmark, you have your final answer.

⊘ Predict the Answer

Before you even start looking at the answer choices, it is often best to try to predict the answer. When you come up with the answer on your own, it is easier to avoid distractions and traps because you will know exactly what to look for. The right answer choice is unlikely to be word-for-word what you came up with, but it should be a close match. Even if you are confident that you have the right answer, you should still take the time to read each option before moving on.

General Strategies

⊘ Tough Questions

If you are stumped on a problem or it appears too hard or too difficult, don't waste time. Move on! Remember though, if you can quickly check for obviously incorrect answer choices, your chances of guessing correctly are greatly improved. Before you completely give up, at least try to knock out a couple of possible answers. Eliminate what you can and then guess at the remaining answer choices before moving on.

⊘ Check Your Work

Since you will probably not know every term listed and the answer to every question, it is important that you get credit for the ones that you do know. Don't miss any questions through careless mistakes. If at all possible, try to take a second to look back over your answer selection and make sure you've selected the correct answer choice and haven't made a costly careless mistake (such as marking an answer choice that you didn't mean to mark). This quick double check should more than pay for itself in caught mistakes for the time it costs.

⊘ Pace Yourself

It's easy to be overwhelmed when you're looking at a page full of questions; your mind is confused and full of random thoughts, and the clock is ticking down faster than you would like. Calm down and maintain the pace that you have set for yourself. Especially as you get down to the last few minutes of the test, don't let the small numbers on the clock make you panic. As long as you are on track by monitoring your pace, you are guaranteed to have time for each question.

⊘ Don't Rush

It is very easy to make errors when you are in a hurry. Maintaining a fast pace in answering questions is pointless if it makes you miss questions that you would have gotten right otherwise. Test writers like to include distracting information and wrong answers that seem right. Taking a little extra time to avoid careless mistakes can make all the difference in your test score. Find a pace that allows you to be confident in the answers that you select.

⊘ Keep Moving

Panicking will not help you pass the test, so do your best to stay calm and keep moving. Taking deep breaths and going through the answer elimination steps you practiced can help to break through a stress barrier and keep your pace.

Final Notes

The combination of a solid foundation of content knowledge and the confidence that comes from practicing your plan for applying that knowledge is the key to maximizing your performance on test day. As your foundation of content knowledge is built up and strengthened, you'll find that the strategies included in this chapter become more and more effective in helping you quickly sift through the distractions and traps of the test to isolate the correct answer.

Now that you're preparing to move forward into the test content chapters of this book, be sure to keep your goal in mind. As you read, think about how you will be able to apply this information on the test. If you've already seen sample questions for the test and you have an idea of the question format and style, try to come up with questions of your own that you can answer based on what you're reading. This will give you valuable practice applying your knowledge in the same ways you can expect to on test day.

Good luck and good studying!

Three-Week LSAT Study Plan

On the next few pages, we've provided an optional study plan to help you use this study guide to its fullest potential over the course of three weeks. If you have six weeks or more available and want to spread out your studying more, spend two weeks on each section of the plan.

Below is a quick summary of the subjects covered in each week of the plan.

- Week 1: Reading Comprehension Test
- Week 2: Logical Reasoning Test
- Week 3: Argumentative Writing

Please note that not all subjects will take the same amount of time to work through.

Four full-length practice tests are included with this study guide (one printed in the guide and three more online). We recommend using the first two as described in this study plan and saving the rest (and any additional practice tests you might have) for after you've completed the study plan. Take these practice tests without any reference materials in the days leading up to the real thing as practice runs to get you in the mode of answering questions at a good pace.

Week 1: Reading Comprehension Test

INSTRUCTIONAL CONTENT

First, read carefully through the Reading Comprehension Test chapter in this book, checking off your progress as you go:

- ❏ The Passages: What's the Deal?
- ❏ The Big Picture: How to Approach the Reading Comprehension Questions
- ❏ One Very Important Tip
- ❏ What Are Your Options?
- ❏ There's a Lot More to Reading Than Just Reading

- ❏ Active Reading: The Mental Aspect
- ❏ Active Reading: The Physical Aspect
- ❏ The Question Types
- ❏ Breaking Down the Questions

As you read, do the following:

- Highlight any sections, terms, or concepts you think are important
- Draw an asterisk (*) next to any areas you are struggling with
- Watch the review videos to gain more understanding of a particular topic
- Take notes in your notebook or in the margins of this book

After you've read through everything, go back and review any sections that you highlighted or that you drew an asterisk next to, referencing your notes along the way.

PRACTICE TEST #1

Now that you've read over the instructional content, it's time to take a practice test. Complete the Reading Comprehension section (Sections II & III) of Practice Test #1. Take this test with **no time constraints**, and feel free to reference the applicable sections of this guide as you go. Once you've finished, check your answers against the provided answer key. For any questions you answered incorrectly, review the answer rationale, and then **go back and review** the applicable sections of the book. The goal in this stage is to understand why you answered the question incorrectly, and make sure that the next time you see a similar question, you will get it right.

PRACTICE TEST #2

Next, take the Reading Comprehension section (Sections II & IV) of Practice Test #2. This time, give yourself **70 minutes** to complete all of the questions. You should again feel free to reference the guide and your notes, but be mindful of the clock. If you run out of time before you finish all of the questions, mark where you were when time expired, but go ahead and finish taking the practice test. Once you've finished, check your answers against the provided answer key, and as before, review the answer rationale for any that you answered incorrectly and then go back and review the associated instructional content. Your goal is still to increase understanding of the content but also to get used to the time constraints you will face on the test.

Week 2: Logical Reasoning Test

INSTRUCTIONAL CONTENT

First, read carefully through the Logical Reasoning chapter in this book, checking off your progress as you go:

- ❏ What's in the Logical Reasoning Section?
- ❏ Logical Reasoning Strategies and Tips
- ❏ Watch Out for Red Herrings
- ❏ Logical Reasoning Basic Concepts
- ❏ Author's Main Point or Purpose

- ❏ Inferences
- ❏ Underlying Assumptions
- ❏ New Information Questions
- ❏ Paradox Questions
- ❏ Flawed Reasoning Questions
- ❏ Parallel Reasoning Questions

As you read, do the following:

- Highlight any sections, terms, or concepts you think are important
- Draw an asterisk (*) next to any areas you are struggling with
- Watch the review videos to gain more understanding of a particular topic
- Take notes in your notebook or in the margins of this book

After you've read through everything, go back and review any sections that you highlighted or that you drew an asterisk next to, referencing your notes along the way.

PRACTICE TEST #1

Now that you've read over the instructional content, it's time to take a practice test. Complete the Logical Reasoning sections (Sections I & IV) of Practice Test #1. Take this test with **no time constraints**, and feel free to reference the applicable sections of this guide as you go. Once you've finished, check your answers against the provided answer key. For any questions you answered incorrectly, review the answer rationale, and then **go back and review** the applicable sections of the book. The goal in this stage is to understand why you answered the question incorrectly, and make sure that the next time you see a similar question, you will get it right.

PRACTICE TEST #2

Next, take the Logical Reasoning sections (Sections I & III) of Practice Test #2. This time, give yourself **70 minutes** to complete all of the questions. You should again feel free to reference the guide and your notes, but be mindful of the clock. If you run out of time before you finish all of the questions, mark where you were when time expired, but go ahead and finish taking the practice test. Once you've finished, check your answers against the provided answer key, and as before, review the answer rationale for any that you answered incorrectly and then go back and review the associated instructional content. Your goal is still to increase understanding of the content but also to get used to the time constraints you will face on the test.

Week 3: The Argumentative Writing Essay

INSTRUCTIONAL CONTENT

First, read carefully through the Argumentative Writing chapter in this book, checking off your progress as you go:

- ❏ How Important Is It?
- ❏ The Argumentative Writing Format
- ❏ Prewriting
- ❏ Writing
- ❏ Some Common Mistakes to Avoid

- ❏ The Opening
- ❏ The Body: Supporting Your Argument
- ❏ The Conclusion
- ❏ Reviewing and Editing

As you read, do the following:

- Highlight any sections, terms, or concepts you think are important
- Draw an asterisk (*) next to any areas you are struggling with
- Watch the review videos to gain more understanding of a particular topic
- Take notes in your notebook or in the margins of this book

After you've read through everything, go back and review any sections that you highlighted or that you drew an asterisk next to, referencing your notes along the way.

PRACTICE TEST #1

Now that you've read over the instructional content, it's time to take a practice test. Complete the Argumentative Writing section of Practice Test #1. Take this test with **no time constraints**, and feel free to reference the applicable sections of this guide as you go. Once you've finished, check your sample against the provided suggestions. For any questions you may have, review the answer rationale, and then **go back and review** the applicable sections of the book. The goal in this stage is to understand how to craft a complete and coherent sample.

PRACTICE TEST #2

Next, do the Argumentative Writing section of Practice Test #2. This time, give yourself **15 minutes** for prewriting and **35 minutes** to complete your essay. You should again feel free to reference the guide and your notes, but be mindful of the clock. If you run out of time before you finish writing, mark where you were when time expired, but go ahead and finish your essay. Once you've finished, check your sample against the provided suggestions, and as before, review the answer rationale and then go back and review the associated instructional content. Your goal is still to increase understanding of the content but also to get used to the time constraints you will face on the test.

18

Reading Comprehension Test

The Reading Comprehension section of the LSAT is designed to test your abilities to understand and interpret written materials. Lawyers daily perform interpretation of written information, much of which can be difficult to understand. Reading comprehension skills are critical for success in law school, as students are required to read and understand massive amounts of material. Even though almost all law school applicants are aware that they'll have to do a lot of reading if they're admitted, many law school graduates still report being shocked at finding out just how much reading is required. The Reading Comprehension section of the LSAT is designed to weed out those applicants who don't have the skills to cope with the reading requirements of law school.

On this portion of the LSAT, you will have 35 minutes to answer approximately 27 questions about four reading assignments. Three of these assignments will consist of only one passage, while one will be a comparative reading test, consisting of two passages. The passages are usually between 400 and 500 words in length, and subject matter can be in any field, but most passages are about a topic in law, science, or the liberal arts. You will not need to know any specialized information to understand a passage, even if it includes technical terms you have never encountered before. You are expected to base your answers only on what is stated or implied in the passage or passages.

One aspect of the Reading Comprehension test that makes it so difficult is that you're expected to read and comprehend a large amount of difficult material in a very brief amount of time. Each passage is hundreds of words long, and is often quite ponderous. Passages are almost always densely written, filled with facts and details that may or may not be important for you to remember. The sheer amount of information in a passage can be quite intimidating and unnerving to test takers.

Then, once you've finally navigated your way through the passage, you're confronted with up to eight questions you must answer. Each question will have four possible answers to choose from, and many of them will be obtuse, having been deliberately crafted to be very hard to interpret. Sometimes it will seem as if several answer choices could conceivably be acceptable. For many questions, two answer choices will be so similar that choosing one or the other would seem to be little different than flipping a coin. You will have less than nine minutes to read each passage thoroughly, mark important information, read each question and all five answer choices, compare and contrast the possible answers with each other, and go back to the passage to find the answer. This is a formidable challenge, to put it mildly. There's no denying that the LSAT Reading Comprehension section is a race against the clock; in fact, it's designed to be that way. However, there's no reason you need to fear the Reading Comprehension test. Yes, it's hard, but we'll show you how you can excel on this portion of the LSAT. You'll learn:

- the main question types
- the best plan for tackling the reading material
- powerful reading techniques
- what to focus on in your reading
- what notes to take
- "red flag words" to watch for
- how these "red flag words" can point you to the correct answer
- other factors that can be important signals
- how to choose between answers that are extremely similar

THE PASSAGES: WHAT'S THE DEAL?

The passages you'll encounter on the LSAT Reading Comprehension test are unlikely to be similar to any of your regular reading material. In fact, it's very likely you have never run across any of these kinds of passages before. They are usually taken from academic journals, and then adapted for use on the LSAT. They have to be carefully edited and rewritten to suit the 400–500-word format used for Reading Comprehension passages. Any parts requiring technical knowledge on the part of the reader are removed.

That's just the beginning. After the removal of any information that is only understandable by a professional in the field, the material then must be rewritten to work around the sentences or paragraphs that were removed. Sometimes the results are less than ideal, which explains why LSAT Reading Comprehension passages sometimes seem jarring and disjointed. The reason the passages are so dense is that the editors at the Law School Admission Council have taken most of the details and facts from an article that was 1,500–2,000 words and forced them into a passage that is only about a third or a fourth the original length.

Topics can be all over the map, but most of the time the subject of the reading passage will not be something you are familiar with, but rather an obscure topic. This is done deliberately to keep the Reading Comprehension test fair. By choosing subject matter that virtually all test takers are unfamiliar with, the test creators make the exam a level playing field where no one has the advantage of knowing the subject better than others.

When you add up all these factors—scholarly writing, three or four pages' worth of material crammed into a one-page article, and subject matter that isn't even on the average person's radar—it becomes clear that the passages you'll be dealing with on this part of the LSAT are not exactly light reading. Knowing these things before you take the LSAT will help keep you from feeling overwhelmed when you begin this section. You can relax knowing that you're not supposed to be familiar with the material, that it's supposed to be extremely dense, and that everyone else is in the same boat you are.

There's more good news—the LSAT doesn't penalize incorrect answers. In other words, if you choose the wrong answer, it doesn't lower your score versus leaving it blank. If you're running out of time, and a question completely stumps you, just pick a letter and fill it in. You may get lucky and get it right; if not, there's no harm done, because a wrong answer is scored the same as a blank answer. It won't raise your score, of course, but it won't lower it either, as your score is based only on correct answers.

Another thing to keep in mind is the fact that the LSAT is not scored the same way as a typical test. It's a scaled score, and that's very good news if you're the kind of person who tends to worry every time you're not completely sure that an answer is correct. Because of the scaled scoring, a person can get over 40% of the answers wrong and still receive a score that's about average. Of course, an average LSAT score is not going to help your application stand out, but that's missing the point. The important thing is that you shouldn't worry too much about getting an occasional answer wrong. Because if you can miss nearly half the questions and still receive a score that's near the average, just think how high your score can be if you diligently prepare for the exam.

THE BIG PICTURE: HOW TO APPROACH THE READING COMPREHENSION QUESTIONS

There are several factors that will contribute to your success on the Reading Comprehension portion of the LSAT, and the first one is having a definite plan for tackling each question from the beginning. Knowing exactly what you're going to do prevents you from wasting time by trying to decide on a plan of attack at the last minute, or even worse, trying out different approaches to each

N

Reading Comprehension Test

question. These are critical mistakes that many test takers make, resulting in a lower score on the LSAT than they could have achieved had they been better prepared.

ONE VERY IMPORTANT TIP

There are several different approaches you could take to the material, but they aren't equally effective. In fact, there's one popular approach that is almost guaranteed to waste time and cause confusion if you follow it. We'll look at the various approaches and compare and contrast their strengths and weaknesses in a moment. Before we do, here's one easy rule to help you save time on the Reading Comprehension section:

Do not waste time reading the instructions.

That's right—you should not read the instructions at the beginning of the Reading Comprehension section. You should familiarize yourself with them right now. The instructions have been the same for decades, and there's no reason to think they're going to change anytime soon. They aren't complicated at all, so just learn them now and you won't lose any time on test day by taking time to read them two or three times to make sure you're not missing anything. Here are the official instructions that appear at the beginning of the Reading Comprehension section on every LSAT.

Each set of questions in this section is based on a single passage or a pair of passages. The questions are to be answered based on what is <u>stated</u> or <u>implied</u> in the passage or pair of passages. For some of the questions, more than one of the choices could conceivably answer the question. However, you are to choose the best answer; that is, the response that most accurately and completely answers the question, and blacken the corresponding space on your answer sheet.

That's pretty simple and easy to remember. So, learn the directions now and save valuable time on the LSAT.

WHAT ARE YOUR OPTIONS?

There are several approaches you can take when you turn to a passage on the Reading Comprehension section. You can start by:

A. jumping right in—reading the passage and then answering the questions
B. skimming the passage, then skimming the questions, answering the easy ones, then reading the passage in full and answering the rest of the questions
C. reading the first and last sentence of each paragraph of the passage, then reading the passage in full and going on to answer the questions
D. reading the questions so that you can look for the answers on your first reading of the passage, then reading the passage and answering the questions

These approaches have their proponents, but there are a lot of reasons to believe that A is the best option. Most people will be more successful if they take a straightforward approach by simply reading the passage and then answering the questions. Now, there's more to "reading" a passage than simply reading it, and we'll get to that. But first, let's look at the different approaches to see how they compare with each other.

We've already told you that *A* is the best, so let's start with *B*. Skimming is often recommended for picking up the gist of material quickly, and in many cases, it works very well. So why don't we recommend it for the LSAT Reading Comprehension exam? There are two reasons: First, because the passages you'll be dealing with on the LSAT, unlike most of the reading material you've encountered before, don't lend themselves to skimming. The second problem amplifies and

Copyright © Mometrix Media. You have been licensed one copy of this document for personal use only. Any other reproduction or redistribution is strictly prohibited. All rights reserved.
This content is provided for test preparation purposes only and does not imply an endorsement by Mometrix of any particular political, scientific, or religious point of view.

exacerbates the first one—the correct answers to the questions usually don't involve the kind of information you can pick up by skimming.

Pick up any newspaper and start skimming the main article on the front page, and it's easy to get the gist of it—the President signed a bill requiring better nutritional labeling at fast food restaurants, for example. You may miss the fact that he signed it at an elementary school and not in a Rose Garden ceremony, and you may not notice that the bill only passed by a very slim margin in the Senate, or that three Republican senators broke ranks and voted with the Democrats. But you'll pick up and retain the main information. The same goes for most magazine articles, blog posts, and even many books. In these cases, skimming can be quite effective when you want the big picture and you want it fast.

LSAT Reading Comprehension passages aren't anything like newspaper articles or blog posts, unfortunately. They are so stuffed with information and detail that skimming them is worse than an exercise in futility. Skimming is for articles that use everyday English and contain a few important facts that are easily picked out and remembered. The passages on the LSAT are dense and difficult to follow, they make complex arguments on different levels, and they almost always rely on technical jargon and/or a highly advanced vocabulary to do so. You won't learn a thing by skimming them, because you *can't*. On the contrary, you'll probably find yourself getting lost and going over the same material several times, which defeats the whole purpose.

Also, skimming on tests is best suited for answers to very basic questions. Many exams have questions that simply ask a person to locate information in the text, and don't require any analysis. Questions such as *How old was Beethoven when he wrote his first composition?*, *Which continent has the greatest land mass?*, and *Who was the last person to arrive at the scene?* are easy to answer by skimming. You won't be seeing any questions of that type on the LSAT Reading Comprehension test.

What's wrong with *C* (reading the first and last sentences of each paragraph)? There are a couple of drawbacks to this approach. The Reading Comprehension passages are dense precisely because the individual sentences are dense. If you try to decipher one of these sentences, you're going to run into the same problem as the person trying to skim—to get anything out of a stand-alone sentence at all, you will most likely have to read it more than one time. Even reading it several times, however, is unlikely to be any more effective. That's because each sentence after the first one interacts with and builds on the foundation laid by all the previous sentences. One sentence simply won't make much sense by itself. Trying to glean some insights into the meaning of the passage by reading the first and last sentences of each paragraph won't yield any meaningful information, because without the details and context from the rest of the paragraph, these sentences will be essentially unintelligible.

Just as with skimming, the idea behind the first sentence/last sentence approach is basically sound when it comes to other kinds of reading material. In most kinds of nonfiction writing, the author often puts the main idea of the paragraph in the opening sentence, and often reiterates or stresses it in the closing sentence. However, not only are the LSAT Reading Comprehension passages too dense and complex for this to work, but the LSAT writers are aware of the popularity of this strategy and they take pains to foil it. So, even in the rare cases when a sentence might concisely express the main idea, it's unlikely to be the first or last one of the paragraph.

Option *D* also looks promising at first glance; in fact, reading the questions before reading the passage might well be the optimum strategy on most reading comprehension tests. When the reading material is not very complex, it makes perfect sense to find out what you need to look for prior to reading the passage. This greatly simplifies your task and can be a real time saver.

On the LSAT Reading Comprehension, however, reading the questions first and then the passage is a recipe for disaster. On average, each passage will have seven questions, none of which will be easy. Each one will require careful, focused thought just to make sure you've understood the question precisely. In some cases, merely reading the question won't be enough—you'll need to read, consider, and compare and contrast the answer choices with each other to even have an idea of what you should be looking for when you read the passage.

For example, many questions will be some variation of *What is the author's main point?* followed by five answer choices. The five choices will each be lengthy, and a few of them will be remarkably similar. Since you should be able to understand the author's main point by reading the passage, what would you gain by trying to do so while simultaneously attempting to mentally keep several different and highly nuanced answer choices separate as you read? If that doesn't sound difficult enough, imagine trying to do the same thing for up to eight different questions as you read the passage for the first time. For most people, even remembering all the questions while reading the passage would be extremely difficult. Doing so while keeping a couple dozen answer choices in mind at the same time is simply impossible. It's difficult to see how reading the questions before the passage can increase a person's comprehension of a difficult reading selection. On the contrary, using this strategy on the LSAT would almost certainly diminish a person's comprehension and retention of what he or she has read.

The best option, by far, is *A*: start by reading the passage in its entirely, and only then start answering the questions. Once you've finished the passage, you should start with the first question and answer it before moving on to the next one, and then answer each question in turn. Don't bother skimming the questions to see if there are some easy ones you can answer first before concentrating on the harder ones. That won't work, for the same reason skimming the passage itself won't work. There are very few easy questions on the LSAT Reading Comprehension exam. Most questions are either difficult or extremely difficult. If you encounter a question that's particularly difficult, move on to the next one. Never forget that you're in a race against the clock. If you're running out of time and still have some unanswered questions left, just take a guess and fill in a circle. When you stick with this approach, you'll have a much better chance of answering all the questions—the other approaches simply eat up too much time.

So, when it comes to the LSAT Reading Comprehension, a simple, straightforward approach is best. You should read the passage first. Only after that should you even look at the questions. Any other approach will waste valuable time and make answering the questions much more difficult. We think it's pretty clear why the simple approach of reading the passage in its entirety before even looking at the questions is the best one. However, in case you still have any doubts, the Law School Admission Council—the organization that creates the LSAT—also recommends this approach as being the most effective.

THERE'S A LOT MORE TO READING THAN JUST READING

What is the most important skill for achieving a high score on the Reading Comprehension section? That's easy—it's being very good at "active reading." If reading isn't one of your strong suits, now's the time to start working on that. Anyone with average to poor reading skills simply won't have a chance to succeed on this portion of the LSAT without significant improvement between now and test day. However, even if you possess superior reading skills, that doesn't mean that you can relax or that the Reading Comprehension exam will be a breeze for you. You may have a leg up on someone with mediocre reading skills, but odds are you're not used to doing the kind of reading that's necessary for success on the LSAT Reading Comprehension test.

The kind of reading needed for success on the LSAT, active reading, is much different than the kind of reading most people are used to, and that includes even those very good readers who have high natural or acquired abilities for comprehension and retention. It's far from being the same kind of activity a person engages in when they curl up with a good book. You may have already used a form of active reading when you underlined important passages in textbooks, but active reading involves a lot more than that. Active reading is work, and to get good at it takes practice.

So, what is active reading all about? Let's start by talking about its opposite. How many times have you been reading a magazine, book, or newspaper and had to stop and start over from the beginning because you realized that you had no idea what you'd just read over the last few minutes? This has happened to virtually everyone, and it happens on a regular basis. In fact, it's not uncommon for people to have to start over several times before the material finally starts registering with their brain. That's because our minds have a natural tendency to wander while we're reading. If what we're reading is emotionally gripping, such as a key passage in a mystery novel, or extremely interesting in other ways, our minds tend to overcome this tendency and we have no trouble staying focused on the material.

Of course, most of the time people fall somewhere between these two extremes when it comes to staying focused while reading. We usually comprehend and retain some of what we read without having to force ourselves. That won't be good enough for the LSAT. The passages you'll be reading in the Reading Comprehension portion of the exam will be neither interesting nor emotionally gripping. They will be exceedingly dry and dull, in addition to being extremely dense, which will make for very tedious reading. It will take a strenuous effort to stay focused on the exam.

That's the beauty of active reading—it forces you to mentally dive into the passage and actively involve yourself in the text. There are both mental and physical aspects of active reading. Both aspects are important, but it's the physical part that plays a bigger role in enabling you to come back and find the information you're looking for after reading the questions. However, in this case, the whole is truly greater than the sum of its parts. It's the combination of keeping both your mind and your hand fully engaged in the text that makes active reading so powerful.

ACTIVE READING: THE MENTAL ASPECT

As you read each passage, you'll want to keep several questions in mind:

- What is the author's main point?
- What is the author's point of view?
- What is the author's tone?
- What are some of the author's key arguments?
- What are some other viewpoints the author takes note of?

Keeping these questions in mind isn't difficult, although it might seem that way at first glance. If you think about it, however, most of them are questions that will naturally come to mind anytime a person is reading a text they're unfamiliar with. When we read something for the first time, we tend to automatically ask ourselves what the author is trying to say and where they're coming from, and we take notice of their tone and the points they're making. Unfortunately, we also tend to brush these things away while we're reading, and that's one of the main reasons we find it so easy to get completely distracted.

You can avoid this problem by choosing to deliberately focus on these questions as you read. If you have this as a clear and definite purpose in your mind as you begin, staying focused and on track for the few minutes it takes to read each passage will not be a problem. This is another reason you

should not read the LSAT Reading Comprehension questions before reading the passage. You'll have plenty of questions to be thinking about as you read without adding five to eight more, along with a couple dozen possible answer choices to consider. It will be a challenge to keep the above questions in mind as you read and interpret the passage, but you can do it if you make a serious effort.

There is one more important consideration when it comes to active reading on the exam, and that's how to handle words you're unfamiliar with. These will fall into two categories. The first one is technical jargon that is relevant to the context of the passage, but unknown to the average person. The second category will consist of advanced vocabulary words of a nontechnical nature. Hopefully, most of the unfamiliar words you encounter on the LSAT will fall into the first category. Don't let these worry you, as they will either be explained in the passage, either implicitly or explicitly, or they will be of no importance. As for the nontechnical words you run into, if they're not explained explicitly, you can often infer their meaning from the context. If you do happen to run into a word and you have absolutely no idea what it means, and the context is no help whatsoever, don't stress about it, as it's unlikely that any questions are going to be based on it.

ACTIVE READING: THE PHYSICAL ASPECT

As you have probably surmised, the physical aspect of active reading involves annotation, or marking up the text. In addition to the blank paper provided for notes, you will be allowed to make annotations in the text itself, so you'll want to make effective use of the power of annotation. Making the right kinds of notes and markups in the text will enable you to track down the answers to questions much, much faster.

Now, if you've bought a few used textbooks in your academic career, you're no doubt aware that annotation can be taken way too far. Those unfortunate souls who underline nearly every sentence on a page, or even sometimes in a whole chapter, have done themselves no good at all, and only wasted their time. The whole point of marking up a text is to make a word or passage stand out from the whole. If everything on a page has been highlighted, then nothing has been highlighted. That shouldn't be a problem for you with the Reading Comprehension passages, but you should keep in mind that it's easy to make too many annotations. Just make sure you don't go overboard and slow yourself down. Also, be as legible as possible when writing notes on your scratch paper. Many of your notes will be only a few key words, so make sure you can read them with one quick glance. You don't want to be struggling to decipher your own handwriting when seconds count.

On the topic of annotations, the LSAT provides you with four options: underlining and three colors of highlighter—yellow, orange, and pink. We'll give our recommendation for what to use each of these for, but feel free to use whichever colors make the most natural sense to you. The important thing is to decide in advance what colors you're going to use for what, and then stick to your plan.

What kind of things should you be noting? There are several things you'll want to keep an eye out for as you read. Be on the lookout for certain kinds of words or phrases that can be important guideposts when it comes to answering the questions. They show that something is coming that will emphasize an author's point more strongly, or support their argument, or mark a shift of some sort in the writing, such as contrasting or comparing one thing with another. Think of them as "red flags," because they are often important signals that you ignore or skip over at your own peril.

Here are some of the main ones to watch for:

> **Words that signal emphasis**: additionally, also, furthermore, in addition
>
> **Words that signal support**: because, for example, since, regardless
>
> **Words that signal a shift in thought**: but, after all, in spite of, except, yet, although, admittedly, on the other hand, despite, whereas, still, however, nonetheless, in contrast, even though, nevertheless, unlike

Marking these red flags so they stand out will make it easier to find the correct answer for many of the questions when the answer isn't immediately clear to you. You can **underline** these words.

You also need to mark the author's main point as soon as you come across it. Highlight the main point in **pink**. You could also make brief notes on the author's main point, but that would be more time consuming than highlighting.

Sometimes the author will include a number of supporting arguments, points, reasons, etc. Highlight supporting arguments in **yellow**.

Most passages will feature points or arguments that oppose or conflict with the main point the author is making. Highlight opposing arguments in **orange**.

These won't be present in every passage, but if a definition is given, there's a good chance that the definition will be important. Highlight definitions in **pink**.

Similarly, passages will sometimes employ a compare and contrast structure for an argument and a counterargument. If a passage contains this, it is usually important. Highlight comparisons in **yellow**.

In some parts of some passages, you'll encounter more than one thing that needs to be marked, meaning you'll have several annotations in the same part of the passage. This could be quite confusing, which would defeat the purpose of these annotations. If making the annotations results in the passage being cluttered, use the provided scratch paper to make notes corresponding to specific highlighted or underlined passages, making it clear which color highlighting each note refers to. These notes should be used only when necessary, however, because of the time factor.

THE QUESTION TYPES

The questions you'll have to answer in the Reading Comprehension section will be complex and difficult, just like the passages themselves. Unlike reading comprehension tests you may have taken in the past, there won't be many questions for which only one answer choice will be clearly and inarguably the only possible correct answer. As the official LSAT Reading Comprehension instructions put it:

...more than one of the choices could conceivably answer the question. However, you are to choose the best answer; that is, the response that most accurately and completely answers the question...

Don't make the mistake of thinking that *more than one* means *two*. Sometimes you will encounter questions that have not just two, but several answer choices that could plausibly be correct. It's also a certainty that more than once you will be faced with questions that have two answer choices that seem to be saying almost exactly the same thing, and trying to understand the difference between them in order to choose "the best answer" will seem like an impossible task. Rest assured, however, that in each case, only one answer will be acceptable. LSAT test writers spend a lot of time laboring over the precise wording of questions and answers in order to create this level of difficulty. Their purpose is to measure your ability to pick up on nuance and detail, an ability that will be crucial to your success in the legal field.

Fortunately, Reading Comprehension questions fall into a few basic types, which greatly simplifies the challenge you'll face on exam day. Knowing exactly what you'll be up against allows you to be much better prepared to do well on the exam. Here are the main kinds of questions you'll see on the Reading Comprehension test:

- What is the main point the author is making?/What is the author's primary purpose in writing this?
- What is the author implying in this passage?/What can be inferred from this passage?
- Which of the following supports/weakens the author's argument?
- Based on the information in the passage, which of the following must be true?
- What does the author say about X in this passage?

Those are broad generalizations, of course—most questions won't be phrased exactly like any of the above—but approximately 75% of them will be some sort of variation on one of these themes. Here are some examples of the phrasing you'll see in the actual questions on the Reading Comprehension:

- Which one of the following most accurately expresses the main idea of the passage?
- Which one of the following would be the best title for this passage?
- Which of the following inferences is most strongly supported by this passage?
- The author implies which of the following in lines 17–19?
- Which of the following would most weaken the author's argument?
- The author's response to X would most likely be which of the following?
- In writing this, the author primarily seeks to…?
- Which one of the following most accurately and completely expresses the author's main point?

Most of the remaining questions will be about the author's tone, how the passage is structured, and definitions of words (which can be derived from information supplied in the passage).

BREAKING DOWN THE QUESTIONS

Let's take a deeper look at the main question types.

1. MAIN POINT/PRIMARY PURPOSE

Nearly every passage on the Reading Comprehension will have a question asking about what the author hopes to accomplish by writing this, or what their overriding point is. There is a lot of overlap between what the author's main point is and what the author's primary purpose is, so you can think of these two kinds of questions as essentially the same question, but expressed in a slightly different way. Basically, both of these questions boil down to this: What message is the author trying to communicate?

MAIN POINT

Questions about the author's main point are not always phrased exactly alike, but they are usually pretty straightforward. By this point in your academic career you should be familiar with this kind

27

of question, as it's not only one of the most common ones on the LSAT Reading Comprehension exam, but it's also standard fare on any test of reading comprehension. By *straightforward*, we don't mean to imply that these questions are easy to answer; we're only pointing out that the average test taker will have no trouble ascertaining the point of the question.

Almost all Reading Comprehension passages will contain a sentence that expresses the author's main point. Think of this sentence as the thesis statement of the passage. In a written essay, the thesis statement is almost always found in the last sentence of the first paragraph, but that won't be the case in these passages. You will sometimes find the thesis statement there, but many times you won't. The writers of these passages go out of their way to avoid falling into that kind of pattern, which is why formulaic approaches to the LSAT simply don't work. In fact, in some passages the thesis statement won't appear in the first paragraph at all, but in one of the others.

The biggest difficulty test takers have with Main Point questions is that more than one of the answer choices might be an actual point made by the author, but not their main point. An incorrect answer choice might be a secondary point they made, or it could be one aspect of their main point, without accurately summing up the entire point. In many cases the main difference between a wrong choice and the right answer is that the incorrect one is too narrow, or too broad. Because of the phrasing and sentence construction of the answer choices, it's not always easy to distinguish these plausible-sounding answer choices from the one that best encapsulates the main point. It's important to read all the choices carefully and deliberately before choosing an answer.

PRIMARY PURPOSE

Every author has an overriding goal in mind when they write; this is their primary purpose for writing the piece. Their primary purpose can be any number of things. Here are a few possibilities:

- to provide information about a topic
- to demonstrate opposition to a person or thing
- to evaluate or examine a topic
- to challenge an idea, belief, or practice
- to demonstrate support for a person or thing
- to convince someone of something
- to convert someone to a viewpoint or cause
- to critique or criticize something or someone
- to satirize or ridicule someone or something
- to clear up confusion about something
- to bring about change in some area

Those are just some of the primary purposes an author might have in mind when they sit down to write; obviously, there are many more. Unlike the main point of a passage, however, the primary purpose will rarely be stated overtly. You must be able to infer the author's primary reason for writing the passage even though it isn't spelled out. As they do with questions about the author's main point, LSAT writers specialize in surrounding the correct answer choice with others that are often remarkably similar to the actual answer. We can't stress enough how necessary it is to read all the answer choices before deciding that one is correct.

2. IMPLICATION/INFERENCE

On the Reading Comprehension portion of the LSAT, you will encounter many questions about what the author is implying in the passage, or what may be inferred from the passage. Just as in the Main Point/Primary Purpose questions, they will be phrased in a variety of ways:

- With which of the following would the author most likely agree?
- The author implies which of the following?
- With which of the following would the author most likely disagree?
- It can be inferred from the passage that...
- Which of the following inferences is most strongly supported by the author's argument in paragraph two?
- In paragraph three, the author implies that his critics...
- The passage suggests which one of the following about X?
- The passage most strongly implies that the author agrees with which of the following statements?
- The passage provides evidence to suggest that the author would...

No matter how it is phrased, each implication/inference question is asking you about an idea or opinion that the author most likely believes in or subscribes to, even though they have not overtly said so in the passage. Sometimes the question will be about an implication/inference about a narrow subtopic of the passage. If so, some of the answer choices will be quite similar, with only slight differences between them. They can be so similar that a test taker in a hurry could easily fail to see any differences at all between them. Other questions will be broader, with each answer choice representing a clear and discrete alternative to the others. The latter are generally easier to answer than the former.

3. SUPPORTS/WEAKENS

For these questions, you'll be asked which of the answer choices most strengthens or weakens something the author says in the passage. The question could refer to one of the arguments the author makes, one of the conclusions they state, or even the main point. These questions will require you to consider the idea from the passage or the author's statement in light of information not mentioned in the passage, which would most strongly support or detract from the passage or statement. The phrasing of these questions doesn't vary as much as some of the other question types:

- Which one of the following, if true, most supports the author's statement about X in paragraph three?
- Which one of the following, if true, most weakens the author's statement that...?
- Which one of the following, if true, most supports the author's conclusion?
- Which one of the following, if true, most weakens the author's suggestion that X is the best approach to...?

Notice that the correct answer is the one that *most* supports or weakens the statement or idea in question. Rest assured, one or more of the other answer choices will clearly support or detract from the statement or idea, but not quite as forcefully as the correct answer does. Also keep in mind that you will never have to decide if the new information being considered is correct or incorrect. These questions will always qualify the new information with the phrase *if true*.

4. MUST BE TRUE/CANNOT BE TRUE

Must Be True questions are usually phrased along these lines:

- Based on the information in the passage, which of the following must be true?
- Which of the following is most consistent with the author's conclusion that...?

29

You will encounter all kinds of arguments on the exam. An argument may be logically flawed, or it may be perfectly logical. It may be weak or strong. Your task on this portion of the LSAT will be to rapidly and accurately comprehend the argument, and then analyze it in some way based on the criteria in the question. In some cases, you won't have much trouble doing so, but for most of the questions you'll have to do some serious reasoning to get to the right answer.

If the stimulus contains an argument, then no matter what kind of argument it is, it will consist of two basic elements—the **premise(s)** and the **conclusion**. The conclusion is the point the author is trying to convince the reader of, while the premises constitute the evidence they provide to support their conclusion. In other words, an author's conclusion is the *what* of their argument, and the premises are the *why*. Here's an example of a short, concise argument:

Alice has a 4.0 GPA and she scored in the 99th percentile on the Medical College Admission Test, so she is certain to be admitted to an elite medical school.

The conclusion is that Alice should have no worries about being accepted by an elite medical school. The premises are that she has a 4.0 GPA and that her MCAT score is in the 99th percentile. Now, as we said, this is a very basic argument, so let's add some additional information:

Alice has a 4.0 GPA and she scored in the 99th percentile on the Medical College Admission Test, so she is certain to be admitted to an elite medical school. With her work and study habits, she will be at the top of her class. When she graduates, she'll have her pick of residencies thanks to her prestigious degree and record. Obviously, Alice is going to have a hugely successful career in medicine.

This changes things quite a bit. The new argument, while not highly complex, is definitely more complex than the one in the first passage. Notice that the point the author was trying to express in the first passage is no longer their conclusion. Their new conclusion is that Alice is going to have a very successful medical career. What happened to their previous conclusion? It has now become a **sub-conclusion**, which helps build the case for their actual conclusion. You will run into this kind of argument several times on the LSAT. It's important to be able to distinguish a sub-conclusion from a conclusion, so you must read carefully. Also, there's no rule in logic that says a conclusion must come at the end of the argument. Look at how we can rearrange this argument:

Alice is going to have a hugely successful career in medicine. She has a 4.0 GPA and she scored in the 99th percentile on the Medical College Admission Test, so she is certain to be admitted to an elite medical school. With her work and study habits, she will be at the top of her class. When she graduates, she'll have her pick of residencies thanks to her prestigious degree and record.

This is making the very same argument as before, only worded differently. The conclusion is now in the first sentence, appearing before the sub-conclusion. So always keep in mind that the conclusion can appear anywhere in an argument. Furthermore, there can also be more than one sub-conclusion. Careful reading is just as critical on the Logical Reasoning portion of the LSAT as it is on the other sections.

LOGICAL REASONING STRATEGIES AND TIPS

Here are some brief tips and guidelines for helping you do your best on this section:

DO NOT READ THE QUESTION FIRST

You need to decide on a consistent strategy for attacking each Logical Reasoning problem long before you ever walk into the testing center. In fact, you should do this before you even begin taking practice tests. So, what's the best strategy? *Our strong recommendation is that you should always*

read the argument before reading the question. It's important to note that this is the same approach we recommend you employ on the Reading Comprehension section of the LSAT. In fact, we say that one of the worst things you can do on the Reading Comprehension portion is to read the questions first and the passage second, even though this is a popular strategy. The same holds true for the Logical Reasoning section of the LSAT. Reading the question first will often cause you to be distracted or confused while you're reading the argument, and in almost all cases, you'll wind up having to read the question again anyway, wasting a lot of valuable time. Don't try to read the question first, and then the argument. You'll only slow yourself down, making it even harder to complete all of the questions in the very brief thirty-five minutes.

OPPOSITES

Often, when two answer choices are a pair of direct opposites, one of them is correct. The paragraph or passage will often contain established relationships (e.g., when this goes up, that goes down). The question may ask you to draw conclusions from this and will give two similar answer choices that are opposites.

Example:

*If other factors are held constant, then increasing the interest rate will lead to a **decrease** in housing starts.*

*If other factors are held constant, then increasing the interest rate will lead to an **increase** in housing starts.*

Once you realize there are two answer choices that are opposites, you should examine them closely. One of the two is likely to be the correct answer. Of course, they often won't be as easy to spot as the two answer choices in this example. In many cases the wording of the two choices won't be nearly as similar to each other as is the case above. However, it's the meanings that are important, not the particular phrasing.

WATCH OUT FOR RED HERRINGS

Are you familiar with the term *red herring*? It's a literary device used by writers to mislead people into drawing a wrong conclusion about something or someone in the story. Novelists and scriptwriters often employ this device. For example, in a murder mystery, the dead man's butler may be subtly portrayed as scheming and greedy (the red herring), leading many readers to conclude that he committed the murder. In the end, however, the grieving widow is revealed to be the actual culprit, the butler's putative greed and deceit notwithstanding.

Well, novelists and scriptwriters aren't the only people who regularly use red herrings in their line of work; so do the folks at the Law School Admission Council, who are responsible for creating the LSAT. In fact, creating red herrings is a huge part of their job. The designers of the exam deliberately create wrong answer choices that are very close to being correct. One of the most important duties of their job is to go to great lengths to attempt to convince you to choose the wrong answer, and they wouldn't be very successful if none of the incorrect answer choices sounded plausible. If that were the case, you could just go down the list and eliminate the four choices that are clearly implausible, and the only one left would be the correct answer. That kind of exam wouldn't be much of a challenge.

However, on most Logical Reasoning questions there will be three answer choices that aren't all that close to being correct, and only one that could really trip you up. That's because there simply aren't very many ways of coming up with an answer choice that sounds *almost* right, but isn't. An

33

answer that's almost right but *not quite* has to strike the test taker as extremely plausible, and that makes it very difficult to create wrong answers that appear to be correct. So, for the most part, you should have no trouble picking out the blatantly incorrect answers. Once you've eliminated the obviously wrong answers, then you only have to choose between two possibilities. That's the good news. The bad news is that while eliminating three answer choices may make it a bit simpler to select the correct answer, it certainly doesn't make it a snap, because you'll now have to decide which of the two remaining answers is correct, and which one is an artfully constructed red herring.

There are several kinds of red herrings. Here are some that LSAT designers employ most often.

1. TAKING THINGS TO AN EXTREME

In many arguments, the LSAT writers will include an answer choice that takes a point made in the passage to an unjustified extreme. Consider this passage:

> Many so-called conservatives are eager to have America go to war, while at the same time they condemn President Jones for running up massive federal deficits. This makes no sense. One of the historic foundational principles of conservatism is opposition to deficit spending on the part of the government. Well, President Jones is not to blame for these huge budget deficits; they are actually the fault of his allegedly conservative predecessor, President Smith, who hastily started a long and very expensive war without first exhausting all other options.
>
> Given the statement above, which of the following must be true?
> (A) President Jones is not a conservative.
> (B) The author of the passage is a liberal.
> (C) President Smith was a Republican.
> (D) People who are true conservatives should not be eager to go to war, because wars lead to budget deficits.
> (E) Many people calling themselves conservative think going to war is more important than having a balanced budget.

As we mentioned earlier, on most arguments you should expect to find three answer choices that you can quickly dismiss. Let's look at each answer, starting with A. If the argument is correct, must it also be true that President Jones is not a conservative? No, not at all. We know that many professing conservatives are condemning Jones for the large deficits, but that doesn't mean that Jones is a liberal or a moderate. Many political partisans are more strident about condemning politicians of their own persuasion who fail to please them than they are about condemning politicians in other camps. Thus, there is absolutely nothing in the passage that means it must be true that President Jones is not a conservative. Therefore, A is out.

How about B, then—is it necessarily true that the author of the passage is a liberal? Again, the answer is no. There is nothing in the passage that requires us to draw the conclusion that the author is a liberal. They might well be, but they could also be a frustrated conservative. For that matter, they could be a moderate, or even an apolitical person, and this argument could be part of a larger "a pox on both their houses" article. So, B is easily dismissed.

Moving on to C, does it logically follow from the passage that the former president was a Republican? No, it does not. Now, of the three answers that are more obviously wrong, this is the one that would be most likely to trip a few people up due to careless reading and mentally bringing in real-world facts to solve the problem. We know from the passage that President Smith was

Logical Reasoning Test

allegedly conservative. However, we know nothing of his party affiliation. While in the real world of American politics most people rightfully associate the label *conservative* with the Republican Party, that doesn't mean that there aren't some Democrats who call themselves conservatives. In fact, in the 1992 election, Bill Clinton and Al Gore won by selling themselves as conservative Democrats, in contrast to liberals such as Michael Dukakis and Walter Mondale. So, *conservative* does not have to mean Republican. Furthermore, the passage doesn't mention Republicans or Democrats at all. It could be describing a hypothetical future America in which neither party exists any longer. Thus, C is incorrect, too.

So, we have two answers left to choose from. Is D the right choice? Can we conclude from the passage that wars lead to budget deficits? Many people would select this answer. Would you? You should not, as the reasoning is faulty. In fact, it's a great example of how LSAT designers trip people up. Let's look at it more closely.

In this red herring, the test designers take a specific point, but then make far too much of it. They start with an inarguable fact from the passage—the author stated that President Jones shouldn't be blamed for the huge federal budget deficits during his tenure; the blame should actually be assigned to the man he succeeded, President Smith, who started an expensive war while he was in the White House. This is a perfectly reasonable argument because wars usually *are* very expensive, and in the recent history of America, they have certainly led to massive deficit spending. Also, for the purposes of the LSAT, we should assume the truth of the facts presented in an argument, unless instructed otherwise.

Furthermore, most conservatives favor fiscal restraint and generally oppose running up deficits. So, a very good case can be made that people who are true conservatives should have opposed President Smith's getting America into an expensive war before all other options had failed.

However, answer choice D goes much further than that. It says that *wars lead to budget deficits*. It doesn't say that wars *tend to* result in budget deficits, or that *most* wars in history have led to deficit spending. It makes a categorical statement that wars result in budget deficits. This is an If/Then statement. Remember, If/Then statements rarely appear on the Logical Reasoning exam in their pure form. They are usually implied. In this sentence, the phrase *because wars lead to budget deficits* contains this implied If/Then statement:

If a country goes to war, then it will experience budget deficits.

However, this does not logically follow from the information we have in the passage. There's nothing in the passage that tells us that all wars in history have caused budget deficits, or that all wars in the future will do so, let alone that war always leads to budget deficits. All we know from the passage is that huge federal deficits under President Jones followed a war started by President Smith. Does this mean that all wars, everywhere, at all times, lead to budget deficits? Is it possible to imagine a scenario where a country goes to war and doesn't experience budget deficits as a result?

Couldn't the government of a country conceivably fund a war without running up deficits by using budget surpluses left over from previous years, or by raising taxes, or a combination of both? Yes, it could. Isn't it also possible that if Nation A goes to war with Nation B, Nation B could surrender almost immediately, resulting in a very short and very inexpensive war, the cost of which could be entirely covered by Nation A's current military budget? Yes, that's certainly a possibility, too.

So, based on the information in the passage, we cannot say categorically that wars lead to budget deficits. The fact that President Smith's wars resulted in budget deficits does not mean that all wars *must* have that same effect. Therefore, D is incorrect, even though it seems to make sense. It's wrong because it goes to an extreme, by taking one occurrence of something and making it into a hard-and-fast rule.

Notice that this tactic of going to extremes works in the opposite direction, too. Instead of making a leap from something happening *in one case* to a rule about it happening *in every case*, the answer choice could just as easily call for the illogical conclusion that because something *didn't happen* in a specific case, it *never happens* in any cases.

Watch carefully for categorical words in arguments and answer choices, such as *always, all, must, never, none, can't, only, absolutely,* and *certainly*. If one of these words shows up in an answer choice, it's usually incorrect, unless the argument also makes a similar categorical claim, either expressed or implied. If one of these kinds of words appears in the argument itself, then look for an answer choice that aligns with it.

Keep in mind, however, that a categorical statement can exist without using any of these tipoff words. In the example above, the word *all* doesn't appear in the critical phrase *because wars lead to budget deficits*. It is clearly implied, however, because there are no modifiers such as *some* or *most* in the phrase that would limit the statement as applying only to a number of wars less than all.

The correct answer is E. Notice that it uses the word *many* as a modifier, just as the author does, and doesn't make a blanket statement about all conservatives. If we assume the argument is true, that means that the first sentence of the argument must be true, which logically leads to the conclusion found in E.

2. IRRELEVANCE, SIMILAR LANGUAGE, AND PARALLEL REASONING

You will run across many answer choices that seem to be correct, but which are actually completely irrelevant to the argument. You will also find answer choices that attempt to trip you up by using language that is similar to some of the language used in the passage. You'll also come across incorrect answers that seem right because they employ parallel reasoning.

Sometimes you'll encounter answers that combine two or more red herrings. Here's an example combining Irrelevance, Similar Language, and Parallel Reasoning.

Let's return to the same argument, but change it up a little at the end:

Many so-called conservatives seem eager to have America go to war, while at the same time they condemn President Jones for running up massive federal deficits. This makes no sense. One of the historic foundational principles of conservatism is opposition to deficit spending on the part of the government. Well, President Jones is not to blame for these huge budget deficits; they are actually the fault of his allegedly conservative predecessor, President Smith, who hastily started a long and very expensive war without first exhausting all other options. So-called conservatives who support rushing into war are not real conservatives.

Now, suppose the question was:

Which of the following, if true, would most strengthen the argument?

And suppose this was one of the answer choices:

Historically, conservatives have strongly condemned homosexuality, but today many so-called conservatives actually support the legalization of same-sex marriage.

Would this statement strengthen the argument? At first glance, it might seem to. The fact that people who support same-sex marriage would not have been regarded as conservatives in past generations certainly seems to go along with what the author is saying. Didn't the author assert that many so-called conservatives have moved away from their foundational principles? If conservatives used to strongly oppose homosexuality, but today many conservatives approve of same-sex marriage, isn't that evidence that many of today's so-called conservatives aren't true conservatives, strengthening the author's argument? Many people would select this answer choice.

However, the author's argument isn't that many so-called conservatives aren't true conservatives because they have moved away from *some* foundational principles. The author only mentions one foundational principle of conservatism—opposition to deficit spending—and that is the only standard they employ for determining if someone is a true conservative. Here is their argument in syllogism form:

The recent war led to budget deficits.

True conservatives oppose budget deficits.

Anyone who is eager to go to war is not a true conservative.

The author's argument is very narrowly focused, and does not address any other aspect of conservatism besides opposition to deficit spending. We have no idea if they believe that self-described conservatives have moved away from any other foundational principles of conservatism, or if they even believe that opposition to homosexuality is a foundational principle of conservatism. So, this answer choice doesn't strengthen the author's argument at all. What conservatives believe now or used to believe about homosexuality or same-sex marriage has absolutely no bearing on the author's argument, which is that anyone who is eager to go to war is not a true conservative. This answer choice not only fails to strengthen the argument, but it is completely irrelevant. Nonetheless, it would fool many test takers.

Why is this answer choice so deceptive? Why is it that many people would think it strengthens the author's argument when in fact it is completely irrelevant? There are several reasons this answer would fool many test takers. For one thing, it's factually true—nearly all conservatives of past generations regarded homosexuality as immoral, but these days many reject that view and even endorse same-sex marriage. This is enough by itself to trick many examinees into choosing this answer.

We can't stress enough that you must not take real-world factual accuracy into consideration at all on this portion of the LSAT; you must think of yourself as being in a self-contained universe while you answer questions on the Logical Reasoning section of the exam. Ignore everything outside of that universe, because the only facts that matter are the ones you're dealing with on the test, and some of them would be wrong in the real world. You must constantly be on guard against this tendency to work factual accuracy into the answer selection process, because it's very easy to fall into it without even realizing it.

Another reason the answer choice is so deceptive is that it uses some of the same language the author uses when it mentions *so-called conservatives*. This is the exact same phrasing that the author of the passage uses in the first sentence. Many test takers would not even catch this, but their brains would nonetheless make a connection between this answer and the argument without realizing it, simply because it uses the same phrasing.

37

Furthermore, the phrasing is pejorative, as *so-called* is used only to describe someone we don't regard as authentic, as the real deal. No one would use the phrase *so-called expert* to describe someone they regard as a real expert. Using this phrasing, both the passage and the answer choice convey the idea that there are a lot of phony conservatives running around out there. Because our minds look for reasons to make connections, and because when there's one connection there are often more, it's easy to mistakenly conclude that since the answer choice supports the author's view that many people calling themselves conservatives are no such thing, it also supports his or her main argument. (Again, this would not necessarily be a conscious thought process.)

Finally, the wrong answer employs parallel reasoning. Both the answer and the passage say that many people calling themselves conservatives aren't actual conservatives, and they both do so based on what the writer sees as a failure or refusal on the part of these people to measure up to a certain standard, by not taking a position that all (or nearly all) conservatives used to take. Because our brains are constantly looking for patterns and connections, and because these two arguments are so similar in their logic, many people will conclude that the answer choice strongly supports the passage, but that's not true. It is a similar argument in its form, but it does nothing to strengthen the author's conclusion.

BENCHMARK

After you read the first answer choice, decide if it sounds correct or not. If it doesn't, move on to the next answer choice. If it does, make a mental note of it. This doesn't mean that you've definitely selected it as your answer choice; it just means that it's the best you've seen thus far. Go ahead and read the next choice. If the next choice is worse than the one you've already selected, keep going to the next answer choice. If the next choice is better than the choice you've already selected, make it your tentative answer. Repeat this process until you've gone through all five answer choices.

The first answer choice that you select becomes your standard. Every other answer choice must be benchmarked against that standard. That choice is correct until proven otherwise by another answer choice beating it out. Once you've decided that no other answer choice seems as good, do one final check to ensure that it answers the question posed.

NEW INFORMATION

Correct answers will usually contain only information contained in the paragraph and/or question. Rarely will completely new information be inserted into a correct answer choice. Occasionally the new information may be related in a manner that LSAT is asking for you to interpret, but this is rare.

Example:

> *The argument above is dependent upon which of the following assumptions?*

> *A. Scientists have used Charles's Law to interpret the relationship.*

If Charles's Law is not mentioned at all in the referenced paragraph and argument, then it is very unlikely that this choice is correct. All of the information needed to answer the question is provided for you, so you should not have to make guesses that are unsupported or select answer choices that refer to unknown information that cannot be analyzed.

LOGICAL REASONING BASIC CONCEPTS

Both Logical Reasoning exams on the LSAT contain a variety of problem types, each with its own nuance and ideal solution strategy. Even so, a thorough comprehension of certain foundational

concepts will make it much easier to correctly answer the questions regardless of the argument type.

CONCEPT #1: CONDITIONS

The first foundational concept involves understanding how LSAT test writers make use of two types of conditions: **necessary conditions** and **sufficient conditions**. You'll need an understanding of these two concepts, and the differences between them, in order to do well in Logical Reasoning.

Necessary conditions are those that *must* be present in order for a certain outcome to occur. For instance, in order for a forest to catch fire and burn down, there must be an ignition source. So an ignition source is a necessary condition for a forest fire. A necessary condition is anything that's absolutely required to be present in order for something else to be present. In other words, if *B* can't exist unless *A*, then *A* is a necessary condition for *B*. Here's another example of a necessary condition:

All pregnant people are females.

Since a person cannot be pregnant without being a female, being a female is a necessary condition for being pregnant.

On the other hand, a sufficient condition is enough to bring about an outcome, but may not be the only condition that can do so. Returning to the case of forest fires, for example, lightning strikes can cause forest fires. So, a lightning strike is enough, in and of itself, to cause a forest fire. It's not a necessary condition, however, because it's not the only way a forest fire can be started. So, while a lightning strike is not a necessary condition of a forest fire, it is a sufficient condition.

Going back to our second example, is being a female a sufficient condition for being pregnant? No, because other conditions must also be present, such as having undergone puberty and having been inseminated. So, while being a female is a necessary condition for being pregnant, it is not a sufficient condition.

Of course, on the actual Logical Reasoning exam, few conditional statements will be expressed as clearly and succinctly as our example statement about being pregnant. In most cases, there won't be a sentence that directly states *All members of A are members of B*, or something similar. In fact, there probably won't be any part of the argument that makes any kind of direct conditional statement. If an argument contains a conditional statement, it will usually be implied, meaning you'll have to reason it out for yourself. The arguments that have conditional statements, whether expressed or implied, will include them as part of a larger passage. You will need to ignore the noise, or the nonessential details of the passage, so you can distill the argument (or the answer choice) down to its essence in order to find the underlying conditional statement.

IF/THEN STATEMENTS

Conditional statements can be easily understood and analyzed when put into If/Then form. Doing so can also help you spot logical fallacies, which is what the Logical Reasoning exam is all about. Here's an example of an If/Then statement.

If it's raining, then Mr. Jones will be indoors.

The first part of the statement (the If part) is called the hypothesis. The second part (the Then part) is called the conclusion.

Logical Reasoning Test

The statement is straightforward and uncomplicated. It's easy to understand, and hardly anyone would have any trouble with it. Things can get tricky, however, when we change some of the elements up. For example:

If Mr. Jones is indoors, then it's raining.

This is the *converse* of the original statement. But does it logically follow from the original statement? In other words, can we reason logically from the first statement and come up with this statement? No, we cannot. There could be any number of reasons Mr. Jones is indoors. He may be ill. He may be sleeping. He may be surfing the internet. We cannot say with certainty, based on the original statement, that because Mr. Jones is indoors it must be raining. It does not say that rain is the only condition that causes Mr. Jones to stay indoors. In other words, rain is a sufficient condition for Mr. Jones to be indoors, but it's not a necessary condition. *The converse of a conditional statement may or may not be true.*

Now let's look at the *inverse* of the original statement:

If it's not raining, then Mr. Jones will not be indoors.

Once again, the question we need to answer is this—does this logically follow from the initial conditional statement? No, it does not. Just as with the converse, there are a multitude of reasons Mr. Jones might be indoors. If this inverse conditional statement were true, then Mr. Jones would be required to be outside any time it's not raining, no matter what time it is, or what activity he's engaged in. *The inverse of a conditional statement may or may not be true.*

Now, let's look at one more change to the elements of the statement.

If Mr. Jones is not indoors, then it's not raining.

This is the *contrapositive* of the original conditional statement. Does it logically follow from it? Yes, it does. If Mr. Jones is indoors every time it's raining, then if he is not indoors it cannot be raining. *The contrapositive of a conditional statement is always true.*

Now, when we say that the inverse and converse of a conditional statement may or may not be true, and that the contrapositive of a conditional statement is always true, we're using *true* in the sense that you'll need to understand it for the Logical Reasoning exam. Obviously, it's hard to believe that there could actually be a person alive who has never been caught in the rain, and for the rest of his life will never be outside when it's raining. We're simply taking for granted that the conditional statement itself is true, so when we say that the contrapositive is true, we mean that it logically follows from the conditional statement.

We're not at all concerned with the real-life factual accuracy of a statement, nor should you be when you take the LSAT. *Do not fall into the trap of measuring Logical Reasoning arguments by their factual accuracy.* You must judge them only on their logical consistency. Forget the real world when you sit down for the LSAT. Don't underestimate your tendency to go into fact-based mode. It's easy to think you won't fall into this trap, but we're so used to fact-based exams that it's very difficult for some people to avoid falling back on their experience and knowledge on the Logical Reasoning exam.

CONCEPT #2: REASONABLENESS

Not all arguments on the Logical Reasoning exam will involve If/Then statements. In many cases, you will need to evaluate an argument on the basis of how reasonable it is. That is, you will need to

ask yourself if the conclusion makes sense based on the evidence presented. Or is the author making an untenable argument, because they didn't present sufficient evidence to support their conclusion? This represents much of what you'll be doing on the Logical Reasoning portion of the LSAT.

This is what juries in criminal trials do. A prosecutor makes a case against a defendant, and the jury weighs the evidence he or she presents. If they believe that the evidence is strong enough that there can be no reasonable doubt that the defendant committed the act, they find the defendant guilty. In most *civil* trials, though, the burden of proof is not as heavy—there only needs to be a preponderance of evidence in order to assign liability. In other words, in a civil trial, the plaintiff only has to present evidence that indicates that it's more likely than not that the other party committed the act he or she is accused of.

On the other end of the scale, we all run across people making completely unwarranted leaps of logic on a regular basis, especially while we're surfing the internet or watching cable news talk shows. In those environments, it's common to see people making outlandish claims based on very little evidence, or none at all:

The federal government's response to Hurricane Katrina proves that politicians are uncaring, lazy, and greedy.

Anyone who supports raising the minimum wage is a Communist who wants to destroy the American way of life.

Of course, most of the arguments we encounter on a daily basis fall somewhere in the middle of the two extremes of being beyond a reasonable doubt and being utterly nonsensical. Consider this:

Jenny said the new Italian café is fantastic. We should go there for lunch tomorrow.

Many people would not consider that to be an argument, but it is. Your friend has reached a conclusion (we should eat lunch at the new restaurant tomorrow) and is trying to convince you that his conclusion is correct by presenting the evidence he bases it on (Jenny raved about the place). Is this a reasonable argument? That depends on a lot of different factors. How long have you known Jenny? Do you trust her judgment when it comes to food and restaurants? How much does she know about Italian food? Does her cousin own the Italian café? Is the speaker telling the truth about what Jenny said?

If you trust the person who told you this, and you think Jenny has a good track record when it comes to restaurant recommendations, then this argument would probably strike you as quite reasonable. The fact that Jenny vouched for the place would be enough evidence for you to agree with your friend's conclusion that you should have lunch there tomorrow.

Now, consider this argument:

Jenny knows good food, and she loves that Mexican restaurant on 23rd street that's for sale. We should buy it and franchise it.

Is this a reasonable argument? In other words, has your friend presented enough evidence to support his conclusion? Even if Jenny is something of a connoisseur, is the fact that she likes the food at a restaurant sufficient evidence for agreeing that it's a good idea to put tens or hundreds of thousands of dollars into an extremely risky business venture? No, not really. Now, the idea behind the argument is not completely illogical—after all, people generally buy or start a business in hopes

41

of making a lot of money; popular restaurants tend to make a lot of money; good food is one of the main factors in why restaurants become popular; and Jenny, who is a very good judge of food, says the restaurant's food is very good. So, there certainly might be some legitimate reasons to *consider* the idea of buying the restaurant.

However, there are many other factors to consider—that your friend hasn't even mentioned—before making such a decision. Why is it for sale? What do you and your friend know about running a restaurant? How much is the asking price? Even if you were to decide that buying the restaurant is a good idea, do you really want to be in a business partnership? If so, would your friend make a good business partner? These are just a few of the dozens of questions you would need to answer before agreeing to buy the restaurant with your friend. So, while there might be a good idea at its root, the argument isn't reasonable, because your friend hasn't presented nearly enough evidence to support it.

CONCEPT #3: CAUSALITY

Examining causality, or what most of us refer to as cause and effect, should help you determine the relative strength or weakness of a particular argument. Given that it is possible that *A* caused *B*, you then have to determine whether it is likely that *A* caused *B*, or if there are other causal agents that are more likely to have caused *B*. For example:

The store that burned down didn't seem to be doing well. I'm sure the owner torched it for the insurance money.

Is this a reasonable conclusion as to what caused the fire that burned the store down? No, it really isn't. It is an awfully long logical leap to say that because a store that burned down didn't appear to be doing well, the owner probably set fire to it.

For one thing, how do we know what kind of financial condition the store was in? Let's say we arrived at the conclusion that the store was struggling because we rarely saw customers going in or out. Well, there could be a lot of reasons for that. Maybe the only time we passed the store was on our way to and from work every weekday, and the store's peak sales occurred at night and on the weekends. It's also quite possible that, like many brick-and-mortar businesses these days, the store made far more money from selling merchandise over the internet than it did from walk-in traffic, but still had enough local customers that it was profitable to keep the doors open.

It's also quite conceivable that the business was only somewhat profitable but, for whatever reason, the owner didn't need the store to make a lot of money and was quite content with the income he was bringing in. There are a great number of reasons why our notion that the store was in bad financial shape might be mistaken. However, even if our opinion about the financial health of the store is actually correct, it's still extremely unreasonable to conclude from that fact that the owner burned the store down to collect the insurance money. Tens of thousands of businesses go under every year in America, but commercial arson is pretty rare.

Now, let's add some more information:

The store that burned down didn't seem to be doing well. I'm sure the owner torched it for the insurance money. After all, he did spend three years in prison during the late '90s for hiring a guy to burn down another store he owned.

Hmm...this information certainly makes our conclusion that the owner torched the place look a lot less unreasonable, as the storeowner has a history involving commercial arson. However, while our conclusion is not nearly as reckless as it was before, it's still not entirely reasonable to definitively

conclude that he burned the store down. Many, many people who have been paroled after a conviction for conspiring to commit commercial arson never do such a thing again.

Let's add some more details:

The store that burned down didn't seem to be doing well. I'm sure the owner torched it for the insurance money. After all, he did spend three years in prison during the late '90s for hiring a guy to burn down another store he owned. On top of that, he owes $300,000 in gambling debts to some pretty unsavory characters. Furthermore, several local ex-cons have told the police that the owner offered them money to burn the place down. He also took out commercial insurance policies with three different companies last month. And there's no getting around the fact that surveillance cameras from a nearby business show him carrying what looks like a can of gasoline behind the store just before the fire started.

These new details completely change things. Assuming that the information is all true, is it still possible that the owner had nothing to do with his store burning down? It may be theoretically conceivable, but it's virtually impossible for a rational person to believe. Based on the new information, it's not only reasonable to believe that he torched the place, it would be unreasonable to doubt it. The more evidence we have that supports a conclusion that *A* caused *B*, the more reasonable that conclusion is. At first, we had very little evidence to support the idea that the store's owner burned it down. However, as we were presented with more evidence, the link between *A* and *B* became pretty much indisputable. The cause-and-effect relationships you'll encounter on the Logical Reasoning section will be somewhere between these two extremes, but you'll use the same kind of reasoning process to analyze them.

In many instances, the test preparers will link a certain progression of evidence with a conclusion the evidence doesn't entirely support. The information given may be factual and reasonable up to a point, yet somewhere in the argument the examiners have made a leap beyond the bridge they were building with the evidence—or have loaded that bridge with more weight than it can support.

Consider this argument, remembering that you are only meant to determine whether, in this instance, the argument supports the conclusion (regardless of your personal opinion about the topic):

In the United States, over six million middle and high school students read significantly below grade level. American fifteen-year-olds rank twenty-eighth out of forty countries in mathematics and nineteenth in science. Clearly, Americans are not spending enough on public schooling for their children.

For a multitude of reasons, many people would take this argument at face value, accepting the underlying assumption that all systems work better when they are given more financial support. That would be unreasonable, however, because there is very little evidence provided to support the conclusion. How much are we spending per student currently? How does that compare to what higher-ranking nations are spending? How is that money apportioned within the system? If the amount of money being spent isn't the issue, what are other countries doing that we are not? Has our ranking ever been higher and, if so, what were we doing then that we are not currently? In short, is lack of funding ultimately the primary cause of our poor scoring? If you were told that the United States is tied for first in terms of spending per student, would you begin looking for other causes? These are all questions that must be considered before deciding that America doesn't spend enough on public schooling, and there are many more.

Logical Reasoning Test

In the end, there may or may not be a link between the money we're spending on education and the test scores our students are achieving. The point is that accepting the argument requires you to make a huge mental leap in order to justify a conclusion that is not fully supported by the supporting statements. Also note (once again) that the LSAT designers count on the fact that you'll have a certain amount of ingrained bias in favor of a widely held point of view. They take advantage of this to try to keep you from noticing the logical relationships that have been left out. Many test takers unintentionally supply the missing logical connections as a result of personal bias and lazy reasoning, and thus answer the question incorrectly.

CONCEPT #4: ACKNOWLEDGING THE UNKNOWN

In our everyday verbal exchanges with others, it's quite common to pretend to know more than we do. There are several reasons we do this, among them a desire to avoid admitting ignorance of the topic at hand. We're not comfortable admitting that we're unable to connect all the dots someone else is presenting as a complete picture. Sometimes we're afraid we may have missed something, particularly if everyone else is nodding along in agreement, and we feel like we're the only one who doesn't know what is going on. You're eating lunch with a group of friends in the dining hall when another friend walks up and says, "Oh, man, have you heard Adele's new song? Isn't it her best one yet?" All your friends are chiming in about how much they love it, and you're nodding and making statements to the same effect, despite the fact that you had no idea Adele even had a new single out. For that matter, some of your friends are probably faking it, too. We all do this sort of thing, and we do it constantly.

Well, that skill may work in conversation, at least occasionally, but it will get you nowhere on the LSAT. In fact, part of what the Logical Reasoning section of the LSAT is testing for is the ability to recognize and acknowledge what you do not know—to be fully aware of missing links, disconnected information, and facts that are irrelevant to the key issues.

Take a look at the following example:

Maude hates the city. Last year she moved her family to Montana.

The connection of statements makes it easy to conclude that Maude's reason for moving to a wide-open state like Montana is her hatred of the city. But is that really correct? Do you have enough evidence to conclude that is the case?

Casually linking the ideas in conversation is fine, but it will get you in trouble on the LSAT. Consider instead the universe of facts you don't know in this scenario. Using the analogy of a circle, what we do know fits inside the circle. What we don't know is everything outside the circle.

First, what we do know: Maude's strong dislike of the city, where she moved, that she has a family of some sort, and very general timing of the move.

What we don't know: That's a much, much longer list. Does she hate all cities or one particular city? Why does she despise them (or it)? Was her move to Montana related to this preference, or to some other reason, such as a job change or an urgent family situation? Is she trying to put distance between herself and someone from a failed relationship? Is she happily married, but seeking lots of room for her seven children to run around? Did she feel an urge to hop from state to state alphabetically and she just finished Missouri? What is her family made up of (kids, husband, cats?) and does its relevance in this statement go beyond the incidental? Obviously, we could go on and on.

The point is that there are many, many unknowns between the two statements above. Although some assumptions may be fairly reasonable given the information, and others may be a complete reach, it is still important to comprehend that they are assumptions and are not, in fact, *known*.

CONCEPT #5: SPOTTING INCOMPLETE ARGUMENTS

One aspect of LSAT problem-solving that we run into over and over is an argument that is somehow incomplete. This can lead to leaps in logic and incorrect assumptions—filling in the blanks. To the test preparers, any specific subject knowledge you may have is substantially less important than the mental skills you will use to identify underlying assumptions and missing pieces. So they will often deliberately pair a statement with a conclusion that doesn't quite match the given evidence, just to see how you deal with it.

First, you should bring to bear skills noted in Basic Concept #4: Be aware of what you don't know in a given scenario. Don't assume facts. But here we take that skill one step further. Not only should you recognize what information is missing, you should also be able to identify the underlying assumption attempting to link the two. The following statement is presented to illustrate the point:

Merla's fingernail was chipped, so she stopped at the library.

Huh? In this case, it's obvious that there are missing links between the initial statement and the accompanying conclusion. What do Merla's nails have to do with stopping at the library? If we were provided additional information—for instance, that a nail-care seminar is taking place at the library—this might make more sense, but there is certainly no obvious link between the two thoughts.

However, it is unlikely the LSAT will employ such an obviously unrelated pairing. Try a more subtle example, like the one shown below:

A well-educated citizenry is required to maintain a free society. Robert has perfect attendance at school, so he must be well educated.

As above, it's important to first realize what you do not know. It may be reasonable to assume, or it may even be true, that Robert is well educated. However, you can't deduce that with any certainty from the above information. We would additionally need to know what is meant by a good education, the steps involved in procuring one (presumably it requires more than merely showing up for school), and how Robert measures up against those standards.

One way the LSAT may test your skills in spotting incomplete arguments is by asking you to identify the assumption in the given passage. In this case, you'd be looking for an answer choice like this:

b. Consistent school attendance results in a good education.

Or you might be asked which statement would most weaken the assumption underlying the author's conclusion. In that case, the correct answer could be something like this:

d. Some of our nation's founders, who were very learned men, never formally attended school.

First, identify what is incomplete in the argument. Dealing with the rest of the problem is easy after that.

Logical Reasoning Test

The Most Common Question Types

AUTHOR'S MAIN POINT OR PURPOSE

You should expect to see some questions about the author's main point or purpose on the Logical Reasoning section of the LSAT, as they are quite common. (Sometimes you'll be asked about the main idea; this is the same thing as the main point.) They are also among the easiest questions to answer correctly. In part that's because the passages in Logical Reasoning are so short; there's really no way to express several important ideas in so few words. Some of them might be harder than others, but in general, they're usually the questions that test takers have the least amount of trouble with in this section. It's also because the question itself is so straightforward and easy to understand. Every argument you'll come across on the exam has essentially two parts—a conclusion and one or more premises. Premises are what the author bases their conclusion on. They're the facts or opinions the author marshals in support of their conclusion. The conclusion and the main point are always the same thing, so once you've found the author's conclusion, you've found the main idea. The *main point* is what the author is trying to say, while the *primary purpose* is what they hope to accomplish by saying it.

> **Review Video: Understanding the Author's Intent**
> Visit mometrix.com/academy and enter code: 511819

Here's an argument that features a Main Point question.

Professional sports associations must make some major changes if they want to stay in business. Drug use, violent crime, and irresponsible behavior are rampant in the NFL, NBA, and MLB, and have been for years. It used to be that when people would think of professional athletes, they thought of outstanding people like Willie Mays, Hank Aaron, Roberto Clemente, Oscar Robertson, and Walter Payton. Now they are more likely to think of Mark McGwire, Jose Canseco, Barry Bonds, O. J. Simpson, Ray Lewis, and Rae Carruth. If something isn't done to get people like this out of professional sports, many fans will stop buying tickets.

Which one of the following is the main point of the passage?

(A) There are a lot of people of bad character in professional sports.
(B) People expect professional athletes to be good role models for children.
(C) Pro sports leagues must take drastic action against illegal and immoral conduct of athletes.
(D) Steroid use continues to be out of control in professional sports.
(E) Today's athletes don't possess the same moral caliber as past generations of athletes.

The author clearly believes, and provides some evidence to back up their belief, that *there are a lot of people of bad character in professional sports*. Is that their main point, though? Let's not decide just yet, and keep going.

Does the author say that *people expect professional athletes to be good role models for children*? No, they do not, although one might reasonably infer that this is something the author believes. The author's main point can sometimes be implied as opposed to clearly stated. However, although this does seem like something they would feel strongly about, it isn't the main point.

How about the statement that *steroid use continues to be out of control in professional sports*, or that *today's athletes don't possess the same moral caliber as past generations of athletes*? Clearly the

author strongly believes the latter, and probably believes the former, but he or she doesn't mention steroids specifically, only drugs in general. At any rate, neither one is the main point.

The author's main point is that *pro sports leagues must take drastic action against illegal and immoral conduct of athletes*. This is almost a simple restatement of the first sentence of the passage, but not quite. The first sentence says that professional sports groups need to make major changes if they want to stay in business, while the next section of the article is about illegal and immoral conduct by athletes. It's clear that the major changes the author recommends revolve around the bad behavior of athletes.

INFERENCE

Inference questions are also common on the Logical Reasoning section of the LSAT. They are more nuanced than Main Point questions, as they require you to read between the lines or put two and two together. They might ask you to determine what the author would agree or disagree with, based on the passage, even though there are no direct statements in the stimulus either for or against the position in an answer choice. Or they might ask you what a reasonable reader could infer from the passage, or what the author implied in the passage. *Imply* and *infer* are flip sides of the same coin—an author implies something by suggesting it without saying it directly. A reader infers something by forming a conclusion about something the author has not actually stated, by making logical deductions from one or more things the author *has* stated. These questions can be phrased in various ways:

The researchers would most likely concur with which one of the following?

The senator would be least likely to agree with which one of the following?

The argument most strongly supports which one of the following?

Which one of the following can be properly inferred from the passage above?

> **Review Video: Inference**
> Visit mometrix.com/academy and enter code: 379203

Here is an argument followed by a typical Inference question:

When you get right down to it, there are only two basic approaches to playing no-limit hold 'em poker tournaments—long ball and small ball. Long ball is based on playing very few hands, but making large bets to either drive out opponents when bluffing or to build a huge pot when holding a strong hand. Small ball players take the opposite approach—they get involved in lots of pots by making small bets before the flop, hoping to make a great hand and trap their opponents or to bluff them out of the pot with nothing. Both approaches have their advantages and disadvantages. Choosing which one to use comes down to personal preference.

The author would most likely agree that:

(A) The World Series of Poker tournament has gotten too large and takes too long.
(B) All poker players need to be skilled at both approaches to the game.
(C) Long ball players tend to win more tournaments.
(D) Small ball play is better suited for introverts.
(E) Bluffing is an essential skill for poker tournament success.

The first answer is obviously wrong because it's completely irrelevant—the author says nothing about the size or length of the World Series of Poker or any other poker tournaments, and there's nothing in the passage to justify this inference.

How about *all poker players need to be skilled at both approaches to the game*? No; nothing like this is either stated or implied, either.

Does the author believe that *long ball players tend to win more tournaments*? No; if they did believe that, why would they say that choosing a style depends on personal preferences? If the long ball approach led to more success in tournaments, surely they would believe that that should be a major factor in choosing a playing style, and would recommend that approach to the game.

Would the author likely agree that *small ball play is better suited for introverts*? So far, this is the only answer that merits any consideration at all. After all, the author does say that choice of playing styles comes down to personal preference. However, they say absolutely nothing to indicate that they believe that small ball is better suited for introverts. This answer would trip a lot of people up because introverts tend to be shy and quiet, and the long ball style is highly aggressive, so it's natural for our minds to think the long ball style would be a poor match for introverts. However, there's no necessary correlation between personality and playing style, and since the author doesn't say that they see any connection between the two, we can't conclude that they would agree with this statement.

By process of elimination, that leaves *bluffing is an essential skill for poker tournament success*, which is the correct answer. We know that this is the right answer because all the others are wrong, but we can also verify it using logical deduction. The author says that there are only two basic approaches to playing poker tournaments, and then he or she describes each one, and both include bluffing. In other words, there are no playing styles that don't include bluffing. This means that he or she would have to agree that bluffing is an essential skill for poker tournament success.

UNDERLYING ASSUMPTION

Another common question you'll encounter on the Logical Reasoning exam will ask you to select the answer that contains an assumption the author is relying on to make their argument. It's important to note that an assumption is *not* one of the author's stated premises, or the reasons they give in support of their conclusion. Assumptions will never actually appear in the passage. Think of them as the unwritten premises standing alongside or behind the author's stated premises, which are the reasons they give in support of their conclusion.

For example, in the argument, the author may conclude *D* based on *C* and *B*. However, *B* or *C* actually hinges on *A* being true, even though the author never mentions *A*. So, *A* is an assumption the author is relying on in order to make their case. It's important to keep in mind that assumptions are always unstated, because on most of these kinds of questions, at least one of the answer choices will be a slight rewording of one of the author's stated premises. It will be incorrect, because if the author is stating something, then by definition, they are not assuming it. Also, while you will only be asked to pick out one, there will always be many, many assumptions underlying an argument. Consider this argument:

O. J. Simpson is a murderer. Murderers don't deserve recognition and honor. Simpson should be removed from the NFL Hall of Fame.

What assumptions is the author relying on? Several, actually, but here are just a few:

- Media accounts of Simpson's activities just prior to and immediately after the murders of his ex-wife and her companion can be trusted.
- Simpson wasn't framed for murder by racists in the Los Angeles Police Department.
- He wasn't framed for murder by a corrupt prosecuting attorney's office.
- The 12 jurors who found him not guilty were either incompetent or dishonest.
- The author has the capacity, at least in this case, to determine that someone is guilty of murder even though a jury has acquitted him.
- Simpson is still in the NFL Hall of Fame.
- Being in the NFL Hall of Fame is an honor.

We could go on and on, but that's plenty. These are all assumptions the author is relying on to be true if their argument is to hold water, even if they aren't consciously aware of all of them. If any of the above assumptions are wrong, then the author's argument falls apart.

That will always be the case if you have chosen the correct answer on an Assumptions question—making the assumption false should tear down the author's argument; if it doesn't, then the answer is incorrect.

Because anytime an argument *relies* on an assumption, if the assumption is turned on its head, then the argument *must* fall apart.

Let's return to a previous argument, using exactly the same stimulus as before:

> Professional sports associations must make some major changes if they want to stay in business. Drug use, violent crime, and irresponsible behavior are rampant in the NFL, NBA, and MLB, and have been for years. It used to be that when people would think of professional athletes, they thought of outstanding people like Willie Mays, Hank Aaron, Roberto Clemente, Oscar Robertson, and Walter Payton. Now they are more likely to think of Mark McGwire, Jose Canseco, Barry Bonds, O. J. Simpson, Ray Lewis, and Rae Carruth. If something isn't done to get people like this out of professional sports, many fans will stop buying tickets.
>
> Which one of the following is an assumption on which this argument relies?
>
> (A) A large number of professional athletes are criminals or drug users.
> (B) Sports commentators are getting increasingly fed up with bad behavior by pro athletes.
> (C) In the past, the media helped cover up the immoral behavior of famous athletes.
> (D) Many people who buy tickets for sporting events base their decision to do so in part on the good behavior of athletes.
> (E) No athletes who use steroids have legal prescriptions for them.

Let's examine each answer choice.

A large number of professional athletes are criminals or drug users. Is this an assumption the author relies on? No, because the author states it expressly in the argument when they say that drug use and violent crime are rampant in the three big professional sports. An assumption, by definition, cannot be something that is stated in the argument.

Is the author assuming that *sports commentators are getting increasingly fed up with bad behavior by pro athletes*? Well, if so, there's really nothing in the argument to indicate that they're doing so. They don't mention sports commentators, writers, or analysts, and there's nothing in the passage that implies sports writers in general are getting tired of immorality and criminality on the part of the athletes they cover. While it's certainly possible that the author is personally a professional sports commentator, even if they are, they don't claim to be speaking for sports commentators in general, and the passage gives us no basis for inferring that other commentators share this view. Also, when in doubt, you should always run the reversal test of an assumption. So, ask yourself this—if this statement is wrong, would the author's argument fall apart? In other words, if sports commentators *aren't* getting more and more fed up with immoral and criminal athletes, would it ruin the author's case? No, it would not, because their argument is about the leagues losing revenue due to fed-up *fans,* not sports commentators. Reversing the assumption doesn't destroy the argument, so this cannot be the correct answer.

In the past, the media helped cover up the immoral behavior of famous athletes. Does the author assume this in making their argument? No, they do not. If anything, they take the opposite view, because they seem to believe that athletes of yesteryear really were better behaved than today's athletes, not that those athletes were just as immoral but the media covered it up.

Many people who buy tickets for sporting events base their decision to do so in part on the good behavior of athletes. Does the author's argument rely on this assumption? Well, this answer certainly looks promising. The author argues that the major sports leagues must take serious action concerning the rampant bad behavior among their athletes if they want to stay in business. The author says that, unlike in the past, when people today think of athletes, they think of drug users and violent criminals, and then the author asks how long fans will continue buying tickets to see such players. So, clearly, the author must be assuming that a large number of fans will stop buying tickets if something isn't done to crack down on the athletes' bad behavior, because fans don't want to pay to see a bunch of drug users and criminals. In other words, many fans buy tickets based in part on the good behavior of athletes. Now, let's reverse the argument: *Few people who buy tickets for sporting events base any part of their decision to do so on the good behavior of athletes.* Does this destroy the author's argument? Yes, it does—if few people make decisions about buying tickets based on the good behavior of the athletes, then the presence of a large number of athletes who don't practice good behavior won't necessarily lead to significantly lower ticket sales. So, this must be the correct answer.

Just to be sure, though, let's look at the last choice. *No athletes who use steroids have legal prescriptions for them.* Does any part of the argument rely on this assumption? No. In fact, the author doesn't mention steroids at all, but only drugs in general. It's a reasonable assumption that the author is referring, at least in part, to major steroid scandals of the past. However, most people upset about steroid use in sports find their use scandalous regardless of whether or not the athlete has a legal prescription for their use. Even if every infamous steroid user in professional sports had acquired the drugs legally, using them is still against the rules of their leagues, as they give athletes a powerful, unfair advantage over their teammates and competitors who don't use them. Thus, even if the author is objecting to steroid use, they haven't said anything at all to indicate that they're against steroid use only if not legally prescribed. If we run the reversal test, we come up with *all athletes who use steroids have legal prescriptions for them.* Does this destroy the argument? No, because the author is denouncing rampant drug use in general, not simply the use of steroids for which they don't have legal prescriptions. In addition, drug use is only one of three factors mentioned. The author's argument also involves violent crime and irresponsible behavior.

NEW INFORMATION QUESTIONS

Another very common question type on the Logical Reasoning test requires you to analyze or reconsider the argument in light of new information. (This is the exact opposite of Inference questions, which require the test taker to *analyze new information in light of the argument*.) There are a few different types of these new information questions on this section of the LSAT. The two most common are Strengthen questions and Weaken questions. They come in two forms. The first form simply asks which answer choice supports or weakens the argument or conclusion. The second one, however, asks you to select the answer that *most* strengthens or weakens the argument. In other words, you will have two or three answers that support/weaken the argument in some way, and you will need to select the one that does so most powerfully.

This second kind of question is usually phrased along these lines:

Which one of the following, if true, most strengthens the argument?

Which one of the following, if true, offers the most support for the conclusion?

Which one of the following, if true, most weakens the argument?

Which one of the following, if true, most undermines the author's conclusion?

Each of the following, if true, offers support for the argument EXCEPT: (This is actually a Weaken question.)

You will see these sorts of questions on arguments where the premises don't strongly support the conclusion. In other words, the evidence is somewhat lacking—the premises make a case for the conclusion, but not one that is airtight and wholly persuasive. You'll be faced with five answer choices that each contain new information; at least one of them will definitely make the argument stronger or weaker, as the case may be.

It's important to note, however, that exactly how much the correct answer strengthens or weakens the argument can vary considerably. With one question, the correct answer might slightly damage the persuasiveness of the argument, and with another, the new information contained in the right answer would cause the argument to fall apart completely. So, the force of the new information is not an issue, in and of itself. It's only important when you have a *most* question, and new information in one answer is contrasted with the new information in other answer choices. For example, if you're looking for the answer that most strengthens the argument, don't simply choose the first answer that strengthens the argument in some way. It could very well be wrong, as there may be another answer that lends even more strength to the argument. Never forget the *most* in a question.

Also keep in mind that the LSAT designers like to trip test takers up on these kinds of questions by inserting answer choices containing information that seems powerful and relevant, but in reality has nothing to do with the author's actual conclusion, meaning that it's actually completely irrelevant because it doesn't affect the argument at all.

MOST WEAKENS QUESTION

Many people believe that advertising plays a major role in how people choose whom to vote for in presidential elections in America, but our recent study proves that this belief is a myth. We selected 5,000 people, chosen from all 50 states in proportion to each state's percentage of the US population, and divided them into two groups. People in Group A each watched between 10 and 20 hours of television a week, while no one in Group B watched any television at all. Three months before the last election, we asked each person in both groups which presidential candidate they favored. Then, after the election was over, we asked each person whom they had voted for. At the beginning of the experiment, members of Group A favored the Republican candidate by a 51/49 margin, but wound up voting for him by a 56/44 margin. Group B favored the Republican candidate by a 52/48 margin at the start of the experiment, but voted for him by a 57/43 margin. So, in both groups, the percentage of actual votes for the Republican candidate was exactly five percentage points higher than the level of support at the beginning of the study, and the level of support for the Democratic candidate was exactly five points lower, proving that advertising does not make a big difference in presidential elections.

Which one of the following, if true, most weakens the argument?

(A) The average number of years of college education in both groups was exactly the same.
(B) The Democrats didn't spend quite as much as the Republicans on television ads.
(C) Members of Group B spent an average of 15 hours a week listening to the radio.
(D) Both candidates had high disapproval ratings.
(E) Two television stations in Alaska refused to run any ads for political candidates.

Does the fact that *the average number of years of college education in both groups was exactly the same* weaken this argument? On the contrary, it would tend to strengthen it, since it reduces the likelihood that a difference in the demographics of the two groups influenced the results.

Let's look at three of the remaining answers together:

The Democrats didn't spend quite as much as the Republicans on television ads.

Both candidates had high disapproval ratings.

Two television stations in Alaska refused to run any ads for political candidates.

Do any of these weaken the argument? Given the results of the study, it's not likely that the fact that *the Democrats didn't spend quite as much as the Republicans on television ads* was much of a factor, but theoretically it could have made a slight difference. If so, that would weaken the argument. Let's hang on to this answer.

Does the fact that *both candidates had high disapproval ratings* weaken the argument in any way? No, it doesn't. In fact, this answer is completely irrelevant. We can reject this answer choice out of hand.

What about the fact that *two television stations in Alaska refused to run any ads for political candidates*? Does that weaken the author's case for claiming that advertising *doesn't* play a major role in how people vote? It's very unlikely, because the people in Group A were proportionally distributed across America. Alaska makes up a tiny percentage of the US population, meaning that

very few (if any) members of Group A were affected by the lack of political ads on these two stations. So, while it theoretically could have had a miniscule effect, it's very unlikely that it did, and even less likely that it had even the impact that lower spending on the part of the Democrats might have had. So, we can discard this answer, too.

Let's examine the remaining answer choice. Would the fact that *members of Group B spent an average of 15 hours a week listening to the radio* weaken the argument? Yes, it would, since it would represent a huge blind spot in the study. The researchers appear to be assuming that the only way Americans can be exposed to ads for presidential candidates is by watching television. However, since the argument doesn't stipulate that fact, we have no reason to assume it's true while analyzing the author's case. Since it's common knowledge that radio stations run a lot of campaign ads during presidential campaigns, and there is nothing in the argument to the contrary, we can use this knowledge in our reasoning. When we do so, it's obvious that it would logically follow that people listening to the radio 15 hours each week would hear a large number of ads for presidential candidates. Since the author based the argument on the assumption that people in Group B weren't exposed to ads for presidential candidates, this information demolishes the case, making it the correct answer.

MOST STRENGTHENS QUESTION

Public awareness campaigns have reduced the number of alcohol-related traffic fatalities in the US. One major factor in this reduction is the fact that many states now require persons convicted of driving under the influence of alcohol to install ignition interlock devices (breath analyzers) on their cars. These devices make it impossible for a car to be started when they detect alcohol on a person's breath. However, even after decades of efforts to reduce drunk driving, tens of thousands of Americans are still killed every year by drunk drivers, so more must be done. If Congress passed a law requiring car manufacturers to include ignition interlock devices on every new vehicle sold in America, eventually thousands more lives would be saved every year.

Which one of the following, if true, most strengthens the argument?

(A) The number of alcohol-related traffic deaths dropped sharply in the late 1980s, but has since plateaued.
(B) Rapidly improving technology is making it increasingly difficult for people to evade or defeat ignition interlock devices.
(C) Because of the economies of scale, requiring ignition interlock devices on all vehicles would add less than $100 to the price of a new car.
(D) Seven percent of alcohol-related traffic deaths are caused by people previously convicted of driving under the influence.
(E) In a few years, iris recognition and vein matching technology will be incorporated into most ignition interlock devices, giving prosecutors extremely persuasive evidence in DUI cases.

The correct answer is D. Let's examine the answer choices in order:

The number of alcohol-related traffic deaths dropped sharply in the late 1980s, but has since plateaued. Does this strengthen the argument? No. The focus of the argument is the conclusion, which in this case is that a law requiring breath analyzers on all new cars would save thousands of lives every year. This statement *does* back up the sub-conclusion that more needs to be done about

Logical Reasoning Test

the number of traffic fatalities, but it provides no support for the idea that breath analyzers on every new car would save thousands of people's lives.

Rapidly improving technology is making it increasingly difficult for people to evade or defeat ignition interlock devices. Does this statement strengthen the argument? Yes, it does. If interlock devices are getting more and more effective, then that would make the impact of installing them on all new cars even stronger. However, the statement found in D does much more to strengthen the argument.

Because of the economies of scale, requiring ignition interlock devices on all vehicles would add less than $100 to the price of a new car. If true, this statement would probably make the law more popular with the public and therefore easier to pass, but it does nothing to strengthen the notion that installing breath analyzers on all new cars is an effective way to dramatically reduce the number of people killed by drunk drivers.

Seven percent of alcohol-related traffic deaths are caused by people previously convicted of driving under the influence. This is the statement that, by far, does the most to strengthen the author's conclusion. How so? Well, if seven percent of alcohol-related traffic deaths (about 1 in 14) are caused by people who have already been found guilty of driving under the influence, that means that 13 out of 14 deaths are caused by drivers who have *not* previously been convicted of DUI, and therefore don't have interlock devices on their vehicles. Since we know from the argument that interlock devices have been a major factor in reducing the number of traffic deaths from DUI, and now we posit that at least 93% of the vehicles involved in DUI fatalities don't have one, it logically follows that installing them on all new vehicles would eventually dramatically reduce the number of drunk driving deaths in America.

In a few years, iris recognition and vein matching technology will be incorporated into most ignition interlock devices, giving prosecutors extremely persuasive evidence in DUI cases. Does this strengthen the argument in any way? No, it doesn't. The argument is about reducing the number of DUI fatalities, not about making it easier for prosecutors to convict people charged with driving under the influence. The statement neither strengthens nor weakens the argument; it is completely irrelevant.

PARADOX QUESTIONS

We've been referring to the stimuli on the Logical Reasoning exam as arguments, but not all of them actually are. Sometimes a stimulus will merely present a few facts without drawing a conclusion from those facts. If there's no conclusion in the text, there's technically no argument, and the stimulus is merely a reading passage. For simplicity, however, we will continue to refer to all the passages as *arguments*.

Paradox questions take this form. Two or more facts are presented, and some of the facts will seem to be at odds with each other. The question will ask you to resolve the problem by choosing the answer that resolves the paradox.

Example:

Medical researchers exploring the obesity epidemic in the US have made an intriguing discovery. With the cooperation of several restaurant owners, they observed and recorded thousands of diners eating lunch over the course of several months. As expected, they found that on average, seriously overweight people consumed far more calories while dining out than did people of average weight. However, when they compared calorie counts only among the seriously overweight diners, they were surprised to find that obese diners who were considered well-dressed consumed significantly fewer calories than did diners of the same weight who were considered casually dressed, even while eating at the same restaurant.

Which of the following statements, if true, would provide the best explanation of the seeming paradox found by the researchers?

(A) Well-dressed diners tend to be more affluent and can more easily afford higher-quality, less-fattening food.
(B) In all weight categories, casually dressed people tend to eat more food when dining out than well-dressed people.
(C) Casually dressed diners tend to be less educated and therefore less informed about what constitutes healthy eating.
(D) Well-dressed diners tend to be more image conscious, so they eat less in public, but make up for it by eating more at home.
(E) The researchers had unconscious prejudices against people who are overweight, and this affected their findings.

Before we examine the answer choices, let's consider the passage. Obesity researchers who studied thousands of lunchtime restaurant patrons over a period of several months discovered what seems to be a paradox. What is the intriguing finding? It's the fact that, on average, well-dressed obese people ate fewer calories than casually dressed obese people who weighed about the same.

What makes this a paradox? It's a (seeming) paradox because one would reasonably assume that in a study involving thousands of people, on average, people who weigh a certain amount would consume about the same number of calories as other people of the same weight. Yet, among obese people of approximately the same weight, there was a significant difference in the caloric intakes of well-dressed people and casually dressed people. Something doesn't add up here. How can casually dressed obese diners take in significantly more calories than well-dressed obese diners while weighing the same? It's your task to decide which one of the answer choices resolves the problem. Let's look at each one.

Well-dressed diners tend to be more affluent and can more easily afford higher-quality, less-fattening food. As a stand-alone statement, this makes perfect sense. It's common knowledge that when it comes to food, the lower the price, the more unhealthy and fattening the food tends to be. Keep in mind, however, that we're not concerned with whether the statement in any of these answer choices makes sense or not, because for the purposes of answering the question, we have to accept it as true.

So, assuming the truth of this statement, does it do anything to resolve the paradox? No, it does not. If well-dressed obese people are eating fewer calories because they have the means to afford less

55

fattening food, then why do they weigh as much as casually dressed obese people who don't have that option? So, the paradox still stands, and this answer is incorrect.

How about the next answer choice? *In all weight categories, casually dressed people tend to eat more food when dining out than well-dressed people.* Is this the answer we're looking for? No. It simply takes one part of the paradox—casually dressed obese people eat more calories when dining out than well-dressed obese people do—and applies it to everyone in general, irrespective of weight. This explains that, when casually dressed obese people eat more calories while dining out than well-dressed obese people do, it is simply part of a larger pattern that holds true across the board. But it does nothing to explain why two groups of obese people with different eating patterns weigh about the same.

Casually dressed diners tend to be less educated and therefore less informed about what constitutes healthy eating. This has a lot in common with A, and it's just as unsatisfactory when it comes to resolving the paradox. Instead of implying that casually dressed people eat poorly because they can't afford to eat healthy food, this answer states that they eat poorly because they're not educated enough to understand the principles of healthy nutrition. While this could be true, it does nothing to resolve the paradox. After all, if well-dressed people make healthier food choices because they're better educated, then why are they just as heavy as their less-educated counterparts?

Well-dressed diners tend to be more image conscious, so they eat less in public, but make up for it by eating more at home. Right off the bat this looks more promising than the first three choices. Why? Because it includes a factor outside of the environment the researchers observed the diners in. That's in its favor, because logically there are very few factors within that environment that could explain how two groups of people can weigh the same despite significantly different calorie consumption patterns. However, that doesn't necessarily make this the correct answer. We have to decide if it resolves the paradox. Yes, it does, and it does so very well. The well-dressed obese diners eat less than their casually dressed counterparts in restaurants because they're self-conscious about their image, but at home, when no one's watching, they eat enough to make up for the caloric gap between themselves and the other group. This explains the paradox of why both groups weigh the same. It's the correct answer.

The researchers had unconscious prejudices against people who are overweight, and this affected their findings. Not only does this answer fail to explain the paradox, it doesn't even make sense. However, since we're required to grant the truth of the statement in order to see if the answer is correct, let's think about it. The paradox involves two groups of overweight people, so if the researchers had been biased against the overweight, whether consciously or unconsciously, they would have been equally biased against *both* groups, which, in effect, would mean that they would be treating both groups pretty much the same way. So, this statement does nothing to explain why they found a discrepancy between the groups. Had the researchers been biased against well-dressed people or casually dressed people, that fact certainly could have played a role in the findings, but the notion that they were biased against the overweight explains nothing.

Keep in mind that the correct answer only needs to be the best explanation of the paradox out of the five choices given. It doesn't have to be the best explanation that's theoretically possible. For example, it's certainly possible that the average well-dressed obese person engages in more exercise than his or her casually dressed counterpart. This could explain the paradox, and might even do so better than D above. However, it's not one of the choices. Of the five answer choices we're given, D offers the best explanation of the paradox.

FLAWED REASONING QUESTIONS

With most of the questions you'll run into on the Logical Reasoning section of the LSAT, the reasoning in the stimulus will be basically sound. The author won't make any logical errors, and the premises will lead directly to the conclusion. Everything will work nicely together to form a solid argument. However, that won't be the case with every stimulus. In some cases, the reasoning found in the stimulus will be illogical in some way, and your job will be to figure out exactly what's wrong with the author's argument. These are Flawed Reasoning questions.

Sometimes the flaw will be fairly easy to spot, but in a lot of cases it will be much more subtle. In fact, many times it will be so subtle that if it weren't for the question asking you to name the flaw, many people taking the LSAT would never realize that the reasoning was illogical.

By the way, this is one of the main reasons that some people recommend reading the question before reading the stimulus. They say that if you know there's a reasoning flaw in the stimulus before you start reading it, you can look for it as you read. They're right about that, but for other types of questions it's better to read the stimulus first, and because the vast majority of questions on the Logical Reasoning section aren't Flawed Reasoning questions, you'll come out way ahead if you read the stimulus first.

There are many different kinds of logical errors an author can make, but they all basically boil down to relying on a false or unjustified assumption: reasoning from only one case to a large number of cases, confusing correlation with causation, assuming that current conditions will continue unchanged, imprecision in numbers or measurement, making poor analogies, etc.

You'll be presented with five answer choices, only one of which will be the actual reasoning flaw in the argument. Remember, it's likely that one or more of the answer choices will be red herrings— one of those wrong answers that have been carefully and deliberately designed to trap you into selecting it as your answer. On Flawed Reasoning questions, LSAT designers often trip people up by offering one or two answer choices that mention something the author actually does in the argument, but isn't illogical—it's actually valid reasoning.

Another common technique is to have one or more answer choices that refer to an error of logic that is common and well known, but isn't part of the author's argument. For example, an answer might say the author appeals to authority or the author assumed what they set out to prove, when the author has done no such thing. This second technique isn't as tricky as the first one, but you should definitely be on guard against it, too.

Here is an example of a Flawed Reasoning question:

> It has been clearly demonstrated that the average married man earns more income than the average single man. Over two hundred scientifically rigorous studies have been done on this subject, starting nearly fifty years ago and continuing today, by such highly respected institutions as Harvard University, Yale University, and the University of Chicago. All told, these studies have included millions of men, from every level of education, all over the country, in hundreds of different occupations, and every one of them found that the average married man is paid more than the average single man. Obviously, there is widespread blatant discrimination in the employment market against men who aren't married.
>
> Which one of the following best describes the flaw in the reasoning in this passage?
>
> (A) The author appeals to authority to make his case.
> (B) The author assumes what he is supposed to be proving.
> (C) The author fails to consider other possible causes than discrimination.
> (D) The author relies on insufficient or irrelevant data to make his case.
> (E) The author fails to use exact figures with respect to average incomes.

Let's look at the argument and consider the answers.

The author points us to over two hundred studies by highly respected organizations that compare the incomes of married men to the incomes of single men, which all found that married men are paid more than single men. He points out that this applies across the board, for pretty much all jobs and education levels, all over the country, and has been going on for a long time. He draws the conclusion that single men are being discriminated against by employers. We know from the question that there is a flaw in his reasoning. We have to determine what the flaw is.

Is it that *the author appeals to authority to make his case*? This sounds promising. A well-known logical fallacy is the appeal to authority, and the author relies on studies for his evidence, and points out that some of them have been conducted by elite universities. So he's guilty of committing the appeal to authority logical fallacy, right? Well, not so fast. While this would trip up a substantial number of test takers, it is not the correct answer.

While the author does cite some authorities, he is not committing the appeal to authority fallacy. Some people who have heard that appealing to authority is a logical fallacy seem to think that one can never cite an authority to back up an argument. This is nonsense. Appealing to an authority is only a logical fallacy if the authority has no expertise in the topic under discussion, or in a case where many other equally knowledgeable authorities disagree on the matter.

For example, if we're having an argument over Roman Catholic theology, and you quote a well-known Catholic theologian to back up your point, that is not a logical fallacy, because a Catholic theologian should certainly understand Catholic theology. However, if we're discussing which baseball player was the greatest ever, and I say, "It's Babe Ruth because my priest said so," then I've committed the appeal to authority fallacy. Only an appeal to authority outside the subject matter, or a quote from one authority on a topic that is disputed among experts on the subject, is a logical fallacy. Citing authorities who know what they're talking about is perfectly logical. So this answer is wrong.

Is it true that *the author assumes what he is supposed to be proving*? This is another logical fallacy, known formally as *begging the question*. Here's a simple argument that begs the question: *Cigarettes are unhealthy because they're bad for you.* This argument begs the question because the conclusion is nothing but a restatement of the premise. It's like if a little boy says his dad is always right, and when his friend asks him how he knows, and the boy replies, "Because Dad said so." This is known as a circular argument. Does the author commit this logical fallacy? No, he does not. His premise, that married men make more money than single men, is not the same as his conclusion, which is that employer discrimination against single men is the cause of the disparity.

How about *the author fails to consider other possible causes than discrimination*? This one sounds like it might have some merit. Because it's the LSAT, we have to assume that the facts in the author's premise are correct, and that hundreds of studies have established that married men make more money than single men as an irrefutable fact. However, does it necessarily follow that discrimination against single men in the marketplace is the cause of this? Are there any other factors that could possibly be causing this phenomenon?

Couldn't experience be one factor that might be involved? Older men are more likely to be married than younger men, and older men are more likely to have more experience than younger men. Since employers usually prefer workers with more experience over those with less, it seems logical that they would pay them more. Another possible factor is motivation—doesn't it make sense that a man with a wife, and possibly kids, might be motivated to work longer hours than a single man, and thereby earn more income? These are just two possible explanations of the pay disparity that don't involve discrimination, and the author didn't consider either one, let alone any others. So this is the correct answer.

What about *the author relies on insufficient or irrelevant data to make his case*? Why is this wrong? Well, if the author had mentioned only one study, he would not have much of a case. Instead, he pointed to over 200 studies by elite universities, involving millions of men from all walks of life, in hundreds of occupations, over a 50-year span, all of which came to the same conclusion. Assuming that the facts that the author cites in a stimulus are true, as we must do on the LSAT, it is clear that there is sufficient, relevant data to establish scientific consensus on this matter.

That *the author fails to use exact figures with respect to average incomes* is true, but completely irrelevant. The 200+ studies have established that there's a pay disparity between single and married men, and he is arguing that the mere existence of the disparity, not its size, is proof that there is widespread discrimination against single men in the workplace. Nothing in the argument requires exact figures to be stated.

PARALLEL REASONING QUESTIONS

Parallel Reasoning questions are very common on the Logical Reasoning section of the LSAT, and you should expect to see a few of them when you take the exam. They can be more difficult to answer correctly than many of the other question types, so they typically eat up more of the clock you're racing against. That's because with Parallel Reasoning questions, you're not just analyzing one argument, you're analyzing six—each of the answer choices is an argument, too. Because of this, we're going to spend more time discussing these questions than we spent on the other question types.

On Parallel Reasoning questions, the stimulus will be a very concise argument, comprising only a few lines. After digesting the argument, you will then be asked to read the five answer choices and select the one whose argument most closely parallels the reasoning in the stimulus. LSAT designers have several ways of phrasing this, but they are all very similar, so there won't be any doubt that you're dealing with a Parallel Reasoning question. Analyzing and comparing five arguments to the original can take quite a bit of time, and this is another reason some LSAT guides recommend that you read the question before reading the stimulus. They suggest skipping all Parallel Reasoning questions, and only coming back to attempt them after answering all the other questions first.

It's your decision, of course, but we think you'll do better if you stick with our suggestion of reading the stimulus first. For one thing, you won't need to read the question in order to decide that you're looking at a Parallel Reasoning question. That will be obvious since the stimulus will be an argument that's only a sentence or two long. And, for that very reason, reading the stimulus first won't take much time at all, so how much time would you have saved anyway?

This is not to say that you should never skip a question and come back to it later. At times, that might be the wisest approach. It depends on how hard the question is. Some Parallel Reasoning questions are pretty tough to untangle, but frankly, many are not that hard. If you get bogged down on one of these questions, by all means skip ahead and only come back to it if you've answered all the other questions. (You should always skip ahead if you get seriously stuck on *any* question on the LSAT, no matter what type of question it is.) It's inadvisable, however, to have a blanket policy that you're going to skip all Parallel Reasoning questions until the end, because many of them are not particularly difficult. Since other kinds of questions can also be very hard, you could very well be skipping a question you could have easily answered only to run into another question that completely stumps you.

On Parallel Reasoning questions, as the name implies, the correct answer must use the same kind of reasoning as what is found in the original argument. In other words, the two arguments must be similar in logical structure. If the original argument makes an analogy, then the correct answer will contain an analogy. If the stimulus relies on circular reasoning, the correct answer will, too. If the original argument reasons inductively, you'll be looking for an inductive argument in the answer choices.

In some cases, the method of reasoning used in the argument won't be all that obvious or easy to discern, but that usually isn't a problem. The much bigger problem is that some of the answer choices will be so similar, or so opaque, that deciding which one best matches the reasoning in the original argument will seem extremely difficult. To find the right answer, you'll need to consider and compare several aspects of the two arguments.

The first factor is validity. Sometimes the argument in the stimulus will be valid, in which case the correct answer must also contain a valid argument. Sometimes the stimulus argument will contain a logical flaw. In that case, the argument in the correct answer must also be invalid. You can know for sure if the argument in the stimulus is valid or invalid because if it's invalid, the question stem will say so. If the question stem doesn't use a word such as *flawed*, *illogical*, or *questionable* to describe the stimulus argument, then the argument is valid.

However, don't put too much weight on validity. It's definitely a requirement, but it's only one factor you must consider when looking for parallel reasoning. Or, to put it in formal logic terms, the correct answer matching the validity or invalidity of the original argument is a necessary but not sufficient condition. Plus, it's very unlikely that only one answer choice will match the stimulus in being valid or invalid.

Next, you'll want to compare the conclusions in each argument. Remember, the stimulus and the five answer choices are all arguments, so they all *must* have conclusions (and at least one premise). The conclusion in the correct answer should have a lot in common with the conclusion in the

original argument. This doesn't mean that the subject matter will be the same, or even similar. Nor does it mean that the two arguments must have the same placement of the conclusion with respect to the premises. The premises could come before the conclusion in the stimulus, and after the conclusion in the answer (or vice versa), and they could still be a match.

Two of the kinds of similarities you're looking for in conclusions are scope and certainty. These are functions of the language used in the arguments. When the conclusion in the stimulus contains broad, all-encompassing absolutes such as *all*, *always*, *must*, *cannot*, or *never*, then the conclusion in the correct answer must have the same scope, even if it's not expressed exactly the same way. For example, compare these two conclusions:

People over the age of 50 never win a marathon.

No person over the age of 50 ever wins a marathon.

These are saying the exact same thing, even though only the first one uses the word *never*, and one sentence refers to *people*, while the other one uses *person*. So, these conclusions are a match.

Now consider these two conclusions:

People over the age of 50 never win a marathon.

People over the age of 50 hardly ever win a marathon.

Are these two conclusions saying the same thing? No, they are not. The first one is making an absolute, categorical statement that a person over the age of 50 winning a marathon never happens. The second one is saying that it's rare for anyone over 50 to win a marathon, but it does not say it never happens. These conclusions do not match up.

So, scope, or extent, is a very important clue when determining the correct answer for Parallel Reasoning questions. Certainty is another factor to consider. Consider these two conclusions:

Eating too much might cause you to get diabetes.

Smoking cigarettes will stain your teeth.

In the first one, it is stated that *A* could possibly lead to *B*, while in the second, it is asserted that *A* definitely results in *B*. One conclusion is certain, while the other is indefinite, so these conclusions are not a match. Of course, there is quite a bit of overlap between scope and certainty; the main thing is to be on the lookout for any kind of an absolute. If the conclusion in the stimulus has an absolute, then the correct answer must too. If the conclusion of the original argument has an indefinite modifier, then an answer that contains an absolute is wrong. Because conclusions must match in scope/certainty, it's often the case that the argument in the correct answer contains some words or phrases identical to the original. This isn't always the case, and it also shouldn't be treated as a smoking-gun level of proof by itself, but it can certainly be an important clue.

So, tackle these questions by first seeing if the method of reasoning jumps out at you. If so, then you should generally be able to select the correct answer with no further analysis. If that's not the case, then consider validity, and eliminate all answers that don't match the argument for validity. If you still aren't sure, compare the conclusions for scope and certainty. In most cases, if you need to compare the conclusions in order to determine the right answer, doing so should be enough to enable you to pick the winner. However, if you're still unsure, then compare the premises in the stimulus with the premises in the answer choices, using the same principles just described above. If

Logical Reasoning Test

61

you're still unsure of the correct answer after that, then it's probably time to move on to another question.

Here is a sample Parallel Reasoning question:

Great college professors love to read. Bob has over a thousand books on his e-reader, so he would make a great college professor.

The flawed reasoning in which one of the following arguments most closely parallels the flawed reasoning in the argument above?

(A) People with analytical minds are good at chess. Everyone in the accounting department has an analytical mind. Zelda works in the accounting department, so she would make a good chess player.
(B) All baseball players can learn to switch-hit if they practice long enough. Jose Ramirez was the American League MVP last year, so he would be able to master switch-hitting in only a couple of weeks.
(C) Everyone who works for an airline loves traveling. Derek has been an airline reservations clerk for seven years, so Derek loves traveling.
(D) When the sky is red in the morning, it usually rains by the end of the day. The sky is red this morning, so it will rain today.
(E) The best restaurant managers like to cook. Zoe throws some terrific dinner parties, so she would be a very good restaurant manager.

Let's look at this in depth.

First, why is this argument flawed? It's illogical because, if great college professors love reading, that doesn't mean that all people who love reading make great college professors. In other words, loving to read is a necessary condition for being a great college professor, but it's not a sufficient condition.

Is *A* the correct answer? In other words, does it have the very same flawed reasoning as the argument in the stimulus?

People with analytical minds are good at chess. Everyone in the accounting department has an analytical mind. Zelda works in the accounting department, so she would make a good chess player.

Let's break it down. It boils down to *all members of A are B, and all members of C are members of A, and D is a member of C, therefore D is B*. Is this reasoning flawed? No, it's not; it's perfectly valid. There's an extra step in there that might conceivably throw some people off, but it's a logical argument. Therefore, it cannot be correct, as the correct answer must contain flawed reasoning.

Moving on to *B*:

All baseball players can learn to switch-hit if they practice long enough. Jose Ramirez was the American League MVP last year, so he would be able to master switch-hitting in only a couple of weeks.

Is this argument valid or invalid? It's invalid—while the premise says that all baseball players can learn to switch-hit, there's nothing that says that the better a player is, the faster they'll learn, let alone anything that puts a time limit on the learning curve. This argument takes the premise too far

and comes to an unwarranted conclusion. However, that is not the same kind of illogical reasoning the stimulus contains, so this answer is incorrect.

How about *C*?

Everyone who works for an airline loves traveling. Derek has been an airline reservations clerk for seven years, so Derek loves traveling.

This is a valid argument: *All members of A are B. C is a member of A, therefore C is B*. The logic is fine, but we're looking for an illogical argument, so this answer is incorrect.

Next, we have:

When the sky is red in the morning, it usually rains by the end of the day. The sky is red this morning, so it will rain today.

This is pretty obviously flawed—it turns a likely outcome (*usually rains*) into an absolute certainty (*will rain*). But it's not the kind of flawed reasoning we're looking for, so it's out.

By process of elimination, we know that *E* must be correct, but let's look at it to find out why.

The best restaurant managers like to cook. Zoe throws some terrific dinner parties, so she would be a very good restaurant manager.

First, notice that the language and structure are very similar, but not identical. This is a good sign. More importantly, though, if we break the logic down, we'll see that it has the same flawed reasoning. Just because the best restaurant managers like to cook, it doesn't necessarily mean that people who like to cook would make great restaurant managers. Enjoying cooking is a necessary condition for being a great restaurant manager, but it's not a sufficient condition. This is the same illogical reasoning found in the stimulus, so it's the correct answer.

LESS COMMON QUESTION TYPES

The majority of the questions you'll encounter on the Logical Reasoning section of the LSAT will fall into one of the question types we've just discussed. That's why we spent so much time dissecting these particular types of questions and explaining how to solve them. However, there are many other kinds of questions used far less frequently by the test designers. You won't see a question from each of these categories on the LSAT when you take it, but you'll definitely run into some of them. It's not necessary to spend nearly as much time prepping for these questions, but you should make sure you're familiar with them before taking the exam. So, here are some other Logical Reasoning question types you can expect to see when you take the LSAT.

PASSAGE COMPLETION QUESTIONS

On a Passage Completion question, the last part of the final sentence of the passage is left blank, and the question stem asks you to choose the answer that best completes the passage. On these, the correct answer should not only make logical sense, but also fit with the rest of the passage structurally and stylistically. Because of this, it's usually not very difficult to select the right answer. At least two of the choices won't make much sense as an ending for the passage, and the other incorrect choice(s) won't be a good fit when it comes to structure or style.

MUST BE TRUE & DEDUCTION QUESTIONS

While these are phrased differently, they are essentially asking the same thing as Inference questions. Just follow the principles for solving Inference questions when you run into a question

asking you something like, *Based on the passage, which one of the following must be true?* or *Which one of the following statements can be deduced from the passage?*

POINT AT ISSUE QUESTIONS

Two brief, conflicting statements will be given, each from a different person, and the question stem will ask you to choose the answer that properly conveys the point at issue between the two. The key here is to ignore the noise in the arguments, such as extraneous details, and boil each statement down to its essence. When you do that, the dispute will become clear, and it will reveal the correct answer.

CONCLUSION QUESTIONS

Every now and then you'll see a question asking you to identify the author's conclusion. Don't let the wording on these questions fool you. Remember, the conclusion is the main point the author is making. In other words, these are simply Main Point questions. Follow the principles described in that section and you'll be fine. Always keep in mind that the test designers like to include a premise or two as answer choices, which trips many people up. Don't let that happen to you; make sure you don't choose an answer simply because it contains a reframing of a statement from the argument—the statement that is restated must be the conclusion.

ARGUMENT PROCEEDS BY & METHOD OF REASONING QUESTIONS

These questions ask you to choose the answer that best describes the method of reasoning employed by the author, or best shows how the argument proceeds. In other words, the conclusion is not the focus, nor is any inference or deduction that can be made on the basis of the argument. The validity of the argument is also not a factor. The only thing that matters for these questions is how the author makes the argument. Once you identify how the argument is structured, the key to answering these questions correctly is to mentally eliminate the fluff in the answer choices and focus on essentials. Because there aren't very many ways of coming up with incorrect but credible answer choices that can deceive many test takers if written in straightforward language, the LSAT designers tend to employ verbosity and bombast as distractions. That is, they use too many words, or intellectual-sounding language, or both, to dress up the answer choices to make the wrong answers sound more appealing. When you strip away all the fancy verbal footwork, you'll find that choosing the correct answer is often fairly easy.

SYLLOGISM QUESTIONS

A syllogism is a classic argument structure used in formal logic. It contains two premises and a conclusion. Here's a basic syllogism:

When the sun is up, it is daytime.

The sun is up.

It is daytime.

You will likely encounter a question or two featuring syllogisms on the Logical Reasoning section of the LSAT. The stimulus will present a syllogism, and then ask which of the answer choices must be true if the syllogism is true. Syllogism questions are probably the most straightforward and easy-to-understand questions you'll come across in Logical Reasoning. For that reason, they are also some of the easiest to solve. You may find it helpful to draw a diagram illustrating the syllogism, but in most cases that won't be necessary.

OTHER QUESTION TYPES

Every now and then, the folks at the Law School Admission Council come up with a new question type, so it's possible you may run into a kind of question that's never before been seen on the LSAT exam. Plus, we have omitted a few question types from this guide because they only rarely appear on the test, and many of them are very close to fitting into one of the categories we've discussed. So, if you encounter a question that doesn't fit into one of the listed categories, there's no need to panic. Logic is logic; if you've used this guide to practice, and you've mastered the skills necessary to tackle the kinds of questions discussed at length in this book, you'll be ready for any curveball the LSAT designers throw your way.

Logical Reasoning Test

The Argumentative Writing Essay

HOW IMPORTANT IS IT?

Reading and writing are a daily part of life for law students and for lawyers. An ability to express your thoughts concisely, clearly, and persuasively in a number of styles, from court briefs to personal letters, is critical to doing well in the profession. This need for attorneys to possess a mastery of writing skills was ostensibly the primary reason for adding a timed writing section to the LSAT. Another reason often cited is that a writing sample gives the admissions committee a more well-rounded picture of a law school candidate, allowing them to make more holistic decisions about who gets in and who doesn't.

However, many people believe that the Argumentative Writing portion is nothing more than window dressing, a sort of diversionary tactic. Law schools have been widely criticized in the past for focusing too much on numbers (i.e., test scores and grade point averages) in making admissions decisions. Critics asserted that this was unfair to many deserving candidates who are perfectly qualified to do well in law school but don't do well on standardized tests, and that law schools' narrow-minded focus on test scores and GPAs resulted in an imbalanced pool of new lawyers, which was stultifying the legal profession.

Law schools dug in their heels for years and resisted changing the test, but they eventually gave in. However, the Argumentative Writing portion is unscored, and it is difficult to determine its effect on admissions decisions. Some observers insist that it can have a small effect, but almost no one believes that the Argumentative Writing portion is essential to getting into law school.

Nevertheless, many people who are preparing to take the LSAT have a lot of anxiety about the Argumentative Writing portion of the exam. But they don't need to. The importance of the writing portion for law school admissions falls somewhere between "not very important" and "not important at all." If you've been stressed about the Argumentative Writing portion, this should help relieve your anxiety.

Another thing to keep in mind is that if you have what it takes to get good grades in college and a high score on the LSAT, then you almost certainly possess all the skills you need to do well on the Argumentative Writing. On the other hand, if you lack the skills necessary for success on the other sections of the LSAT, then it won't matter how well you do on the essay. Also, you will not be expected to produce the kind of writing that appears in magazines or wins literary prizes. Nor will you be trying to craft persuasive arguments for why you'd make a great law school student, as this is not an admissions essay.

Although the whole Argumentative Writing section is 50 minutes in total, it is split into two parts. You will be given 15 minutes to prepare your thoughts and make notes about the subject, and then 35 minutes to write a two-page essay taking a position on a key question and explaining the reasoning behind your argument. Your writing will demonstrate that you have the ability to think on your feet, look at problems from various angles, organize your thoughts, and express yourself clearly and concisely. These are all skills that will be vital to your success in law school and as a working attorney, and which you should be very good at by this stage in your academic career. So, there is really no reason you should be filled with anxiety about the writing portion of the LSAT. However, you should be prepared to do your best on this part of the exam, if for no other reason than that there is an off chance that your essay might be the tiebreaker in a close admissions decision.

66

Do not misunderstand—it is not acceptable to leave the Argumentative Writing portion blank, to turn in a humorous essay, or to put only a half-hearted effort into writing it. You also should not choose a different writing topic from the one assigned. Law schools can and do reject applicants for this kind of behavior, and you should strive to do your very best on this section of the exam. We're simply saying that you should not stress yourself by worrying about the writing portion, because in the vast majority of cases, it simply isn't a decisive factor in the admissions process. If you're prepared and give it your best on test day, you should do just fine. In this section, we'll show you what you need to know in order to be fully prepared for success on the Argumentative Writing portion.

THE ARGUMENTATIVE WRITING FORMAT

Argumentative writing isn't the typical kind of essay most people have in mind when they think of an essay. Often, an essay is fairly open ended. There is usually an assigned topic or subject, but the essay writer is allowed a lot of leeway when it comes to choosing how to address the topic. That is not the case with the Argumentative Writing portion of the LSAT. It has a very specific format, one that has been deliberately designed to test some of the most important skills a person will need to succeed in law school and a subsequent legal career.

First, you will have 15 minutes to complete all of your prewriting activities. You will be given a subject, an introduction to the topic, a key question, and a selection of short written perspectives on the issue. Along with this, you will be given some prewriting questions and recommendations to help you organize your thoughts on the topic. Even though you can skip ahead to writing the essay after 5 minutes, it is in your best interest to take the full 15 minutes to prepare as much as you can. You do not get additional time to write the essay if you cut your prewriting short.

Once you advance from the prewriting phase, you will have a 35-minute time limit to complete your essay. You will also have access to the notes you wrote during the prewriting part. Your task in the Argumentative Writing portion will be to write an argumentative essay in response to the Key Question. Always keep in mind that there is no right or wrong answer; it doesn't matter what argument you make. This aspect of the essay trips many people up, as they see it as yet another test of logic and reasoning. They believe that an important part of doing well is choosing the "correct" perspective, and that, if they give it enough thought, one will clearly stand out as the best choice.

In fact, the opposite is true. It will be clear that each of the given perspectives has both strong and weak points. Your job is simply to come up with a response to the Key Question and make the best case you can for it. The perspectives given in the prompt are meant to provide additional context for the issue. Your response does not need to be in alignment with any of them. However, you can use them to help build your argument or simply react to them directly within your argument.

The following are excellent guidelines for your essay:

- **It should be completely focused on responding to the Key Question.** You may include ideas or facts that aren't mentioned in the prompt as long as they have a bearing on the decision-making process. Any information that isn't germane to the argument should be left out.
- **It should come across as an organic whole.** In other words, even though it is only two pages long, the separate components should work together so that the essay strikes the reader as a well-organized and consistent piece of writing that flows logically. It should have a distinct opening, a main body, and a clear conclusion.

- **It must be a strong argument, backed up with facts and sound reasoning.** You want to state your case persuasively, and to do so, you need to bolster your argument with solid logic and clear statements.
- **It should incorporate the characteristics of good writing.** As we pointed out earlier, your essay doesn't need to be a masterpiece, but it should be well written. That means it should hold the reader's interest. You should use proper grammar and spelling, of course. You should also try to demonstrate a great command of vocabulary, while making sure not to misuse any words in an effort to impress. It's also important to use a variety of sentence structures. An essay with mostly long sentences is boring and hard to follow, while one with mostly short sentences is jarring and unpleasant.

Argumentative Writing: Your Action Plan

PREWRITING

Carpenters have a saying that can help you craft a great argumentative essay—measure twice, cut once. The meaning is that measuring only once often leads to having to make two cuts, wasting time and possibly material. In other words, it's better to play it safe by measuring twice, even though doing so takes longer than doing the bare minimum. This adage is a pithy expression of the critical importance of taking enough time to properly prepare for a task. Of course, unlike carpenters, who can start over with another piece of wood if they make a mistake, you won't get a second chance, so it's even more imperative to take some time to plan your essay before you start writing it.

Start by reading the debatable issue and the associated perspectives all the way through, taking your time and not rushing. Then do it again. Use the digital scratch paper provided to make a note of things that will be important for you to incorporate into the essay. You should really concentrate on the different perspectives given to guide you in your choice, as these will be the key points you need to cover in your essay.

While it's important not to rush the planning of your essay, you should decide as quickly as possible the perspective(s) you wish to address. It may be that you're able to decide which direction to go immediately after your first reading of the issue and perspectives. If so, you're off to a great start. If you're still having trouble making a choice even after your second reading, there's no need to panic, because there is an easy way to make your decision, which we'll get to in a moment.

Whether or not you've made a clear choice as to which argument you wish to make, it's time to make a couple of lists. On your digital scratch paper, make a separate heading for each choice. Under each heading, quickly list all the pro and cons you can think of regarding that option, based on the given perspectives. Don't spend too much time thinking about this step. It isn't complicated; most of the pros and cons should be pretty clear from your reading. If you've already made your choice, then once you have your lists of pros and cons for each perspective, you can begin the writing process. If you haven't yet been able to make your decision, now is the time to set course and pick the direction you want to go.

How? It's very simple—when you have finished making your lists, one is likely to have more pros than cons. If so, make that the one you argue in favor of. If all options are close to being equal, then you can just choose one at random and stick with it. The point is to write about the one you think it would be easier to make a case for. If they're relatively equal, then that becomes a moot point, because you should be able to make a good case for either of them. We can't stress enough that **there is no right answer**, and it's important to keep that in mind. It will be very easy to get distracted and make the all-too-common mistake of trying to determine the "correct" perspective. Don't let it happen to you. Any perspective is fine; it's how you make your case that counts.

While you may move on to writing your essay after 5 minutes of prewriting, you will still only get 35 minutes to write. It is best to use as much of the prewriting time as you can to organize your writing and enable you to just get into it when the essay part begins.

Once you've chosen the argument you wish to make, it is time to begin prewriting. You should have a plan for the type of notes or outline that works best for you. Common prewriting formats include:

- **Cluster or concept map**—This is a main topic or word with a set of words that branch off and additional branches off of those words to group ideas.
- **Structural outline**—This is typically a bulleted or indented list of the flow of ideas that the essay will follow.
- **Questions and answers**—This is identifying pertinent questions and writing simple answers in short sentences or lists. (This is a good way to make use of the prewriting questions provided on the exam.)

WRITING

The clock will be ticking, and you will need to create two pages' worth of solid reasoning and writing in a very short time. This will be a real challenge, but there's no reason you can't accomplish it, especially if you've built a solid foundation by going through the planning steps outlined above. It will take between 400 and 600 words to fill two pages. This is not a lot of words; it adds up to about 4–6 short paragraphs. The challenge for most people will be the quality of their writing, not the quantity.

SOME COMMON MISTAKES TO AVOID

While writing your essay, you should assume that you're writing for a person who is familiar with the prompt you're writing about. There's no need to begin by rehashing the scenario, or outlining the main facts or questions. Doing so would not only be redundant, but might also be viewed as attempting to pad your essay with nonessential material. There's absolutely no need to restate the problem, and doing so can only weaken your essay. (Of course, when you're giving reasons for your argument, feel free to refer back to the topic and the given perspectives to support or contrast your reasoning. That isn't padding your essay with fluff; it's giving proof to back up your argument.)

Another thing to avoid is the generic open, which is a commonly used method of padding a written piece. Don't begin your essay by stating obvious facts that have only a tenuous connection to the prompt and do nothing to advance your argument. Here are some examples of a generic open:

- "In today's economy, it's critical that companies promote the best candidate…"
- "Taking care of the elderly is expensive, and the aging of the Baby Boomers means…"
- "Choosing which college to attend is one of the most important decisions a person…"

Along these same lines, do not write about how difficult it is to argue for a given perspective because each would make a good choice, has strengths and weaknesses, etc. As the prompts are written to provide a framework around a given issue, this would only be stating an obvious fact that does nothing to help persuade the reader that your view is the correct one.

Do not be informal. The tone of your writing should be semi-formal. It does not need to be as formal as a doctoral dissertation, but neither should it read like something you wrote to a friend. Also,

The Argumentative Writing Essay

write your essay in the third person. *I* and *you* are two words that should never appear in an LSAT Argumentative Writing essay.

THE OPENING

For many people taking the LSAT, coming up with the opening is the most difficult part of writing a good essay. It's easy to waste a lot of time trying to think of a good opening, and time is precious on the LSAT. Each minute you spend thinking about this is one less minute you will have for the actual writing, so you need to be ready to start writing as soon as the prewriting portion is finished.

The format of the prompt makes this easy to do, fortunately. Your essay should essentially be a piece that argues for a particular view, offering support for it and adequately addressing counterpoints in a reasonable manner. Because you are so constrained in the way you should handle the subject matter, there is much less room for error when it comes to stylistic choices. There is no need to attempt to be creative or open with some elegant rhetoric. Instead, you should simply get right to the point and state your argument.

At first glance, this suggestion that there is one ideal way to begin your essay may sound limiting. It *is* limiting—deliberately so. However, limitations are not always negative, and they can prevent a lot of bad things from happening. Many of the law school hopefuls sitting for the LSAT will turn in a poor essay because they spent far too much time trying to decide how to get started. Indecision is a luxury that a person cannot afford on the LSAT. That's why it's best to decide right now that you're going to begin your essay by declaring your argument. That's also the opening style that is best suited to the format of the Argumentative Writing, which makes the decision even easier.

There are several effective ways of phrasing your opening, but it will always be some version of *This is the best response to the Key Question, and here is the broad reason why.* (The body of your essay will flesh out the why.)

THE BODY: SUPPORTING YOUR ARGUMENT

After a brief opening in which you declare your main argument, you will move into the heart of your essay, which will consist of the reasoning behind your argument. In other words, you'll be backing up the claim you made in your opening with actual evidence. You will do this by contrasting given perspectives, demonstrating how the strengths of your argument outweigh others' strengths, and showing how others' weaknesses outweigh the weaknesses of your argument. This will be somewhat subjective, of course, because that is the point of this essay.

You will have more leeway in writing the body of your essay than you did in writing the opening. There are several ways you can effectively structure your argument, and none of them is necessarily better than the others. No matter which structure you choose, you will be ready to start writing immediately because of the planning you did in the prewriting stage. Now you will take those ideas and expand on them. You may introduce elements that aren't mentioned in the prompt, as long as they are common knowledge. You could use the fact that gas prices are of growing concern, for example, if that were germane. However, extraneous information should always take a back seat to the given criteria.

One good approach is to thoroughly cover all the strengths and weaknesses of opposing viewpoints, followed by an examination of the strengths and weaknesses of your argument. If you decide to use this structure, it's best to start with the opposing views and end with your perspective, as this makes for a stronger essay.

Another variation is to begin by comparing the weaknesses of several perspectives along with your own, and then going on to compare their strengths. You should end with the strengths for the same reason you should end with your viewpoint in the previous structure—it makes for a stronger essay.

Any of these structures will work well, and there are other ways of organizing your argument. Whichever format you choose, it is best to decide on the structure you will use before sitting down for the actual test. Otherwise, there is a high likelihood that your essay will come off as disorganized and ineffectual. Plus, it will be one less thing you have to think about during the LSAT. You cannot afford to waste any time trying to decide how to format your argument, so make sure you know which one you will use before you walk into the testing center, and stick with it.

THE CONCLUSION

Your essay will only be 400–600 words long, which doesn't leave a lot to work with when it comes to writing a conclusion. This is not really much of a problem, though, because the format of the Argumentative Writing doesn't require a particularly strong conclusion. Unlike a thesis or a research paper, this essay is essentially nothing but one long conclusion. You begin by saying *This is the best response to the Key Question, and here is the broad reason why.* You then go on to flesh out the why in the body of your essay. After that, having a powerful conclusion set off from the rest of the essay would be difficult to pull off. Even if you could make it work, it would be redundant. All you really need is an effective way to end the essay. Something along the lines of *These are the reasons my argument is the best response to the Key Question* will be just fine. The last thing you want to do is simply repeat what you've just said in the body of your essay.

Remember, your essay should consist of 4–6 paragraphs, and you should spend 25–30 minutes drafting it.

> **Review Video: Drafting Conclusions**
> Visit mometrix.com/academy and enter code: 209408

REVIEWING AND EDITING

Once you've finished writing your essay, you should have about 5–10 minutes left. Use that time to proofread it and correct any errors that you find. Misspelled words are common, but they are hardly the only thing to be concerned about. Other errors to look for are vague or mismatched pronouns, dangling modifiers, lack of subject/verb agreement, wrong verb tense, etc. Do your best to find and correct all errors, while keeping an eye on the clock. You do not want to be in the middle of making a correction when the time limit is reached.

> **Review Video: Revising and Editing**
> Visit mometrix.com/academy and enter code: 674181

LSAT Practice Test #1

Want to take this practice test in an online interactive format?
Check out the bonus page, which includes interactive practice questions and much more: **mometrix.com/bonus948/lsat**

Section I: Logical Reasoning

Time – 35 minutes

25 Questions

Directions: The questions in this section are based on the reasoning given in brief statements or passages. Some questions may have more than one answer that is true or correct. However, you are to choose the **best answer**—that is, you must choose the response that most accurately and completely answers the question. You should not make assumptions that are by commonsense standards implausible, superfluous, or incompatible with the passage.

1. **Nutritionist: Obesity is becoming a very serious problem in this country, and we must actively pursue a means of combating it. I have recently conducted a 12-week weight loss study to see which is the best method for obese adults to lose weight. My study shows that the consumption of a healthy, balanced diet and the incorporation of exercise were highly successful. All patients who participated in my study lost weight by eating the recommended diet and by adding a little exercise each day.**

   Which of the following statements, if true, most seriously undermines the statement above?
   (A) The nutritionist's income is subsidized by a government agency committed to encouraging people to lose weight by adding daily exercise.
   (B) All of the patients had a very similar physical makeup and metabolic rate, two significant factors that affect the ability to lose weight.
   (C) The nutritionist has been unable to come to an agreement with a colleague on what constitutes a healthy diet.
   (D) All of the nutritionist's patients incorporated exactly the same form of exercise to their daily routine.
   (E) There were only 80 patients who participated in the nutritionist's weight loss study.

2. **A company specializing in the sales of industrial flooring has been hit hard by the recent economic downturn. Mike has worked for this company for 15 years and now holds a senior sales position. In recent years, his sales record has been stellar, but over the last few months, his sales have been low due to the slowdown. His boss has asked to meet with him next week. Mike is convinced that the company will not fire him: "I've been working with the company for well over a decade, and I have an excellent sales record. If anyone can find a way to boost sales and benefit the company, I'm the person. Therefore, I have no doubt that my job is safe."**

   The flaw in Mike's reasoning is that he:
   (A) Believes that his loyalty to the company will guarantee that he keeps his job
   (B) Does not realize that the company is already bankrupt and has to lay off many employees
   (C) Equates his past success at the company with future opportunity, regardless of the economic conditions
   (D) Is a close friend of his boss and knows that his boss would not risk firing a friend
   (E) Assumes that the company cannot find a better salesperson and so will keep him on despite the recent downturn

Questions 3 and 4

The vast majority of extant music from the medieval period is recorded on manuscripts. The production of medieval manuscripts was very costly because all manuscripts were painstakingly copied by hand onto an expensive form of parchment. As a result, few people were able to produce or own them, and the Catholic Church, which had literate scribes as well as considerable wealth, produced and maintained most manuscripts during the Middle Ages. Any medieval music not recorded on manuscripts has now been lost to history. Most of the medieval music still in existence is sacred music.

3. **The claims made in the above passage, if true, best support which of the following statements?**
   (A) The greatest music of the medieval period was sacred music, and for this reason, it was recorded on manuscripts.
   (B) Because the Church did not value popular music, the scribes were not allowed to copy it onto manuscripts.
   (C) As the Catholic Church was the center of medieval life, popular music paralleled sacred music very closely.
   (D) In addition to the Church, many wealthy aristocratic households held large numbers of music manuscripts.
   (E) Because the Church primarily recorded sacred music on manuscripts, historians are unable to confidently describe medieval popular music.

4. **The passage above implies all of the following EXCEPT:**
   (A) The parchment on which medieval music was copied was difficult to produce.
   (B) Few were qualified for the time-consuming task of copying manuscripts.
   (C) The Church was selective about what music was copied down.
   (D) The copying of manuscripts was limited to people who knew how to read.
   (E) Most of the non-sacred music from the medieval period has been lost to history.

5. **Lito: The island of Kauai features a number of one-lane bridges that are potentially very dangerous. Kauai has recently seen a rise in the number of tourists visiting the island, and most tourists are not familiar with navigating the one-lane bridges. Over the last year, the number of car accidents has increased, and most of these accidents have occurred at the one-lane bridges. These bridges need to be widened to accommodate tourists and prevent future accidents.**

   Miteki: Kauai has a traditional commitment to environmental integrity. The one-lane bridges were installed to minimize the impact on the island environment. To widen the one-lane bridges could have a dangerous effect on the native plant and animal life.

   As a response to Lito's argument, Miteki's comment is flawed because she:
   (A) Relies on faulty information to support her argument
   (B) Uses circular reasoning to make her main points
   (C) Focuses on a minor issue instead of a more important one
   (D) Responds to a supporting point instead of a main point
   (E) Fails to address the substance of Lito's claim by making a secondary argument

6. **Art scholar Herbert Read has asserted that Impressionist artist Pierre-Auguste Renoir was the final painter representing the artistic tradition that started at Rubens and ended at Watteau. Peter Paul Rubens, the Flemish artist who flourished in the 17th century, is renowned for his creative choice of subject matter, from landscapes to allegory. Antoine Watteau, the French-born painter who died in the early 18th century, is generally remembered for his ability to interweave themes from Italian theatre into his paintings. During the late 19th century in which he thrived, the French artist Renoir was particularly renowned for his application of light and shading, his use of vibrant color, and his ability to create an intimate scene.**

   Which of the following best summarizes the main conclusion of the passage above?
   (A) Like Rubens and Watteau, Renoir selected subject matter that was creative and theatrical.
   (B) Read believes that Rubens, Watteau, and Renoir are among the greatest painters in Western history.
   (C) Read believes that apart from Renoir, no great artist of note has arisen since the early 18th century.
   (D) Relative to other painters of Renoir's era and later ones, Renoir best carried on the tradition of individual style that defined earlier artists.
   (E) The painters who had the greatest impact between the 17th and late 19th centuries were either Flemish or French.

7. **School principal: Recent testing indicates that students in our school are struggling in math. At this time, the students are spending only 45 minutes each day on math lessons. However, the testing also indicates that students are excelling in reading. The students currently spend 90 minutes each day on reading. Therefore, we need to increase the amount of time spent on math in order to improve the math skills of students in our school.**

The weakness in the school principal's argument is similar to the weakness in which of the following arguments?

(A) Family psychologists have found that the children with the best speech development are those whose parents read to them at an early age, which ensures that they are exposed to more formal grammar than may be present in everyday conversation. Therefore, all parents should read to their young children in order to enhance their speech development skills.

(B) Travel agents routinely see that families who have the most relaxing vacations are those who stay in three- or four-star resorts. Therefore, any family hoping to have a relaxing vacation should restrict accommodation choices to three- and four-star resorts.

(C) Research has shown that traders who put their money in options tend to be more likely to suffer from losing trades. Research also suggests that traders who put their money in stocks, which require a larger investment up front, tend to be more successful. Therefore, traders should put their money into stocks if they hope to have winning trades.

(D) Studies suggest that students who attend advanced placement classes in high school are better-prepared for the rigors of college than students who do not attend advanced placement classes. Therefore, students who hope to be the most successful in college should strive to be accepted into advanced placement classes.

(E) Caitlyn and Moira discovered that Caitlyn was spending a little more than Moira at the grocery story each month. However, Moira usually stopped at the grocery store several times each week, while Caitlyn never shopped more than once a week. Therefore, Caitlyn and Moira are actually spending the same amount because Moira must pay the extra cost of gas for several trips to the store.

75

8. The CEO of a major fast-food chain just released a statement indicating that the chain has revamped its ingredient list and revised its menu options so that all selections on the menu are now healthier than any of the menu items from competing fast-food chains. Among the changes that will be made, the fast-food chain will be eliminating unsaturated fats and downsizing portions. He claims, "We've heard the request of our customers for healthier meals, and with the changes we're making, we'll be offering our customers better choices. Our customers will now have healthy fast-food options that put all other fast-food chains to shame."

   Which of the following, if true, most seriously undermines the CEO's claim of offering healthier selections to customers?
   (A) While the fast-food chain is improving certain ingredients, the menu items still include additives that tend to make customers addicted to the fast food.
   (B) The CEO is receiving a large bonus for the potential boost in sales that the new menu options are expected to bring.
   (C) A focus group unanimously complained that the food was bland and not as tasty as items on the previous menu.
   (D) The fast-food chain has begun marketing heavily to children, encouraging children to ask for the healthier options when ordering in a restaurant.
   (E) The fast-food chain has not removed many of its previous menu items but has instead simply replaced the unhealthy ingredients with healthier options and reduced the portion sizes.

9. Head of a regional psychiatric association: As an organization, we have found that patients over the last two decades are increasingly likely to suffer from depression, which can lead to an early death in some cases. At the same time, we have found that those patients who already practice some form of spirituality tend to be less likely to suffer from depression and thus live longer and healthier lives. A recent study in a major psychological journal confirms this experience. As a result, we suggest that our members begin encouraging their patients to explore spirituality in the hopes that it will provide them with longer and healthier lives.

   The primary argument made by the head of the regional psychiatric association depends on which of the following assumptions?
   (A) All of the patients being treated by psychiatrists in the regional psychiatric association are suffering from depression.
   (B) All patients noted for their longer and healthier lives were practicing the same form of spirituality.
   (C) All members of the psychiatric association must also pursue spirituality in order to make educated recommendations to their patients.
   (D) When untreated, depression is a serious condition that always leads to death.
   (E) All forms of spirituality are equally healthy, and any form of spirituality will provide patients with longer and healthier lives.

10. Economists have noted in recent weeks that the price per barrel of crude oil has decreased sharply over the last few months, dropping as much as 70 percent. They have also found, however, that the price of gasoline at the pump has not seen a similarly sharp reduction, and gasoline prices have dropped only about 50 percent.

Given the statements above, which of the following most helps to explain the difference between the drop in the price of crude oil per barrel and the drop in the price of gasoline at the pump?

(A) The demand for crude oil worldwide has suddenly decreased; this has led to a drop in the price of crude oil.

(B) While crude oil prices were high, refineries that processed crude oil into gasoline absorbed a large part of the cost; these refineries are now recovering some profit by not yet passing the decreased price in crude oil to customers at the pump.

(C) Oil companies have recently discovered a large and previously untapped oil reserve; this discovery immediately sent crude oil prices plummeting.

(D) A major wind energy company unexpectedly announced plans to provide a large-scale alternative energy option to citizens in several nations; this created a competition for crude oil that negatively affected its price.

(E) Due to the decreasing cost of crude oil, the cost of production now exceeds the return in value; this has forced some oil production companies to go out of business.

11. It is generally assumed that, although some restrictions exist on the freedom of speech or expression—restrictions that usually forbid any speech or expression that might be described as hateful or dangerous—no restrictions do or can exist on freedom of thought or conscience. In fact, the Universal Declaration of Human Rights guarantees that all people have the right to the freedom of thought, the freedom of conscience, and the freedom of religion. However, although thought cannot successfully be controlled through laws, it can be controlled through propaganda or even through an educational system: If children are taught from an early age to think or believe a certain way, it might not be possible for them to have real freedom of thought or conscience as adults, as they may have no real ability to think for themselves.

Which of the following best summarizes the argument implied within the passage?

(A) Freedom of thought or conscience cannot really exist, despite international laws that guarantee it.

(B) Freedom of thought or conscience is controlled in the same way as freedom of speech or expression.

(C) In some cases, thought might be controlled to such an extent that genuine freedom of thought does not exist.

(D) The Universal Declaration of Human Rights is necessary for the guarantee of freedom of thought or conscience.

(E) Restrictions on freedom of speech or expression should be eliminated in order to guarantee real freedom of thought.

12. **Conrad: The town of Ecoville is a leader in the green movement and is establishing excellent standards for all citizens, standards that will make the town one of the greenest in the country. By the year 2030, all residents in the town of Ecoville will be required to drive vehicles that adhere to certain environmental standards, such as standards regarding reduced emissions and better gas mileage. These new standards will improve the air quality and environmental health of Ecoville.**

    Eloise: The new environmental standards for vehicles in Ecoville are good, but they should be delayed or revised until funding for the standards can be established. As currently planned, the standards will place undue burden on lower-income families, many of whom do not have the extra income to meet the requirements. Even the greenest town will have lower-income residents, and these residents might not have the means to buy new vehicles or convert current vehicles to adhere to the standards.

    Eloise counters Conrad's argument by doing which of the following?
    (A) She acknowledges the reasonableness of his argument but presents a counterargument that shows the difficulty of implementing the new requirements.
    (B) She agrees with the substance of his conclusion but suggests alternative reasons for that conclusion.
    (C) She points out a flaw in his reasoning and offers a different perspective that is more logical.
    (D) She disagrees with his argument entirely by proving that the established standards will accomplish very little.
    (E) She overlooks the substance of his argument and redirects the attention to a secondary point.

13. **The largest public health organization in the country has raised concerns about the herbal sweetener stevia, claiming that it has conducted extensive testing and that, in its opinion, the dangers of stevia outweigh its potential benefits. The organization claims that people who consume stevia are at risk for cancer or other life-threatening health problems. As a result, the public health organization has recommended that the FDA recognize the dangers of stevia and ban it for human consumption.**

    Which of the following, if true, most seriously undermines the public health organization's claim that stevia is dangerous?
    (A) The head of the largest artificial sweetener manufacturer in the country has financed the studies exploring the health dangers of stevia.
    (B) It is common knowledge that stevia is widely used in Japan, and no negative side effects have been reported there.
    (C) The head of the public health organization is currently on the short list for a senior position in the FDA.
    (D) A large national diabetes association has publicly supported stevia as a safe sugar alternative for diabetics.
    (E) No tests conducted by the public health organization indicate that stevia has ever caused cancer or any other health problems in human beings.

14. The primary hospital in the town of Riverton has been criticized for declining to accept patients who do not have insurance or who have insufficient insurance to cover their medical care at the hospital. Responding to the criticism, the mayor of Riverton has denounced the hospital for discrimination and demanded that the policy be revised. The mayor has also encouraged the city council to pass an ordinance requiring hospitals to accept all patients, regardless of insurance coverage. The city council has declined, however, arguing that as a private business, the hospital has the right to refuse customers who are unable to pay for hospital services.

Which of the following assumptions can be inferred from the city council's argument that the hospital has a right to decline treatment to patients?

(A) The majority of residents in the town of Riverton have sufficient insurance coverage, so there will be very few patients who are refused service.

(B) The city council believes that anti-discrimination laws do not cover a hospital refusing service to patients who are unable to pay for their medical services.

(C) The uninsured and insufficiently insured patients will be covered by state and federal funding, so the hospital will ultimately not need to turn patients away.

(D) There is a large hospital in a town very near to Riverton that accepts all patients regardless of their insurance coverage.

(E) The mayor is a member of a different political party than most members of the city council, so they tend to oppose him on every recommendation he makes.

15. Scientific journal: Recent testing was conducted to examine the health benefits of drinking milk and what effect it has on calcium levels in women over the age of 40. The test was conducted on 200 women in similar states of health over the course of three months. The women were asked to drink two eight-ounce glasses of milk each day. All participants followed this stipulation closely. Results show that 75 percent of the women showed a mild increase in calcium levels, whereas 25 percent of the women showed a sharp improvement in calcium levels.

Which of the following, if true, most explains the inconsistency among study participants in their testing results?

(A) Twenty-five percent of the women drank whole milk each day, whereas the other 75 percent chose to drink low-fat milk.

(B) Seventy-five percent of the women had previously been treated for a vitamin D deficiency and thus did not absorb as much of the calcium from the milk.

(C) Seventy-five percent of the women were over the age of 50, whereas the other 25 percent were under the age of 50.

(D) Twenty-five percent of the women began taking a multivitamin with added calcium in addition to drinking two eight-ounce glasses of milk each day.

(E) Seventy-five percent of the women had given birth, while the other 25 percent had never had children.

16. Traditional regional performing arts groups across the country provide an important service to small communities. Most of these groups focus on the performance of time-honored material and offer people within the communities an opportunity to experience excellent traditional performances without having to travel far. Unfortunately, federal funding tends to support *avant-garde* groups whose focus is largely on progressive material. Although these groups are unquestionably an essential facet of the performing arts, they do not generally draw as wide of audiences and thus are receiving an undue amount of federal funding for the service that they provide to a community and the return on the federal investment. Those responsible for providing federal grants to performing arts groups should reconsider the allotment of funding in order to favor traditional performing arts groups with respect to their service to a community.

The argument in the passage above proceeds by:

(A) Presenting a general statement, developing it with details, and suggesting an action to be taken
(B) Demanding attention for a cause, citing potential dangers for ignoring it, and insisting upon change
(C) Undermining the opposition, calling previous activity into question, and drawing a conclusion
(D) Beginning with a call to action, pointing out problems with those who oppose it, and concluding with a general remark
(E) Publicizing a concern, discussing possible alternatives to address it, and encouraging action

17. Editorial within local Williamsburg newspaper: Here in Williamsburg, we have an amazing educational opportunity in the form of the extraordinary colonial project that takes visitors back in time to the early days of American history. It has come to my attention that very few local schools take students on field trips there, and I believe that students are missing out on this opportunity. All local schools should be required to take the students to the colonial center, and funding should be provided to make this recommendation a reality. A visit to this wonderful place will benefit all school children and will offer them an experience they will cherish for years.

Which of the following, if true, most seriously undermines the argument made in the editorial?

(A) Williamsburg schools focus heavily on field trips with hands-on activity, and the colonial center in Williamsburg provides such opportunities for students.
(B) The writer of the editorial is the head of the marketing department at the colonial center and has been charged with increasing student traffic there.
(C) Local schools have polled the families of students, and it has been found that 99% of students have already visited the colonial center with their families.
(D) The colonial center at Williamsburg already offers significant discounts to school groups, and the city has little money to provide additional funding.
(E) Gasoline prices have risen sharply in the last few months, causing schools to cut back on field trips and focus on projects that can be completed in the classroom.

18. A large airport in a major city has proposed certain changes intended to improve the ease of flying for domestic passengers. However, these changes will have the negative effect of creating burdens for travelers flying internationally. A number of travelers who frequent the airport for international flights have signed a petition requesting that the airport alter the proposed plans. The airport considered the petition carefully but has decided to proceed with the original plans, despite the fact that many of the travelers who use the airport for international travel have announced that they will begin booking their flights through a different airport.

Which of the following can be inferred from the decision made by the airport to continue with the changes?

(A) The nearest airport that offers international flights is too far for many of the travelers to switch.

(B) Other airports offering international flights are just as burdensome for travelers.

(C) The airport has already spent a large sum on the proposed plans, and it is not cost-effective to give them up.

(D) The benefits from the changes for domestic travelers will bring in enough new domestic passengers to outweigh the loss of the international travelers.

(E) Although the changes will negatively affect international travelers in the short term, the airport has a long-term plan to improve international travel.

19. Conservative voter: Universal healthcare is a very controversial issue in our country that conservative voters have traditionally opposed because of the cost to the taxpayer. Conservative voters should support universal healthcare, however, because under such a healthcare system, the government would actually spend fewer tax dollars than at present. In other countries with universal healthcare, the governments spend less tax money per patient than our government currently spends for a healthcare system that is not universal.

A weakness in this argument lies in the fact that the voter:

(A) Gives an inconsistent definition of universal healthcare

(B) Assumes that universalizing is the only way to reduce the cost per person

(C) Makes unfounded claims in order to establish a conclusion

(D) Deviates from a partisan position to make a policy recommendation

(E) Couches an *ad hominem* (or personal) insult in constructive criticism

20. Language development specialists have discovered that most children learn languages best before puberty. During the years leading up to puberty, children's brains are capable of absorbing new languages with less effort than the brains of children who are post-pubescent. As a result, pre-pubescent children are able to think in a new language far more quickly than their post-pubescent counterparts, and children prior to puberty are also able to retain those languages more easily than if they learn the languages after puberty. Funding is limited for second-language programs, so schools in this country tend to delay the study of modern languages until high school, but young children would benefit from second-language programs in the elementary years.

Which of the following best summarizes the main point of the passage?

(A) Children learn languages best before puberty because their brains absorb new languages more easily than the brains of those who are post-pubescent.

(B) There is currently not enough government funding to provide second-language programs at the elementary level.

(C) Because of a difference in brain development, children before puberty can learn to think in a new language more quickly than children after puberty.

(D) It is a mistake to delay the teaching of second languages until high school, as there is little chance that students will be able to retain a second language.

(E) Because children learn languages more easily before puberty, schools should adopt second-language programs at the elementary level.

Questions 21 and 22

The village of Eyam in central England is often referred to as the "plague village." In the summer of 1665, an outbreak of the plague was discovered in the village, and the people of the village cut off all outside contacts to avoid infecting others, letting the disease run its course internally. For almost a year and a half, the plague touched families throughout Eyam, and when villagers finally reopened the village to outsiders, over 75 percent of the population had died. More interesting, however, was the fact that nearly 25 percent of the population was still living. In some cases, the plague carried off all but one member of a family: Elizabeth Hancock is remembered for having lost her husband and six children, but she never contracted the plague, even while nursing them. Hancock's story is not unique; most of the survivors proved to be immune to the infection altogether. Some researchers have found that a large proportion of the descendants of plague survivors from Eyam carry a mutation of a gene known as delta 32.

21. **Which of the following conclusions can best be inferred from the information in the passage?**

(A) The delta 32 mutation was limited to residents of the village of Eyam and now appears only in their descendants.

(B) The current population of the village of Eyam displays a disproportionately high rate of the delta 32 mutation.

(C) Since the descendants of many of the plague survivors carry the delta 32 mutation, some researchers believe this gene helped people resist contracting the plague.

(D) The plague survivors from the village of Eyam developed the delta 32 mutation in response to the outbreak of plague and are thus immune to future outbreaks.

(E) The people of the village of Eyam were wrong to isolate themselves during the outbreak of the plague because it guaranteed death for so many residents.

22. **Which of the following, if true, most undermines the implications made by the passage?**

(A) In laboratory studies with rats, other researchers have discovered that the delta 32 mutation does not contribute to resisting contraction of the plague.

(B) The delta 32 gene has been found in people throughout Europe, as well as in America in people of European ancestry.

(C) Some researchers believe that the delta 32 gene also protects individuals against the contraction of HIV.

(D) During the 17th century, it was believed that vinegar stopped the spread of plague by killing off the disease.

(E) The plague that struck Eyam (in Derbyshire) also struck London around the same time.

23. **When first presented on the market, the now-ubiquitous microwave oven was anything but a hit with consumers. Percy Spencer, an employee with Raytheon who discovered the potential for cooking with microwaves, first presented the Radarange in 1947, a massive oven that weighed over 700 pounds and was around six feet tall. Over the next few years, Raytheon made some minor improvements to the microwave oven but was unable to elicit a positive reception from the public. It was not until Raytheon's competitor, Litton, began developing microwave ovens of its own in the 1960s that the public embraced the new technology on a wide scale. Litton's new oven jumpstarted the craze for microwaves, and by 1975, about a million of them were in American homes.**

Which of the following, if true, best provides an explanation for why Litton was more successful at selling microwave ovens in the United States than Raytheon?

(A) Litton marketed the microwave oven at a large trade show in Chicago, thereby gaining more consumers through publicity.

(B) Litton expanded its marketing to Japan, where the microwave ovens proved to be very popular.

(C) Litton made the microwave so popular that more than 90 percent of families in the US now have a microwave.

(D) Litton's model redesigned the microwave oven to its now-familiar compact size so that it was affordable and fit easily into a kitchen.

(E) Litton had long been developing the technology for microwave ovens and had surpassed the technology used by Raytheon.

24. The English scientist Edward Jenner (1749–1823) is usually credited with the discovery of vaccines in the late 18th century when he began vaccinating against cowpox (hence the term "vaccine," which derives from *vacca*, meaning cow). But at least 100 years before Jenner's discovery, the Ottoman Turks were already using methods of inoculation to prevent disease. Lady Montagu, wife of the British ambassador to Turkey during the early 18th century, records that she had her son vaccinated in Istanbul using a method that the Turkish had been employing for decades. The Ottoman Turks, however, were not the first to use vaccines. It is believed that the Chinese had discovered the value of inoculation as far back as 200 BC, and one scholar has suggested that vaccination as a common means of disease prevention might have been widespread in India as early as the 11th century.

Which of the following best summarizes the main point of the passage?

(A) Edward Jenner is mistakenly credited with the discovery of vaccines because Lady Montagu inoculated her son in Istanbul in the early 18th century.

(B) Although Edward Jenner is usually credited with the discovery of vaccines in the late 18th century, research indicates that vaccines were used in the East long before Jenner began using them.

(C) Historians believe that doctors in China and India were using vaccines as early as the 11th century and maybe even as far back as 200 BC.

(D) The Ottoman Turks are wrongly credited for the discovery of vaccines in the early 18th century, as vaccines were used in China and India long before this.

(E) Edward Jenner took credit in the late 18th century for the discovery of a vaccine that Lady Montagu used prior to this to inoculate her son in Turkey.

25. Economist: In a weak economy when the stock market is struggling, the US dollar traditionally falls, and the price of gold rises in response to the declining dollar. Recent economic data indicates that the markets are currently struggling: The key stock indexes are lower than they have been in at least two years, and various market sectors are in decline. At the same time, the value of the dollar is still high, and the price of gold remains low. Therefore, the price of gold suggests that we are due for a market turnaround soon.

Given the information above, the economist's argument is flawed because:

(A) She relies entirely on traditional data without adequately considering anomalies in the market's movement.

(B) She bases her commentary on stock indexes, which are traditionally unreliable for determining market direction.

(C) The price of gold is currently fixed at the government level, so it is impossible to rely on that as an indicator of market direction.

(D) She should be focusing more closely on the movement of certain market sectors instead of the price of gold.

(E) She fails to take other significant market indicators into account and thus comes to a conclusion too quickly about the market's movement.

Section II: Reading Comprehension

Time – 35 minutes

25 Questions

Directions: Each passage in this section is followed by a group of questions to be answered on the basis of what is **stated or implied** in the passage. Some questions may have more than one answer that is true or correct. However, you are to choose the **best answer**; that is, you must choose the response that most accurately and completely answers the question.

Passage 1

Russian novelist Fyodor Dostoyevsky made his mark in literature with his explorations of the human psyche intertwined with difficult moral dilemmas. His novels continue to resonate profoundly with readers and writers, and they have set a foundation that later writers have often found themselves measured against. Dostoyevsky's writing is a mixture of moral conflict, existential despair, and a quest for redemption. His narrative style offers a stark view into the souls of his characters, exhibiting rich psychological depth. The dense psychological dialogues within his novels are fraught with spiritual angst and provide a vivid exploration of concepts such as the search for faith, the nature of evil, and free will.

Dostoyevsky's writing contains a mixture of Christian themes and moral incongruity, and he frequently gives his readers a glimpse into his characters' souls. The philosophical dialogues are full of spiritual agonies, and his novels frequently explore freedom, penury, suffering, and nihilistic sentiments. His narratives often walk a fine line between redemption and despair, forcing readers to experience the tumultuous inner conflicts that drive his characters. In this complex tapestry, Dostoyevsky masterfully weaves existential questions with stark social critiques, reflecting the turbulent era he lived in as well as the timeless human condition.

Dostoyevsky profoundly influenced modern literature with his approach to character and moral dilemmas. His characters are deeply flawed, introspective individuals, not merely protagonists or antagonists. His nuanced character development laid the groundwork for much of the morally ambiguous character development seen in modern literature. His narrative style, often delving far into the psychological realm, has paved the way for the introspective style used by contemporary writers. Dostoyevsky's characters' moral and existential dilemmas are devoid of easy answers or moral preaching, and this has set a precedent for the complicated and unresolved moral problems that appear in modern literature. This intricate portrayal of inner conflict and moral ambiguity invites readers to engage in deep introspection, a hallmark of Dostoyevsky's enduring influence on literature. Such literature includes the works of many celebrated writers, including Leo Tolstoy, Franz Kafka, and Albert Camus.

Leo Tolstoy, a contemporary of Dostoyevsky, approached spirituality and morality through a more structured, almost didactic lens. Dostoyevsky, however, presented these themes in a more introspective, turbulent manner. His characters grappled with existential dilemmas, while Tolstoy's characters found moral certainty. Later writers, including Franz Kafka, seemed to follow Dostoyevsky in his more existential exploration. However, while Kafka's writing included elements of the surreal and existential, his stories were grounded in the real world. Albert Camus also explored absurdism and existential nihilism as a thematic continuation of Dostoyevsky's literary journeys.

1. **The primary purpose of this passage is most likely to do which of the following?**

   (A) Describe Dostoyevsky's themes in writing.
   (B) Explain Dostoyevsky's character development.
   (C) Contrast Dostoyevsky's writing with contemporary authors.
   (D) Highlight Dostoyevsky's impact on literature.
   (E) Relate Dostoyevsky's narrative style.

2. **Which modern character would be reminiscent of a character in a Dostoyevsky novel?**

   (A) Dmitri, a social media influencer, who navigates personal fame where appearance, branding, and connections dominate.
   (B) Pavel, a salesman, who focuses on a proactive stance on societal issues and engagement with the world around him.
   (C) Viktor, a cybersecurity expert, who questions the constant battle between the greater good and personal gain.
   (D) Svetlana, a corporate lawyer, who has a pragmatic outlook and focuses on external achievements.
   (E) Olga, a tech entrepreneur, who is driven by clear ethical values and a commitment to positive change.

3. **The comparison of Dostoyevsky to the authors Tolstoy, Kafka, and Camus is intended to do all of the following EXCEPT:**

   (A) To provide contextual contrast
   (B) To showcase Dostoyevsky's influence
   (C) To describe them as imitators of his style
   (D) To illustrate the evolution of literary themes
   (E) To highlight Dostoyevsky's timeless relevance

4. **Which of these choices best describes this passage?**

   (A) Chronological and biographical
   (B) Narrative and descriptive
   (C) Expository and analytical
   (D) Argumentative and persuasive
   (E) Thematic and comparative

5. **This passage supports the inference that prior to Dostoyevsky's time:**

   (A) Literature may not have delved as deeply into the human psyche.
   (B) Writers may not have written about complex characters in their novels.
   (C) Authors may not have been influenced by their contemporaries.
   (D) Narrative styles may not have been very diverse in nature.
   (E) Characters may not have faced dilemmas in literature.

6. **Which of the following is the most likely reason the author mentions faith and Christian themes in the passage?**

   (A) To relate Dostoyevsky's relationship with religion
   (B) To describe how subsequent authors handle Christian themes in their work
   (C) To contrast Dostoyevsky's style with that of modern writers
   (D) To depict the complexity of his characters' internal conflicts
   (E) To illustrate the author's understanding of Dostoyevsky's breadth of thematic approach

7. **Based on the passage, which is the best meaning for the term** *existential*?

    (A) Having faith in a quest for spirituality and meaning beyond the physical realm

    (B) Believing that free will determines the course of a person's life

    (C) Focusing on the biological aspects of human survival

    (D) Concerning the societal structures and social norms of human interaction

    (E) Relating to an individual's subjective experience of being

LSAT Practice Test #1

Passage 2

From the humble beginnings of the first few plants in the 1950s to the over 400 plants around the world in the 2020s, nuclear power plants have been a reliable way to produce emission-free electricity. At the outset, the primary focus of nuclear research was on developing the atomic bomb for defense, but soon after, the focus of harnessing nuclear power became producing electricity. The path to the many benefits from this power source has had some setbacks, but scientists and engineers have learned and adapted to them along the way.

Beginning in the 1930s, experimentation confirmed that nuclear fission releases an abundance of energy. This led to the development of the nuclear bomb, which used fission to create an uncontrolled nuclear chain reaction, releasing an incredible amount of energy from a relatively small amount of matter. Next, research led to the practical development of nuclear power via more controlled chain reactions. In the 1950s, the first nuclear power plant started generating electricity in the US. By the 1980s, new and more powerful nuclear reactors were being developed at an increasing rate. However, the push for plants has not been without incident.

One of the first major accidents was the partial meltdown of the Unit 2 reactor of the Three Mile Island plant in 1979 in Pennsylvania in the United States. Another was in 1986 when containment failed on the fourth reactor of the Chernobyl power plant in what was, at the time, part of the Soviet Union. This is still considered the worst nuclear disaster in history, and as a response to the incident, a major reduction in the number of nuclear reactors occurred until a renaissance of nuclear energy in the 2000s. In 2011, another nuclear reactor accident occurred in Fukushima, Japan, due to the failure of the emergency cooling system and subsequent meltdown of three reactor cores. Although each of these accidents caused significant damage, subsequent improvements to safety systems and new reactor designs have greatly improved the overall safety of producing nuclear power to the point where only solar power is safer.

Currently, nuclear power yields an array of potential benefits, including the recycling of spent fuel, minimal downtime, low emissions, and low costs. Now regarded as a sustainable energy source, it can decrease the dependency on other sources of energy, including fossil fuels. Due to technological advances, over 90 percent of the spent fuel from generating nuclear power can be recycled to prolong the production of electricity, and commercial nuclear waste is stored in a highly fortified location until the radiation is no longer dangerous. Nuclear plants are not prone to downtime and can operate around the clock. The carbon-free nature of nuclear energy production reduces excess carbon in the atmosphere. It can combat climate change, and proponents claim that nuclear energy should be used in conjunction with renewable energy sources to replace the use of fossil fuels. Nuclear fuel costs are relatively low compared to other sources of energy, and while the construction of nuclear reactors has a high up-front cost, this cost can be distributed throughout a long operating span of time, making nuclear power cost-effective.

Despite some safety and cost concerns, nuclear power holds great advantages for countries transitioning to clean energy. It is clean, reliable, affordable, and safe, and an increase in reliance on nuclear power will benefit future generations. As technology continues to advance, nuclear power can play an important role in the 21st century and beyond.

8. **Which of the following best characterizes the author's attitude toward nuclear energy?**

   (A) Issues with nuclear energy should cause careful consideration before moving forward with its use.
   (B) Risks of using nuclear energy should cause citizens to be wary of the building of new power plants.
   (C) Nuclear energy should be used in conjunction with fossil fuels and other sources of energy.
   (D) There are many benefits to reap from the use of nuclear energy, and its use should be increased.
   (E) Once the safety issues with nuclear energy are addressed, countries should consider building more nuclear power plants.

9. **Which of the following would help the reader develop a more informed opinion about nuclear energy?**

   (A) A detailed description of the advantages of nuclear power over fossil fuels
   (B) An unbiased, in-depth rundown of the drawbacks of using nuclear power
   (C) A retelling from a reliable source of the issues that caused the Chernobyl disaster
   (D) An assessment of the benefits of using nuclear power rather than solar power
   (E) A quantifiable summarization of nuclear energy's potential carbon benefits

10. **Which of the following best describes reasons that nuclear energy might be cautioned against?**

    (A) Carbon output, safety, and cost efficiency
    (B) Nuclear fission research, carbon output, and safety
    (C) Safety, cost efficiency, and frequency of building new nuclear plants
    (D) Safety, cost efficiency, and concerns with nuclear waste
    (E) Potential for nuclear chain reactions, safety, and concerns with nuclear waste

11. **What does the word *renaissance* mean in the context of this passage?**

    (A) An increase in focus on the creation of artwork and sculpture
    (B) A renewed interest in building nuclear power plants
    (C) A decline in the number of power plants built in a time period
    (D) A decision to reconsider the potential of nuclear energy
    (E) A reliance on newer ways to supply energy

12. **Which of the following best describes the author's treatment of the topic of nuclear power plant disasters in the passage?**

    (A) The author describes the disasters in detail, warning of potential future disasters.
    (B) The author relays the gravity of the disasters and cautions against the building of new plants.
    (C) The author discloses the issues that led to the disasters and expresses a preference for ending the use of nuclear power.
    (D) The author specifies the rarity of these disasters occurring but explains that the occurrence of disasters will likely increase.
    (E) The author mentions the disasters but is dismissive of future safety concerns.

Passage 3

Characterized by large-scale, flat fields of solid color covering a canvas, the color field painting movement emerged in the 1940s in New York City. At a glance, color field painting can appear overly simplistic, and some might even dismiss it as undeserving of a place in museums. Artwork can be admired for its surface beauty without awareness of its place within the art world. However, recognition of the movement's role among other art movements and insight into the minds of those creating the artwork can yield a greater understanding and appreciation of it.

A subset of abstract expressionism, color field painting eschewed subject matter and instead focused on both color relationships and people's optical responses to them. The term originated from an art critic's description of work produced by artists such as Mark Rothko, Clyfford Still, and Barnett Newman. The critic used this term to differentiate the new style from abstract expressionist artwork. Art historian Alfred Barr had originated the term "abstract expressionism" in the late 1920s to describe the work of Wassily Kandinsky, a Russian-born painter who is credited as a pioneer of abstract art. Kandinsky embraced the organic forms of Art Nouveau and the bright colors of Fauvism in his artwork, seeking to express emotions through colors, shapes, and the interplay of figure and ground.

Action painting, another subset of abstract expressionism and a contemporary movement to color field painting, placed more importance on the action to create the artwork than on the end result. While abstract expressionists separated themselves from any need to portray objects in their artwork, focusing on expressing emotions through the artwork's aesthetics instead, action painters took it one step further by exploring the role the subconscious has in creating art. Rather than evoking emotions, action painters sought to connect with the viewer's subconscious, and their techniques were inspired by the automatism of surrealist artists.

Color field painting emphasized the flatness of the canvas, creating tension through the interaction of large fields of color on a flat surface. These paintings were meant to be viewed up close so that the colors on the large canvases would seem to extend beyond the viewer's field of vision, engulfing the viewer in color. Any shapes used generally avoided a sense of creating an image versus a background. Exploring new ways of using color and paint, color field painters emphasized the potential of analyzing color relationships. Barnett Newman stated, "The purpose of art is to awaken something in the observer." He sought to transform the viewer's perception of art and evoke emotions through his use of color. Rather than expressing ideas through subject matter, Newman and other color field painters tried to convey spirituality and transcendence to the viewer through their artworks. A second wave of abstract expressionism followed in the 1960s, with artists trying out new ideas that stemmed, but also departed, from the abstract expressionist movement. Artists like Helen Frankenthaler used thinned paint to stain raw canvases, merging the motion of action painting and color techniques of color field painting.

13. Which of these options best describes the author's purpose for writing this passage?

    (A) To persuade the reader that color field painting is superior to abstract expressionism

    (B) To compare the motivations of color field painting with those of the action painting movement

    (C) To explain the significance of abstract expressionism by giving examples of subsets of the movement

    (D) To inform the reader about the background of color field painting and its place in art history

    (E) To contrast abstract expressionism with art movements that followed it

14. Which of these options best characterizes the timeline of art movements in relation to color field painting?

(A) Abstract expressionism and action painting preceded color field painting, and Fauvism occurred after color field painting.

(B) Abstract expressionism and Fauvism preceded color field painting, and action painting occurred at the same time as color field painting.

(C) Color field painting and action painting occurred as subsets of abstract expressionism, and Fauvism and Art Nouveau occurred before these.

(D) Color field painting and action painting occurred after the first and second waves of abstract expressionism.

(E) Fauvism and Art Nouveau occurred before action painting, and both abstract expressionism and color field painting followed them.

15. Which of the following best distinguishes action painting from color field painting?

(A) While action painters prioritized movement, color field painters sought to fill the viewer's field of vision with color.

(B) While action painters approached art in an entirely new way, color field painters were heavily influenced by Fauvism and Art Nouveau.

(C) While action painters tried to connect with the viewer's subconscious, color field painters experimented with various subject matter in their art.

(D) While action painters created artwork that was void of emotions, color field painters tried to provoke the viewer's emotions through the use of color.

(E) While action painters worked with representational subject matter, color field painters focused on color instead of subject matter.

16. Which of these options best describes what the word *eschewed* means in the passage?

(A) Included a large quantity

(B) Deliberately avoided doing something

(C) Transitioned from one period of art to another

(D) Focused on including particular subject matter

(E) Understood the significance of

17. Which of these options best describes the organizational pattern of this passage?

(A) Problem and solution

(B) Compare and contrast

(C) Claim and counterclaim

(D) Chronological

(E) Cause and effect

Passage 4A

The genetic modification of crops has caused increasing debate since its first use. Some people have expressed concerns about the safety of including modified produce in our food supply. Genetically modified organisms, or GMOs, are living organisms that have had their genetic code altered. This technique can be applied to any living organism, including plants, animals, and microbes. Despite this, the term is most commonly associated with crops and produce. Certain crops, such as soybeans and corn, are predominantly available now as GMOs. GMOs are currently used in agricultural practices to increase crop yield, improve resistance to pests, and even enhance nutritional content.

GMOs are engineered to enhance the factors that increase the productivity of a plant, including resistance to pests and droughts. Crops with a higher yield are then used to address food security concerns. When the better production rates of these genetically modified crops are leveraged, progress can be made toward alleviating hunger and malnutrition. Crops with an improved resistance to pests and diseases are less likely to undergo devastating losses. GMO practices can even insert proteins that are toxic to specific pests into plant genes. This modification not only reduces the need for farmers to use chemical pesticides but also saves money and time. Staple crops can also be enriched to increase their nutritional profile to address nutritional deficiencies.

Despite concerns about the safety of these practices, advances in genetic engineering of crops are being used to address agricultural challenges. They are subject to strict safety standards set by several organizations, including the US Food and Drug Administration (FDA). GMO food producers are compelled to label them as genetically modified or containing genetically modified ingredients. The continued use of GMOs can pave the way for increasingly sustainable and resilient agriculture.

Passage 4B

The controversial practice of modifying crops through genetic engineering began in the mid-1990s. Critics have expressed concerns over risks to human health, socioeconomic equity, and the integrity of the environment. Opponents of the use of GMOs argue that the uncertainties surrounding this genetic modification outweigh their benefits and the continuance of GMO practices should proceed with caution.

Genetically modifying organisms changes them in ways that would not happen otherwise. To perform these modifications, scientists sometimes insert genes from one organism into the DNA of a different type of organism. Critics have expressed concerns that this genetically engineered DNA could spread to other, non-modified organisms.

Those wary of GMOs warn of potential adverse health effects despite rigorous safety standards. Genetic modifications have the potential to transfer toxins or allergens into food, and concerns have been raised over long-term consumption leading to health problems. There is also concern over the transfer of antibiotic-resistant genes into the human digestive tract from GMO foods, so the use of antibiotic-resistant genes is limited.

The use of GMOs favors larger agribusiness organizations rather than small-scale farmers since the proprietary GMO seeds fetch a higher price, and those who cannot afford to plant them are forced to spray larger amounts of pesticides. The intellectual rights surrounding GMO seeds prevents farmers from saving seeds from their crops, necessitating the purchase of new seeds each growing season. The cultivation of these GMO crops can lead to unintended environmental consequences, such as "superbugs" and "superweeds"—insects and weeds that are resistant to pesticides and herbicides.

This can then cause the overuse of sprays, resulting in environmental pollution and harm to other organisms.

18. **Which of the following best characterizes the difference in tone between the two passages?**
    (A) Passage A is informational and neutral, while Passage B is critical and cautionary.
    (B) Passage A is enthusiastic and intense, while Passage B is dismissive and scornful.
    (C) Passage A is optimistic and nostalgic, while Passage B is persuasive and sarcastic.
    (D) Passage A is sympathetic and sincere, while Passage B is anxious and urgent.
    (E) Passage A is colloquial and candid, while Passage B is argumentative and defensive.

19. **Which of the following best characterizes the difference between the main ideas of these passages?**
    (A) Passage A shares the concerns raised about GMO crops, while Passage B focuses on the inequities between large farms and small-scale farmers due to GMO use.
    (B) Passage A relays the nutritional advantages of GMO use, while Passage B criticizes the environmental consequences of using GMOs.
    (C) Passage A focuses on the potential that GMO crops have for benefiting society, while Passage B presents a critical view on GMOs, emphasizing the risks and consequences.
    (D) Passage A describes the financial benefits of GMO use for farmers, while Passage B explains the issues raised by intellectual rights and GMOs.
    (E) Passage A emphasizes the availability of certain crops as GMO produce, while Passage B warns of the consumption of these GMO crops.

20. **Which of the following statements is best supported by both passages?**
    (A) Although GMO crops bring numerous advantages for society, some still see them as a potential danger.
    (B) Since GMOs are so pervasive in our food supply, it is important to focus on the positive effects of their use.
    (C) Because GMOs pose several concerns for safety, we should pause their use while investigating their safety further.
    (D) Despite the high safety standards that GMO crops are subjected to, their inclusion within our food supply still causes some concern.
    (E) Though GMOs have been proven to be effective against certain pests, their high cost is likely not justifiable.

21. **The authors of passages 1 and 2 would most likely disagree over which of the following?**
    (A) Whether GMO practices are beneficial to owners of large farms
    (B) Whether GMO foods should be used to address nutritional deficiencies
    (C) Whether the term "GMO" is most frequently associated with crops or animals
    (D) Whether any criticism or concerns exist about GMO practices
    (E) Whether any farmers have used GMOs to their advantage

22. **Which of these statements is supported by one or both of the passages?**
    (A) Most GMOs found in stores are meat and fish.
    (B) Genetic modification mainly uses antibiotic-resistant genes.
    (C) GMOs level the playing field among different sizes of farming practices.
    (D) The use of GMOs is a positive addition to our food practices.
    (E) Genetic modification eliminates the need to use pesticides on crops.

93

LSAT Practice Test #1

23. Which aspect of GMOs seems positive in Passage A but not in Passage B?

(A) Benefits to small-scale farmers
(B) Reduced susceptibility to pests
(C) Intellectual rights
(D) Reduction of greenhouse gas emissions
(E) Increased nutritional quality of food

24. How would the author of Passage A likely respond to the comment in Passage B about the potential adverse health effects of consuming GMOs?

(A) GMOs have been found to affect a person's health negatively, so pausing their use is sensible.
(B) GMOs are subjected to strict safety standards, and the benefits far outweigh any risks.
(C) Since GMOs are so widely used at this time, it is a good idea to find safer options.
(D) Adverse health effects are a reasonable tradeoff for the possibility of addressing food security.
(E) Anyone concerned about the adverse effects of GMOs should be able to easily avoid them.

25. According to both passages, which of the following is a drawback of GMOs?

(A) The costs associated with farming GMO crops
(B) The potential implications for human health
(C) The possibility of creating "superbugs"
(D) The introduction of toxins into the food supply
(E) The use of antibiotic-resistant genes in GMOs

Section III: Reading Comprehension

Time – 35 minutes

27 Questions

Directions: Each passage in this section is followed by a group of questions to be answered on the basis of what is **stated or implied** in the passage. Some questions may have more than one answer that is true or correct. However, you are to choose the **best answer**; that is, you must choose the response that most accurately and completely answers the question.

Passage 1

Until the early part of the 20th century, Federalist No. 10, James Madison's essay on the issue of dealing with factions in a society that seeks to be unified, received very
5 little attention. First published in November of 1787, No. 10 has generally been overshadowed by the more famous No. 51, No. 78, and No. 84, all of which are considered to be highly influential statements about the
10 requirements for establishing a republic that survives and operates successfully. Within the last few decades, however, scholars have given No. 10 more consideration as they apply Madison's arguments to a society now
15 clearly divided by political parties and various individual interests. That being said, No. 10 was just as relevant in its own time, as there was no shortage of partisanship and individual interests. The difference seems to
20 lie in the fact that the partisanship of late 18th-century American politics has long since disappeared and is no longer relevant for the modern reader.

Written in a joint effort by James
25 Madison, Alexander Hamilton, and John Jay (later the first chief justice of the Supreme Court), the 85 Federalist Papers were composed as a rebuttal to the Anti-Federalists. This group, which included such
30 statesmen as Patrick Henry and George Clinton, opposed the ratification of the Constitution out of fear that a strong central government would strip the states of their rights and that a president would ultimately
35 become a monarch. One of the primary arguments of the Anti-Federalists was that a nation formed by states as large and diverse

as the American states could never truly be united. Arguing under the pseudonym "Cato,"
40 the Anti-Federalists claimed that a nation of states as diverse as the American states could never unite fully without requiring that the states compromise sovereign rights for the benefit of the central government; they
45 argued that the "unkindred legislature" recommended by the Constitution would lead to the biblical example of the house collapsing because it had been divided against itself. In essence, the Anti-Federalists believed that
50 factions would always exist and that it would be impossible to forge a union without forcing uninterested factions together in an uncomfortable state of existence. To some extent, the fears of the Anti-Federalists were
55 proven justified: in 1789, the Constitution was ratified (with the inclusion of the Bill of Rights, which Madison suggested as a means of compromise between Federalists and Anti-Federalists), and the Anti-Federalists more or
60 less ceased to exist, its members left with little choice but to accept the system that had been adopted.

With the silencing of the Anti-Federalist faction and the enthusiasm of unity
65 surrounding the ratification of the Constitution, Madison's arguments in Federalist No. 10 seemed to lose their relevance in the latter days of the 18th century. According to historian Douglass
70 Adair, it was his fellow historian Charles Beard who turned scholarly attention on No. 10 by his interpretation of the Constitution as a tool used to exploit the lower classes, an interpretation given at a time when Marxist

95

75 theories were increasingly in vogue and such interpretations were gaining credibility in academia. For his part, Adair chose to see No. 10 as a document that was exclusive in application and in relevance to the time of its 80 composition. However, other historians have recognized the significance of Madison's thesis in Federalist No. 10 for the modern age, especially with regard to his arguments about the need to quell factions for the good of 85 societal unification, and it is now considered to be far more relevant to this era than to its own. What historians have failed to appreciate is that No. 10 has a continuing relevance by speaking to an issue that has 90 always been, and will probably always be, a part of any functioning political system. In this, perhaps, the Anti-Federalists have the last word.

1. **The passage can be described as doing which of the following?**

   (A) Contrasting two viewpoints and then arguing in favor of one of them
   (B) Defending a traditional argument by supporting it with scholarly sources
   (C) Offering a new perspective on an ongoing scholarly argument
   (D) Defining a term and presenting a thesis in defense of it
   (E) Considering a popular academic position and challenging it with new evidence

2. **Which of the following best expresses the author's main point?**

   (A) Federalist No. 10 discusses a political reality that the Anti-Federalists understood and that is not limited by era.
   (B) Federalist No. 10 has been ignored for too long and deserves more attention by scholars.
   (C) Federalist No. 10 had virtually no relevance when it was written and has acquired relevance in recent decades only.
   (D) The Federalists did not appreciate the reality that factions are, and always have been, inevitable.
   (E) The Anti-Federalists were ultimately correct in their understanding of human nature within a political system.

3. **Which of the following can be inferred from the statement by Douglass Adair that Federalist No. 10 was a "document that was exclusive in application and in relevance to the time of its composition"?**

   (A) Adair believed that all of the Federalist Papers applied only to the 18th century and the problems of that age.
   (B) Adair disagreed with Charles Beard about the Federalist Papers as instruments of class exploitation.
   (C) Adair agreed with the Anti-Federalists about the inevitability of factions within 18th-century politics.
   (D) Adair believed that Federalist No. 10 might have contemporary relevance if the current political situation developed problems similar to those in the 18th century.
   (E) Adair did not believe that Federalist No. 10 could be applied directly to the current political conditions.

4. **The passage above suggests which of the following?**

   (A) The Federalist Papers were an essential contribution to America's understanding of the Constitution and its purpose.

   (B) Although the Federalists won the primary argument for the Constitution, the Anti-Federalists were ultimately correct in their belief that the country could not be fully united.

   (C) More 18th-century Americans should have paid attention to the Anti-Federalists because silencing them after the ratification of the Constitution had long-term consequences for free speech.

   (D) It is a great irony of 18th-century America that the ratification of the Constitution, a document committed to establishing freedoms, actually succeeded by quelling the opposition.

   (E) Modern historians are correct in their belief that Federalist No. 10 is a significant contribution to the Federalist Papers, though not as important as some of the others.

5. **The passage implies that the author would agree with which of the following?**

   (A) Federalist No. 51, No. 78, and No. 84 remain the three most important essays of the Federalist Papers.

   (B) The Marxist theories touted by Charles Beard failed to interpret the Federalist Papers accurately or effectively.

   (C) The Anti-Federalists were forced to be quiet about some of their ideas after the ratification of the Constitution.

   (D) Douglass Adair's argument that Federalist No. 10 is primarily of 18th-century relevance is intentionally misleading.

   (E) The Anti-Federalists had a more realistic appreciation of social and political challenges than the Federalists did.

6. **Which of the following best expresses the meaning of the word *unkindred*, as used by "Cato" in line 45 of the passage?**

   (A) Diverse
   (B) Disorganized
   (C) Disparate
   (D) Unique
   (E) Antagonistic

7. **Which of the following best describes the organization of the passage?**

   (A) The author presents several theories, narrows the focus to one, and then defends a primary argument.

   (B) The author suggests a main point, diverts to discuss historical context, and then returns to the main point to summarize.

   (C) The author begins with a wide historical focus and ultimately narrows to a contemporary focus.

   (D) The author states a thesis, defends it with historical research and quotes from leading scholarly authorities, and then restates the thesis.

   (E) The author presents an idea, offers historical context, and then argues a main point.

LSAT Practice Test #1

Passage 2

English language scholars generally agree that the modern English language developed from several sources: the Anglo-Saxon language, or Old English, spoken by the
5   Germanic peoples who migrated to the island of Britain in the 5th century; the Old Norse influences of the Vikings and the Danish kings of England in the 9th and 10th centuries; the French influence of the Norman invaders
10   in the 11th century; and the Latin influences of the earlier Roman inhabitants and the Catholic Church. However, one mystery remains. When the Anglo-Saxons arrived in Britain, there were numerous Celtic
15   inhabitants dwelling alongside what remained of the Roman population. Why, then, did the Anglo-Saxons, and thus the English, not absorb *more* of the Celtic languages? The English language ultimately
20   adopted very few Celtic words, so few, in fact, that scholars are at a loss to explain the reason with any certainty. One thing is certain: the Celtic languages are in no way related to Anglo-Saxon, and indeed developed
25   from an entirely different family of languages. So, what happened? Some scholars have suggested that the Anglo-Saxons already had enough words of their own and thus did not need to borrow from the Celts, even upon
30   arriving in a new place. For instance, if the day-to-day elements of life in Britain were similar enough to those in the Anglo-Saxon homeland, the Anglo-Saxons would not feel the need to make use of foreign words to
35   describe their new life. This theory, however, is inconsistent with evidence that the Anglo-Saxons borrowed everyday words from other languages, such as Old Norse and French. Other scholars have suggested the theory that
40   the Anglo-Saxons chose to avoid the Celtic words because the Celts were essentially a conquered people—an explanation that is strongly supported by the rapid disappearance of Celts from south and central
45   England and their subsequent movement north and west into what would become Cornwall, Wales, and Scotland.

Leading linguistic scholar David Crystal disagrees with this latter hypothesis,
50   however. He points out that among the Anglo-Saxons, it was not uncommon to find children with Welsh names. The great Christian poet Cædmon and Cædwalla, the king of Wessex in the 7th century, were both noteworthy
55   and highly respected Anglo-Saxons who bore Welsh names. From a purely practical perspective, it is unlikely that Anglo-Saxon parents would bestow Celtic names on their children if those names were closely
60   associated with a despised language or a group of people deemed inferior. As a modern example, during World War I, people in England began changing their names to avoid sounding too Germanic. Even the royal family,
65   up to that point bearing the name Saxe-Coburg-Gotha, changed the family name to Windsor due to the long connection of that name with a specifically English history. Additionally, the respected Battenberg family
70   in England, closely connected to the monarchy, felt the need to change their name to Mountbatten, as it had a less decidedly German connotation.

Perhaps more significantly, David Crystal
75   raises the possibility that the word *cross*, steeped in important religious meaning for many English speakers, came from a Celtic background. In Latin, the word is *crux*, and the Scandinavians rendered it *kross*. But there
80   is, on the whole, very little linguistic influence on early English religious terminology from the Germanic languages or the Germanic peoples, who were decidedly pagan upon their arrival to England. On the other hand,
85   the Irish Celts were enthusiastic and thorough in their missionary efforts to England and other parts of Europe, and they rendered the Latin *crux* as *cros* in Old Irish and as *croes* in Welsh. It is highly possible
90   that the English word *cross* and the Old Norse word *kross* were influenced by the Irish missionary work. It is unlikely that the mystery of the missing Celtic words will ever be solved satisfactorily, but what little

95 evidence remains suggests that the mystery can no longer be written off as a case of a

conquered people becoming linguistically obsolete.

8. **Which of the following best states the main idea of the passage?**

(A) Although linguistic scholars do not know why the English language has so few Celtic words, it can no longer be assumed that the Anglo-Saxons avoided Celtic words in the belief that the Celts were inferior.

(B) The possible Celtic derivation of the word *cross* suggests that the Anglo-Saxons interacted more closely with the Celts than was previously thought.

(C) New evidence suggests that the traditional belief about the Anglo-Saxon, Old Norse, French, and Latin influences on the English language is erroneous and misleading.

(D) The actions taken by the English during World War I indicate strongly that their forebears eradicated Celtic words for similar reasons.

(E) The appearance of Welsh names among significant Anglo-Saxon figures indicates that of all the Celtic peoples, the Welsh had the greatest linguistic impact on Anglo-Saxon daily life.

9. **The use of the word *connotation* in line 73 most closely suggests which of the following?**

(A) Clear relationship

(B) Linguistic origin

(C) Theoretical definition

(D) Potential association

(E) Emotional correlation

10. **The discussion of the word *cross* in the passage is intended to show which of the following?**

(A) Although they were previously ignored by scholars, it is clear that many important Celtic words were indeed absorbed into the English language.

(B) Scholars now realize that many Celtic words influenced Old Norse words and not the other way around.

(C) It is incorrect to assume that there was a very great influence on the English language from Celtic words.

(D) Linguistic scholar David Crystal believes that Celtic words make up an important part of the English language.

(E) The significance of the few Celtic words within the English language suggests a more important influence than was previously thought.

11. **The author provides examples of English behavior toward German last names during World War I in order to do which of the following?**

(A) Prove definitely that human nature does not change

(B) Undermine the theory of the Welsh influence on English names

(C) Use a fairly recent event to provide context for a hypothesis

(D) Show that the English changed names because they considered Germans inferior

(E) Suggest that many of the so-called "English" names are really German

LSAT Practice Test #1

12. Which of the following best describes the author's attitude toward the theory that there are few Celtic words in the English language because the Anglo-Saxons viewed the Celts as inferior?

(A) Self-righteous insistence
(B) Scholarly disagreement
(C) Patronizing disapproval
(D) Justifiable concern
(E) Vitriolic dissent

13. The primary purpose of the passage is to do which of the following?

(A) Caution against making a historical judgment without considering further linguistic evidence
(B) Introduce a new theory and support it with linguistic evidence
(C) Defend a scholarly position by citing leading authorities in the field
(D) Dispute a long-held scholarly position by disproving the linguistic evidence in support of it
(E) Compare several theories and argue in support of one of them

14. The passage suggests that the author would probably agree with which one of the following?

(A) There is less Latin and Old Norse influence on the English language than there is Celtic influence.
(B) Although there seem to be few Celtic words within the English language, these words suggest a significant linguistic role.
(C) The possible Celtic derivation of the English word *cross* is enough all by itself to suggest that the English viewed the Celts favorably.
(D) The Anglo-Saxons did not adopt many Celtic words because they had enough everyday words in their own language.
(E) Because some of the Anglo-Saxons gave their children Welsh names, the Anglo-Saxon people unquestionably had a high opinion of the Celts.

Passage 3

The question of beauty has captivated and frustrated artists, writers, and scholars for centuries. What defines beauty, and who can justifiably be described as beautiful? Is there
5 a universal "look" that is beautiful in contrast to one that is not? History and literature are replete with descriptions of women who are said to be the "most beautiful." Greek myth claimed that Helen of Troy was the most
10 beautiful woman in the world, with a "face that launched a thousand ships" as well as a ten-year war between Greeks and Trojans. But there is no clear account of Helen's appearance, and even Hollywood has been
15 unable to agree on this issue, rendering Helen a variety of ways in different movie productions about the Trojan War. Today, scientists are beginning to consider the question of beauty and to devise tests that
20 attempt to quantify attractiveness. The goal is to see whether beauty is simply a subjective perception or if people in general tend to agree on who is beautiful and who is not. In some tests, participants from a variety of
25 cultural backgrounds are asked to compare different faces and to decide who is beautiful and who is not. In the majority of these tests, the participants agree in large percentages that the faces most likely to be considered
30 beautiful are in fact beautiful. Some scientists have even tested infants, showing them pictures of different faces. The tests indicate that the gaze of the infants tends to linger more on the beautiful faces rather than on the
35 faces not traditionally considered beautiful.

Other scientists have found that this potential for a universal appreciation of beauty leads to interesting consequences. As psychologist Nancy Etcoff notes, beauty can
40 affect belief in one's character. That is, beautiful people are often assumed to be better than unattractive people in terms of character or other traits. There is evidence that beautiful children are often scored
45 higher than unattractive or less beautiful children in classroom situations, apparently under the assumption that the beautiful

children *must* be doing well. Scientists are quick to note that this is not a conscious
50 decision on the instructor's part but is an unconscious response to the child's appearance. This effect is also commonly observed in the workplace. When applying for jobs, attractive applicants often receive
55 the desired employment, whether or not they are more qualified than a less attractive applicant. Political analysts also claim that the attractive candidate wins the election, regardless of his or her political platform.
60 Historians have found that during the Nixon and Kennedy debates of 1960, viewers tended to favor Kennedy in the video debates and Nixon in the radio debates, and it has been suggested that Kennedy's attractive and
65 youthful appearance gave him the edge.

Scientists claim that a certain combination of features is universally considered beautiful, but one element that has not been tested to any great extent is the
70 effect of personality on beauty. In the immediate sense, beauty might be associated with character, with beautiful people assumed to be morally or ethically better than others. But perhaps there is a reverse
75 relation to consider. That is, character might affect beauty, and not the other way around. Etcoff hints at the effect of character or personality in determining beauty: She records that upon meeting the writer George
80 Eliot, a woman who was generally considered to be very unattractive, her fellow writer Henry James was immediately struck by her ugly appearance; but in the course of talking with her for only a few minutes, he
85 discovered an inner beauty that completely altered his opinion of her outward appearance. It may be that although physical features are indeed important in determining beauty, beauty itself is not simply "skin deep"
90 and can be defined by more than an arrangement of eyes, nose, and lips. Scientists studying the phenomenon of beauty would do well to turn their attention to the more intangible qualities that define beauty and to

LSAT Practice Test #1

95 consider what lies beneath the skin in
addition to what lies on it.

15. Which of the following best summarizes the central idea of the passage?

(A) Despite society's claim that all are beautiful in their own way, scientific studies show that beauty is quantifiable and some faces are always considered beautiful.

(B) Scientists testing for beauty need to consider more than mere outward appearances to determine what makes a person beautiful.

(C) Beauty is related far more to personality and character than it is to outward appearances.

(D) Beauty is inevitable, and the beautiful will always find more success than those who are less attractive.

(E) Because beauty is subjective, scientists will never succeed in quantifying beauty, despite developing complex tests in an effort to do so.

16. It may be inferred from the passage that the author believes which of the following?

(A) After long ignoring beauty, scientists have finally recognized its importance and have begun to quantify beauty in objective tests.

(B) There is a specific combination of features that is considered beautiful across cultural boundaries.

(C) Beauty should never be associated with a person's character or personality because personality cannot determine outward appearance.

(D) Beauty is determined entirely by cultural standards, and what one culture perceives as beautiful, another might dismiss as unattractive.

(E) Personality might play a significant role in determining whether or not a person will be perceived as beautiful.

17. Which of the following best expresses the reasoning behind the author's main argument?

(A) Beauty is so subjective that much more testing is required to obtain any definitive results about what constitutes it.

(B) Infants can identify beauty because they recognize the qualities of a person's character as well as the features on a person's face.

(C) Given the mystery that sometimes surrounds perceptions of beauty, it is likely that beauty is determined by more than an arrangement of facial features.

(D) Beautiful people have received inappropriate privileges that have created long-term consequences in society.

(E) Because scientists have been able to quantify beauty, it is indeed possible to determine that certain physical features are beautiful.

18. The passage states that in classroom situations, teachers respond differently to attractive students than to unattractive students. This information is intended to do which of the following?

(A) Indicate that beauty sometimes plays a role in the perception of a person's character or qualities.

(B) Illustrate that society gives unnecessary privileges to the beautiful.

(C) Show that the personality or character of the schoolchildren affected their outward appearance.

(D) Suggest that youth is inevitably associated with beauty.

(E) Indicate that this is a phenomenon that appears around the world.

19. **The example of Henry James's meeting with George Eliot is intended to indicate which of the following points?**

(A) There might be intangible qualities that contribute to the perception of beauty.

(B) George Eliot would be considered beautiful today by scientific standards.

(C) It was possible to understand George Eliot's beauty only by interacting with her.

(D) Henry James abandoned his unnecessarily high standard of beauty after meeting George Eliot and coming to know her better.

(E) Standards of beauty are universal, so if George Eliot was considered unattractive then, she would be considered unattractive now.

20. **Which of the following phrases best replaces the use of the word *phenomenon* in describing beauty in line 92?**

(A) Unexpected reality

(B) Intriguing occurrence

(C) Remarkable quality

(D) Abstract experience

(E) Subjective analysis

21. **The passage states that beautiful people are often assumed to be of good character and receive privileges for their appearance. The author's tone toward this claim can best be described as which of the following?**

(A) Combative skepticism

(B) Mocking amusement

(C) Quiet resignation

(D) Informative interest

(E) Righteous anger

Passage 4A

Adam Smith's comments in *The Wealth of Nations* have stood the test of time. Smith claimed that a country should consider its available resources and manufacture those products that are cheapest for it to make at home. If that country finds that another nation can provide products more cheaply than it can make for itself, the country should engage in trade and purchase the products from the other country while applying its workforce to domestic manufacturing.

Roughly 90 percent of Americans support unrestricted free trade and do not oppose the idea of outsourcing by American businesses. Harvard economics professor Gregory Mankiw argues that the majority of economists also recognize the importance of free trade, believing that it improves economic growth as well as the standard of living around the world. In other words, free trade provides comparatively inexpensive products for Americans, which frees them to put more of their money into the economy while also providing jobs for people in countries with smaller, potentially weaker economies; this gives the workers better payment for their work than they might be able to earn with opportunities in their countries. Although some argue that the jobs provided for these workers are hardly up to the wage standards that most Americans would accept, it is important to note that the cost of living is considerably lower in many of these countries; so, the workers are better off with the jobs, even if their wages do not compare to those of workers in the United States. Mankiw also cautions against faulting the free movement of imports into the US during a time of economic weakness because imports are not necessarily to blame for economic weakness. It is not a question of the US importing too much but rather a question of the US exporting too little. The US has traditionally manufactured enough goods to balance its roster of imports, but in recent years has focused more on consumption than on production. Adam Smith argued that free trade allows a nation to import items that it could not manufacture cheaply, but as Mankiw suggests, this does not mean an importing nation should fail to manufacture altogether. A balance of imports and exports is required to maintain a stable economy, and an increase in manufacturing for exports during economic weakness can actually bolster a struggling economy.

Passage 4B

As most economists agree, free trade is a sound economic practice and necessary for the US to function effectively in a global economy, but unrestricted free trade is fraught with potential dangers that few economists seem willing to acknowledge or address. Leading economist Ha-Joon Chang expresses concerns about the disadvantages of free trade in less developed nations. In a global economic system that is constantly changing and evolving, many small businesses will be successful one day and gone the next. In large nations such as the US, there are welfare systems in place and a variety of loans available to support these business owners until they can reestablish their businesses or develop new ones; in smaller nations with weak or less developed economies, the governments cannot support welfare systems, and the workers who lose businesses have little recourse to help them get back on their feet. As a result, the old statement about the poor just getting poorer is often true when workers in smaller and weaker economies fail to withstand a decreased demand for the goods they produce. It is historically significant that the US was heavily protectionist until it became a world leader in the economy. In Sweden, economics professor Peter Soderbaum adds that the issue of free trade is usually discussed only at the level of commodity cost,

but this fails to consider other important issues for economies—issues that include
35 environmental concerns, cultural upheaval, the loss of traditional ways of life, and so forth. These issues incur significant costs on nations and their economies, and to ignore them is to disregard the factors that may
40 contribute to an economy's ability to sustain free trade for long periods of time, as well as the ability of workers to exist within that economy in a gradually improving way of life. As some economists now indicate, what is
45 needed is a new approach to free trade, along with the resources to quantify the cost-value ratio of free trade. This new approach would be an attempt to view free trade from a variety of angles, including angles not
50 traditionally viewed through economic lenses, thereby providing a "big picture" and thus a more accurate perspective.

22. **The authors of the two passages would likely agree on which of the following statements?**

(A) A global economy ensures the economic survival of smaller nations because it improves the quality of life among the workers.

(B) Free trade must contribute to the creation of stable jobs for an economy to survive during an economic downturn.

(C) Although free trade can create controversy at times, most economists agree that free trade is an important part of any economic system.

(D) Free trade runs the risk of damaging one economy while improving another and thus has as many negative qualities as positive qualities.

(E) Export rates in the US must increase if the US economy is to overcome its economic weakness and heavy dependence on imports.

23. **Which of the following best summarizes the main point of Passage A?**

(A) Adam Smith's economic theories about free trade, as described in *The Wealth of Nations*, were sound and remain applicable to contemporary economics.

(B) Free trade can cause economic weakness if a nation fails to generate enough exports in comparison to its imports.

(C) Economic weakness in the US is related to domestic concerns and does not relate to unrestricted free trade.

(D) Free trade is valuable to an economy and does not necessarily need to be restricted, but an economy needs to balance imports and exports.

(E) The outsourcing of US businesses has positive effects on economic growth in the US and is thus strongly supported by Americans.

24. **Which of the following best expresses the main point of Passage B?**

(A) Free trade is essential for any society that hopes to grow in a global economy.

(B) Economists fail to address the real problems with unrestricted free trade by focusing only on the price of commodities.

(C) Unrestricted free trade has the potential for causing serious problems for weaker economies when small businesses fail and they have no governmental support.

(D) A welfare system could provide a fallback opportunity for business owners in weaker and smaller economies by offering support until the business can be reestablished.

(E) Unrestricted free trade has too much potential for causing problems in some economies, so a new approach is needed to address peripheral effects of free trade.

105

25. **Which of the following best describes how Passage B responds to Passage A?**

(A) Passage B points out a logical flaw in the argument of Passage A.

(B) Passage B acknowledges a part of the argument in Passage A but then offers an alternative thesis.

(C) If the author's claims in Passage A are true, they negate the claims made in Passage B.

(D) The details about secondary problems detailed in Passage B undermine the definition of free trade as described in Passage A.

(E) The argument in Passage A proceeds under the assumption that the argument in Passage B is true.

26. **The use of the word *protectionist* in line 28 of Passage B is intended to indicate which of the following?**

(A) Protecting small businesses from unrestricted free trade

(B) Protecting free trade without any restrictions on imports or exports

(C) Protecting a domestic economy from encroaching globalism

(D) Protecting a domestic economy through government intervention

(E) Protecting small businesses through welfare programs and federal loans

27. **Passage B differs from Passage A in that the author's tone concerning the issue of free trade is more:**

(A) Sophisticated

(B) Speculative

(C) Cautious

(D) Debating

(E) Pragmatic

Section IV: Logical Reasoning

Time – 35 minutes

25 Questions

Directions: The questions in this section are based on the reasoning given in brief statements or passages. Some questions may have more than one answer that is true or correct. However, you are to choose the **best answer**—that is, you must choose the response that most accurately and completely answers the question. You should not make assumptions that are by commonsense standards implausible, superfluous, or incompatible with the passage.

1. **It is important to distinguish between criticism and opinion. The purpose of criticism is to direct a commentary on someone or something with the particular goal of change. A person who criticizes the behavior of another is specifically hoping to effect a modification. The purpose of opinion, on the other hand, is simply to offer a viewpoint that does not require a change. A person who shares an opinion is generally providing a perspective that is intended to help another in making a decision. As a result, *criticism* usually has a negative connotation, whereas *opinion* does not. More importantly, not everyone is necessarily entitled to *criticism*, but everyone should be entitled to *opinion*.**

    Considering the statements made in the passage above very carefully, which of the following may be inferred?

    (A) Criticism that is worded as opinion can be both appropriate and effective because it provides the pretense of opinion while still effecting a change.
    (B) Criticism and opinion are often confused with one another because some mistake a negative opinion for criticism.
    (C) Opinion is simply the phase of thought before one reaches criticism, so there is often not a clear distinction between the two.
    (D) Positive, or constructive, criticism is equivalent to opinion, so all are entitled to share constructive criticism.
    (E) The freedom of speech and of thought guarantees that all are allowed opinions, so government cannot and should not restrict the sharing of opinions.

LSAT Practice Test #1

2. **A large department store was looking for a new "face" to represent its brand, with certain clear requirements in mind based on the popularity of the previous representative: The new representative needed to be friendly and articulate, and she must possess a clean image. Several applicants were interested in the position, and one in particular campaigned heavily for the job, expressing to the company her view that she fit the requirements well. The company believed that this woman would be perfect for the job and hired her quickly, deciding that no market research was then required since she had all of the necessary qualifications. Within a few months, however, the company began pushing her aside in favor of the previous representative, who was rehired for her old job.**

   Based on the information in the passage, which of the following, if true, would best provide a reason for why the department store decided to push its new representative aside in favor of the old one?

   (A) The department store performed market research after hiring the new representative and found that she was unpopular among customers.
   (B) A tabloid hinted that the new representative had an unsavory past inconsistent with the clean image she presented to the company.
   (C) A competitor department store hired a new representative who was far more popular than the first department store's new representative.
   (D) Department store staff believed they had made a mistake with the new representative and decided to look for another one to replace her.
   (E) The new representative did not enjoy the position, so she began ignoring her responsibilities.

3. **A snowstorm in the city of Denver is expected to cause considerable delays for people going to work. All news outlets in the city warn that traffic will be very slow, and employers should expect their employees to be late. Therefore, all the employees at First Community Bank of Denver will be late to work.**

   The flawed reasoning in the passage above is similar to the flawed reasoning in which of the following statements?

   (A) Testing shows that food with MSG, or monosodium glutamate, is known to cause migraines in many people; therefore, everyone who eats food with MSG should expect to develop a migraine.
   (B) Theodore is two years older than Ferdinand; therefore, Theodore is taller than Ferdinand.
   (C) A major power outage in Chicago occurred in an area with 300,000 customers; therefore, the majority of these customers were without power.
   (D) Edward accidentally broke an antique vase that belonged to Nina's great-grandmother; therefore, Nina will be angry with Edward for breaking her great-grandmother's vase.
   (E) Lunchtime is served to students at Adams Elementary at noon every day; therefore, some students are hungry at noon.

4. **A major automobile manufacturer is planning to increase its production of vehicles due to an unexpected period of strength in the economy. The company CEO believes that now is the best time to add to the company's supply of vehicles, when the strength in the markets makes this decision economically feasible. At this time, many of the primary supplies needed to build the cars have artificially low prices, and the auto manufacturer hopes to produce the cars while the cost-value ratio is still low.**

   Based on the information contained within the passage, which of the following, if true, most supports the decision by the auto manufacturer?

   (A) The automobile manufacturer's stock is expected to rise within the next few months due to the economic strength.
   (B) A major producer of car batteries is expected to go out of business within six months, leaving few car battery suppliers for auto manufacturers.
   (C) A recent study indicates that the steel used by the auto manufacturer is expected to increase considerably in price over the next few months.
   (D) The auto manufacturer is planning to merge with another auto manufacturer that has a considerable number of surplus vehicles.
   (E) The cost of oil is expected to rise, a factor that will make consumers less likely to buy new cars.

5. **An IT company is planning to open a new office in the large industrial city of Nizhny Novgorod, Russia. The IT industry has, in recent years, become one of the most important industries in Nizhny Novgorod and provides the majority of high-paying jobs for residents. At the same time, the city is currently undergoing a minor economic downturn, and a number of its residents are out of work. Additionally, the IT industry has been struggling to remain strong in Nizhny Novgorod, and many of the original IT businesses, which have traditionally been the city's most successful businesses, are failing. The IT company that plans to open a new office, however, is confident it will be highly successful.**

   Given the passage above, which of the following, if true, would best explain the discrepancy between the current economic situation in Nizhny Novgorod and the IT company's confidence in its likely success?

   (A) The IT company, unlike most of the original IT companies, is at the cutting edge of the IT industry and can keep its costs low.
   (B) The IT company is acquiring the building of a failed IT company, so it will not have to spend funds to build a new office.
   (C) The IT company is expected to bring much-needed jobs to Nizhny Novgorod, and many residents are excited about the new office.
   (D) The IT company is not opening the new office within Nizhny Novgorod, instead locating the office where there is less industrial scenery.
   (E) The IT company has had to take out considerable loans for the construction and maintenance of the office building.

LSAT Practice Test #1

109

6. **Member of a local school board: All classrooms in our school district need computers. A recent poll indicates that our city is one of the few in the state that has not acquired computers for every classroom, and as a result, our schools are suffering. Our school district has actually seen a loss in student body due to parents relocating to other school districts. Adding up-to-date technology to classrooms would encourage parents to remain in our school district. More importantly, though, my research indicates that schools with computers in every classroom have the highest graduation rates and go on to receive higher-paying jobs than students who were not educated with computers. Therefore, we need to put computers in all of our classrooms.**

   The school board member's reasoning is flawed because it fails to establish which of the following?
   (A) Proof that the local school district currently has the funds required to place computers in every classroom in the school district
   (B) Support for the claim that a school district with a decrease in student body should be investing in new technology
   (C) Evidence that the lack of computers alone contributes to the decision by parents to relocate to new school districts
   (D) Information that students who are educated with computers are more likely to graduate and receive higher-paying jobs
   (E) Evidence that computers offer better classroom management opportunities because they keep students occupied and reduce the risk of classroom disorder

Questions 7 and 8

In recent years, the fashion industry has become increasingly unable to ignore the reality of eating disorders among models. Although models are, as a group, thin beyond the "normal" standards of society, many have succumbed to nutritionally deficient eating habits in order to sustain unnatural weights, even for their super-physiques. The fashion industry has, in recent years, begun addressing the issue more openly. Some countries have gone so far as to establish rules that require models to maintain a certain BMI if they expect to walk the runways. Additionally, the industry recently held an international conference on the issue of eating disorders. But the overall mood there was one of resistance, among models as well as designers. Most of the models claim that they are just naturally very thin and are modeling for that very reason. They admit that some do develop eating disorders but claim these disorders are often based on individual problems and not on the industry. Among the designers, the resistance was equally palpable. Most resented the interference and claimed that the fashion world has always relied on thin models and that it is unfair to single out a single industry for eating disorders because eating disorders are connected to personal issues. Overall, the hope within the industry is that there will be awareness about eating disorders but not extra rules: Models should know that help is available should they need it and that the industry will support them as they seek treatment.

7. **Which of the following best expresses the main point of the passage above?**

(A) The fashion industry believes that eating disorders are inevitable and thus cannot be entirely eliminated among models.

(B) The fashion industry does not feel responsible for eating disorders among models, claiming that eating disorders arise from personal situations and should be treated individually.

(C) The fashion industry believes that models need to be thin, and many of the models are naturally and not unhealthily thin.

(D) The fashion industry resents the intrusion because it ultimately hopes that the models will recognize when they have a problem and seek help.

(E) The fashion industry knows that any rules established to combat eating disorders by requiring a healthy BMI will ultimately be ignored.

8. **Given the passage above, the reasoning within the fashion industry is vulnerable to criticism because it fails to consider which of the following?**

(A) The public is tired of the excessively thin image propounded by the fashion industry and would prefer to see models of average weight.

(B) Fashion trends are constantly changing, and the trend for very thin models will ultimately give way to a trend for models of different sizes.

(C) Eating disorders affect people for many reasons, and there are as many people struggling with eating disorders in the fashion industry as there are elsewhere.

(D) The women chosen to model are selected entirely for their height and build and are perhaps naturally thin, rather than suffering from eating disorders.

(E) Models suffering from eating disorders might not have the means or the ability to acknowledge their problem and pursue help.

9. **All of the employees at the Marshalltown Packing Warehouse receive a 3 percent bonus each Christmas. The company owner instituted the Christmas bonus at the company's inception 10 years earlier, and the company handbook includes a guarantee to new employees that they will receive the bonus annually. The company has recently hired a new financial officer whose review of the books indicates that the company's budget might not allow for the Christmas bonus this year due to a decline in advertising revenues for the company. The financial officer sends out a memo to all employees, informing them that the company will be unable to provide the Christmas bonuses this year unless all employees contribute to an improvement in advertising revenues.**

Consider the passage above carefully. If the information contained within it is true, which of the following must also be true?

(A) If advertising revenues are down, the company is not responsible for providing Christmas bonuses to its employees unless the employees are willing to help improve advertising revenues.

(B) By asking the employees to contribute to an improvement in advertising revenues, the company is essentially asking employees to contribute to their own bonuses.

(C) If the company has always been able to provide the Christmas bonus in the past, there is no reason it should be unable to do so in the present, so the financial officer must be falsifying the numbers.

(D) Unless employees contribute to the advertising revenues, the only other choice for the company will be to downsize and lay off employees.

(E) Because the company has guaranteed the Christmas bonuses in the employee handbook, the employees will likely go on strike if they do not receive the bonuses.

10. **Philatelist: The Swedish Treskilling Yellow is the rarest stamp in the world. It was issued in 1855 when Sweden first began issuing postage stamps. The Treskilling, or three-skilling, stamp was originally intended to be printed in blue but was accidentally printed in yellow, the color reserved for the eight-skilling stamp. A number of Treskilling Yellow stamps were printed before the mistake was noticed in 1858. A stamp collector located the first Treskilling Yellow and sold it to another collector. Soon, it became apparent that this particular stamp might be the only remaining variety of the mistaken coloration, and the Treskilling Yellow became a desired item among stamp collectors. In 1996, it was sold for $2.06 million, making it the costliest stamp in the world. Therefore, the Treskilling Yellow is also the most valuable stamp in the world.**

Which of the following statements represents the assumption on which the philatelist's conclusion depends?

(A) If another Treskilling Yellow stamp happens to be found, it will bring in a price as high as that of the current Treskilling Yellow stamp.

(B) It is the unique quality of having been printed in error that makes the Treskilling Yellow stamp as rare and valuable as it is.

(C) Because the Treskilling Yellow stamp is the only one of its kind, it would be worthless if another such stamp were located.

(D) Because the Treskilling Yellow is the only one of its kind and has currently sold for the highest price among stamp collectors, it must have the most intrinsic value.

(E) Most of the finest and costliest stamps in the world have originated from printing errors in Sweden.

11. **When first published in 1867, Karl Marx's massive thesis on capitalism, *Das Kapital*, was anything but a bestseller. In fact, the book hardly made a dent in the public consciousness at first. So little was it noticed that Marx's friend and colleague Friedrich Engels began to write glowing reviews of *Das Kapital* under assumed names. The book received little attention during Marx's lifetime, much to his personal disappointment, as he believed that he was offering hope for the future of politics through economic revolution. After his death in 1883, however, there were growing changes in the international political climate, and *Das Kapital* grew in popularity, ultimately becoming one of the most influential political treatises of the 20th century.**

Considering the above statements, which of the following can be inferred from the passage to explain the reason for the eventual popularity of *Das Kapital*?

(A) *Das Kapital* became popular after people began questioning traditional capitalist values during the late 19th and early 20th centuries.

(B) *Das Kapital* was censored in several European countries and thus was unavailable to the general reading public until the mid-20th century.

(C) *Das Kapital* is about 3,000 pages in full and thus is limited in readership to those willing to undertake such a lengthy book.

(D) Karl Marx was not known as an authority in the field of political philosophy, so the book was poorly received among academics.

(E) *Das Kapital* was originally published in German and was unavailable in translation form until early in the 20th century.

12. Although most scholars agree that the Black Death was a massive blight that killed as much as 60 percent of the European population, some scholars now argue that the plague might have contributed to Europe's social system in unexpectedly positive ways. These scholars point out that the plague saw no social boundaries and affected noblemen as well as serfs; when the noblemen began to die, their serfs were left free and able to work for themselves. The argument claims that the Black Death, by wiping out large portions of the land-owning aristocracy across Europe, contributed to the development of the middle class: The now-freed serfs began developing trades and grew wealthy and powerful over time.

Which of the following, if true, most undermines the claims made by scholars about the positive impact of the Black Death?

(A) The Black Death actually struck very few members of the European peasantry because they had already developed immunity to the infection.
(B) Historians have calculated that more men than women were killed from plague infection between 1340 and 1400.
(C) Some scholars have noticed an increase in pre-industrial productivity immediately after the Black Death, suggesting a rise in new trades.
(D) The Black Death weakened the aristocracy to the point of irrelevance in society, in addition to reducing the value of lands by as much as 70 percent.
(E) Historians have found that a thriving middle class was already in development when the Black Death first struck Europe in the 1340s.

13. Politician: Although our country has traditionally benefited greatly from trade with our chief trading partner, we need to cease any and all trade with this trading partner immediately due to its clear and egregious human rights violations. Reports indicate that our long-time trading partner has been engaging in practices that our country considers utterly insupportable and that the United Nations has frequently condemned. As a nation, we have always stood for clear human rights standards, and we cannot risk practicing a double standard. We must instead set the standard and encourage respect for human rights around the world.

The argument made by the politician depends on which of the following assumptions?

(A) Ending trade with the chief trading partner will help put a stop to the trading partner's current human rights violations.
(B) The human rights violations are closely connected to the specific products traded between the countries.
(C) The need to stand by a standard of human rights is of greater value than the trading loss that will occur by ending trade.
(D) The politician is currently head of a committee that is responsible for keeping track of human rights violations among trading partners.
(E) This country will end trade with the chief trading partner in order to encourage other nations to do the same.

LSAT Practice Test #1

113

14. Letter to the editor of a Dublin newspaper: The traditional Gaeilge language is currently being taught in some Irish schools with funding from the Irish government. This should be stopped at once. Gaeilge is the language of revolution among the Irish and has done more throughout history to contribute to unrest and even open conflict in Ireland than it has done to bring about peace. The teaching of this language will ultimately bring about division in Ireland. The Irish government should rethink its funding and remove it as soon as possible.

Considering the statements above, the reasoning in the letter to the editor is flawed because of which of the following?
(A) The author fails to note that language is an important part of any culture, and the loss of that language will deprive a people of an essential link to their past.
(B) The author assumes that events occurring in history when the Irish spoke Gaeilge will occur once again simply by teaching students the language.
(C) The author relies on obsolete sociological data to derive a conclusion about current events.
(D) The author focuses on an isolated historical event and assumes that it established a trend for the modern day.
(E) The author ignores other traditional languages in Ireland, and fails to explain why they should not be taught as well.

15. A local farmer is hoping to establish a certified organic farm but is concerned about the cost of setting it up. A certified organic farm requires far fewer supplies than a non-organic farm, and most of the supplies are less costly in comparison. Also, because an organic farm does not use expensive pesticides or tools, the cost of maintenance is fairly low in comparison to the maintenance cost of a non-organic farm. However, the set-up of the certified organic farm remains expensive, and the farmer is unsure if the return on his investment will justify the cost.

Which of the following statements best explains the farmer's concern about the high cost of setting up a certified organic farm?
(A) There is little demand in the community for more certified organic food.
(B) Obtaining certification as an organic farm requires hiring expert consultants to ensure that the farm complies with all regulations.
(C) There are three other certified organic farms in the community that are much larger than the farm that the farmer is planning to establish.
(D) The fees for the farmer to acquire certification add considerably to the cost of set-up.
(E) The supplies needed to set up the certified organic farm are unique and must be special-ordered.

16. **Commercial: Men who struggle with hair loss need worry no longer—they can now purchase Extra-Strength Spray-On Hair Growth! This amazing product will stimulate hair to regrow and offer you a full head of hair once again. However, if you don't try our Extra-Strength Spray-On Hair Growth, your chances of having a full head of hair again will vanish, along with your hairline. So, try Extra-Strength Spray-On Hair Growth today!**

    The flawed reasoning in the commercial is similar to the reasoning in which of the following?

    (A) Students who attend universities tend to be more successful in life; therefore, all students should attend a university in order to be successful and not fail in life.
    (B) If you walk in the rain with your head uncovered, you will develop a cold; therefore, you should carry an umbrella.
    (C) Over time, ovens develop a buildup of food residue that gets burned into the bottom of the oven; therefore, ovens should be cleaned annually.
    (D) "Green" products lessen the toxic impact on the environment; therefore, people should purchase green products as one way to help the environment.
    (E) Stan is unpopular among the members of his team because of his temper; therefore, Stan will be removed from the team.

Questions 17 and 18

The state of Hawaii plans to build a nuclear power plant in a town along the leeward coast of Oahu. The nuclear power plant is expected to provide new jobs for people in Oahu. The town in which the power plant will be located, however, is unhappy with the plan. A spokesperson for the town reveals to the local news station that the residents are concerned about the dangers of nuclear power as well as the potential for another accident of the magnitude of the Chernobyl disaster. As the spokesperson notes, Chernobyl was the nuclear power plant in Ukraine where a reactor exploded in 1986, creating extremely unsafe levels of radiation for residents throughout Ukraine and parts of Eastern Europe. The long-term effects of the Chernobyl explosion included permanent health damage for many residents and a variety of birth defects among children. These possible consequences are what the Hawaiian town residents most fear in the event that a nuclear facility in Hawaii suffers a similar accident.

17. **Which of the following, if true, would most undermine the spokesperson's primary argument?**

    (A) The nuclear fallout that occurred at Chernobyl was a one-time historical event, and it cannot be assumed that a similar event would occur in Hawaii.
    (B) The spokesperson is a paid member of an anti-nuclear power organization that frequently lobbies against the building of new nuclear power plants in the US.
    (C) The advances made in nuclear power plants since the days of Chernobyl ensure that the chance of a similar nuclear explosion is almost nonexistent.
    (D) The nuclear power plant will bring high-paying jobs to the community and ensure excellent benefits for all employees.
    (E) The voters of the state of Hawaii have voted overwhelmingly in support of the building of the nuclear power plant.

115

18. **Which of the following statements would, if true, most seriously undermine the state's attempt to build the nuclear power plant?**
    (A) The community is unsure whether the new nuclear power plant can be built within the required budget.
    (B) Many of the jobs that the nuclear power plant would bring are not higher-paying than the jobs that are currently available.
    (C) The state official in charge of granting the permit for building the proposed nuclear power plant is a former employee of the manager of the proposed plant.
    (D) A local builder is planning a neighborhood near the expected site of the nuclear power plant and has already sold 75 percent of the lots.
    (E) Ocean water surrounding Hawaii is too warm to cool a nuclear reactor, so the plant would have to use a considerable amount of extra energy to keep a nuclear reactor cool.

19. **The female earless seal has a gestation period that usually spans 9–11 months, depending on the species. Each female gives birth to only one pup at a time. The mother fasts while she is nursing the pup due to the distance between the breeding ground and the area where the seals feed. As a result, the earless seal mother burns a considerable amount of energy during lactation. During a bad season, as many as three earless seal mothers in a colony will die around three months after giving birth. It is not uncommon, however, for all of the seal pups to survive.**

    Which of the following, if true, most explains the discrepancy between the number of deaths among the earless seal mothers and lack of deaths among the pups during a bad season?
    (A) Female earless seals can nurse two pups at a time, thus ensuring that at least two pups will live.
    (B) During a good season, no female earless seals die, and marine biologists note that there have been more good seasons than bad in recent years.
    (C) Some of the female earless seals do not give birth during breeding season.
    (D) The earless seal pups nurse only for a brief period of time, with the longest nursing period being one month.
    (E) Some of the female earless seals will live as long as six months after giving birth, thus guaranteeing that their pups have a better chance of survival.

20. William Paley was an 18th-century Christian apologist credited with developing what is now known as the watchmaker analogy. This analogy has often come under attack for a logical flaw. Paley's argument followed this reasoning: Suppose a person found a watch lying on the ground and did not know it was a watch. Would the person assume that it simply came into being without some sort of intelligent design? Most likely not. This is because a watch contains a carefully crafted and highly complex series of mechanisms in order to make it work correctly; due to the complexity of its design, it cannot have come into being *ex nihilo*, or out of nothing, and thus it indicates intelligence and a designer. In the same way, the universe exhibits a carefully crafted and highly complex system. As with the watch, the universe cannot have come into being without intelligence and a designer.

Which of the following best expresses the logical flaw in Paley's reasoning?

(A) A red herring, or a strategy used to create a distraction
(B) A premise that assumes the conclusion
(C) An *ad hominem* or personal attack
(D) An appeal to sympathy that uses an emotional quality to make the argument
(E) An appeal to authority that uses the claimed authority of an outside source

21. The climate extremes of the North Atlantic nation of Iceland ensure that little plant growth will be able to survive there. The majority of the island is covered in low grasses, with only one tree species known to exist. Deforestation in previous centuries depopulated the entire island of its trees. Because of both the severe cold and the severe heat, plants require a long period of time to grow in Iceland, and modern residents have only just begun replanting the trees. Plant life in Iceland is also notoriously delicate, and off-road vehicles are allowed only in certain areas; in some cases, hikers are required to walk around certain plants to ensure that the plants will survive even during the extreme weather that constantly surrounds Iceland.

Considering the claims below within the context of the passage above, which claim is most likely to be true?

(A) More developed plant growth exists closer to the island's center, where volcanic warmth allows the plants to survive.
(B) The plants that manage to survive in Iceland are extremely hardy.
(C) The only type of tree capable of growing successfully in Iceland is the northern birch.
(D) Global warming in recent decades has encouraged plant growth, with a corresponding improvement in the development of Icelandic plant life.
(E) Off-road vehicles can cause permanent or long-term damage to the regrowth of some plants.

LSAT Practice Test #1

22. **The short and shaggy Highland Cattle are an iconic feature of Scotland and closely connected to that nation's history. This sturdy, resilient breed is very familiar with the cold rainfall and bitter winds of the mountainous Scottish Highlands, and it has existed in that landscape for unknown centuries. The Highland Cattle are most common in the remote areas of the Highlands, where they live and breed in the wild. They are known for their hardy ability to withstand the elements; in fact, many of them live upwards of 18–20 years, giving birth as many as 15 times.**

    Which of the following assumptions can be drawn from the information in the passage above?
    (A) Due to their stature and tough hides, the Highland Cattle cannot be used for human consumption and are good only for grazing.
    (B) As they are native to the Scottish Highlands, the Highland Cattle are the only breed that can survive in Scotland.
    (C) Having lived in the Scottish Highlands for centuries, the Highland Cattle have adapted to the climate and developed the ability to survive there.
    (D) The shaggy coats of the Highland Cattle have long been used by the Highlanders for a variety of household purposes.
    (E) Scotland's Highland climate severely limits the plant life that can grow and survive there, leaving the Highland Cattle with limited food to eat.

23. **Colorblindness is a vision deficiency that limits the ability of the sufferer to see certain colors clearly. The condition may affect a person in varying degrees, ranging from mild colorblindness with a red or green color deficiency to complete colorblindness with no ability to distinguish any colors beside dim shades of brown. The primary cause of colorblindness is believed to be a mutation on the X chromosome. Men carry a single X chromosome, possessing an XY-chromosome makeup, while women carry two X chromosomes, giving them the potential to combat colorblindness with an extra X chromosome.**

    If the passage above is true, which of the following can be inferred from it?
    (A) Colorblindness is a rare condition that affects very few members of the population.
    (B) Despite the handicap, those who are colorblind might have certain advantages, particularly in seeing camouflage.
    (C) Women alone are capable of passing on a gene for colorblindness.
    (D) Because of the way colorblindness affects the X chromosome, men are more likely to be colorblind than women.
    (E) Colorblindness is entirely inherited and can be tested and identified at birth.

24. **Set on the wild and rugged Bodmin Moor of Cornwall, Jamaica Inn is most remembered for playing the starring role in a story by Cornish-born writer Daphne du Maurier. In du Maurier's book, a young woman moves in with a family member at Jamaica Inn, only to discover that the inn is playing a sinister role in the crime of wrecking, that is, setting up lights along the coastline to draw ships in and wreck them on the rocky coast. Du Maurier's book is hardly a historical textbook; anecdote suggests that du Maurier derived much of the source for her tale from the ghost stories she heard while staying briefly at Jamaica Inn. This being said, wrecking was a real activity in Cornwall during the 18th and 19th centuries, and Jamaica Inn's remote locale made it an excellent place to hide from the law.**

    Which of the following best expresses the main point of the passage above?

    (A) Daphne du Maurier's story *Jamaica Inn* has been overlooked by literary historians for its contribution to the history of Cornwall.
    (B) Daphne du Maurier's story *Jamaica Inn* takes inevitable creative license but reflects with some accuracy the reality of deliberate shipwrecking in Cornwall.
    (C) Lights were lit along the coastline in order to lure ships in and force them to wreck along the coast, giving the residents freedom to plunder the ship's goods.
    (D) Daphne du Maurier frequently used Cornwall, and the Cornish coastline in particular, as a setting for her books.
    (E) The story of *Jamaica Inn* falsely represents the historical details of shipwrecking.

25. **Psychologists have found that there are fascinating differences between children and adults when it comes to learning a new musical instrument. In particular, the piano is an instrument that knows no one age for learning and presents multiple opportunities for the successful attainment of musical skills. It does, however, offer a variety of challenges both to children and to adults—due to the differences in mind development—with children developing certain skills more quickly and more effectively than adults. How quickly children learn is often limited by their motor skills, but they are more likely to remember in detail the pieces they learn and to retain that knowledge over long periods of time. At the same time, adults are more likely to retain the muscle memory of the pieces that they learn and reproduce them blindly, just by allowing their fingers to recall the correct notes.**

    If the passage above is true, all of the following may be concluded EXCEPT:

    (A) Adult minds learn the skills required to play the piano differently than children's minds.
    (B) Adults might not recall the exact details of the piece they learned, but the muscle memory in their fingers makes them very likely to remember the notes.
    (C) The piano is the only instrument that both children and adults can learn to play well.
    (D) Learning the piano is not limited to children because adults can learn to play well.
    (E) Adults are more likely to learn hand and finger movements on the piano faster than children do.

Argumentative Writing

(50 Minutes)

The argumentative writing section of the LSAT exam is meant to assess your ability to construct an argumentative essay in response to a given **key question**. In addition to the key question, you will be given an **introduction to the topic** along with a few **perspectives** debating the issue. This section will include 15 minutes of prewriting analysis immediately followed by 35 minutes for writing your argumentative essay.

The prewriting analysis is meant to give you the opportunity to organize your argument by thinking critically about the issue and generating ideas in response to prewriting questions. During this portion, you will be able to read the full writing prompt, including the perspectives on the issue, and you will be able to write notes on a scratch pad that will be visible during the essay-writing portion.

The official instructions and prewriting questions released by LSAC are as follows:

Write an argumentative essay in response to the Key Question.

The various perspectives are presented to provide additional context for the issue and to give you ideas that you can react to or incorporate into your argument as you develop it. They also serve as a model for the types of arguments that various stakeholders are making as they debate the issue raised in the Key Question.

Your essay must directly address ideas from one or more of the perspectives presented in the task. You do not need to address each of the perspectives—use your own judgment in deciding which ideas to address (and how many), based on what you believe will be most effective for developing your argument.

Use the ideas generated during your prewriting analysis to help you create and develop your argument as you see fit. You may incorporate any knowledge or experiences you might have regarding this issue, your own values, and your critical evaluation of the arguments and ideas contained in the other perspectives. Your position may be in full agreement with any of the perspectives, in partial agreement, or completely different. Whatever the case, your position should be supported with logical arguments and detailed, persuasive examples.

PREWRITING ANALYSIS: GENERATING THE IDEA OF YOUR ARGUMENTATIVE ESSAY

Spend the remainder of your prewriting time working through the prewriting questions presented below. These questions are intended to help you think critically about the issue and generate productive ideas for your essay. Record your thoughts in your digital scratch paper by making notes or lists, or by writing short answers to the questions.

Your notes in response to the prewriting questions will still be available to you while you write your essay, but they will not be evaluated or included as part of your essay. These questions are strictly provided to help guide your analysis of the perspectives and to help you develop your own argument in response to the Key Question.

PREWRITING QUESTIONS
- Which perspective(s) do you find most **compelling**?
- What relevant **insights** do you see in the perspective(s)?
- What **principles** or **values** do you see at work in the perspective(s)?
- What **strengths** and **weaknesses** can you find in the perspective(s)?

Your argument should incorporate or address ideas from at least one of the perspectives provided. In addition, your own knowledge, experiences, and personal values can be valid sources of evidence, and you can include these in your essay:

- What **knowledge** do you already have about this issue? Consider information you have read or heard, including things you've learned at home or school, etc.
- What **values** influence your position on this issue? Consider your worldview or belief system, as well as any guiding principles or convictions you hold.
- What **experiences** do you have that might be relevant to this issue? Consider any personal experience you might have or other relevant lessons learned from your own life.

WRITING PROMPT

Subject: Value of Single-Use Plastics

INTRODUCTION TO THE TOPIC

The prevalence of single-use plastic items is undeniable. The benefits and the hazards that have come from the ubiquity of these items in a variety of venues are both substantial. Industries from healthcare to hospitality have legal regulations on safety and sanitation that require single-use items. As they are relatively inexpensive, easy to manufacture, resistant to degradation, and able to be adapted to a variety of needs, plastics are often components in single-use, disposable items.

Due to the difficulty of breaking down plastics via simple or natural processes, recycling efforts are limited and landfills are saturated. In recent years, some groups have cited these factors as reasons for new or altered legislation regarding the production and availability of single-use plastic items. Others have noted advancements in plastic design and innovations in recycling techniques to mitigate these issues as reasons to repeal current legislation and relax regulations.

KEY QUESTION

To what extent should the production, distribution, and disposal of single-use plastics be regulated?

PERSPECTIVE 1 – AN EXCERPT FROM AN ENVIRONMENTAL ACTIVIST'S BLOG

Nearly 200 million tons of single-use plastics are produced worldwide every year. While the accumulation of that much non-biodegradable waste is problematic anywhere, the most extreme environmental impact is to our oceans, where an estimated 5% of those plastics inevitably make their way. This accumulation in our oceans is already believed to cause the deaths of over 1 million marine animals every year, and is only going to get worse over time as the buildup of waste continues to increase.

Congress must act now to regulate and limit the production of single-use plastic items, starting with a tax. This tax will serve the twofold purpose of naturally reducing the volume of production and providing a source of funding to begin cleaning our oceans of the waste from years past. As we lead the way, we must also call upon our fellow citizens of the world to do the same, petitioning their governments to enact similar legislation so that together, we can preserve our oceans for future generations to enjoy.

PERSPECTIVE 2 – AN EXCERPT FROM A REPORT ON THE PLASTICS INDUSTRY

In the US, the market for single-use plastics is approximately $26.96 billion as of 2024. The single-use plastics industry employs approximately 100,000 people, 10% of those employed in the plastics industry overall. Industries and businesses that rely on single-use plastics, including healthcare and grocery stores, do so because there are no viable alternatives.

The need to develop more-sustainable products is undeniable, but simply banning or severely restricting single-use plastics before these alternatives are ready would cause economic devastation as entire industries find themselves unable to function, and the single-use plastics industry would collapse overnight. Regulations must be introduced in manageable pieces and should be based on incentivizing a move away from single-use plastics rather than punishing continued use. Carefully crafted regulations should provide grants, tax breaks, and other positive incentives for developing and manufacturing new materials, allowing economic stability through the transition period followed by growth once the new materials are in production.

PERSPECTIVE 3 – AN EXCERPT FROM A PUBLIC HEALTH BROCHURE

Due to their harmful impacts to public health, single-use plastics should be placed under a higher level of scrutiny in the development of public policies. Chemicals found within single-use plastics have been proven to have significant health risks to the population. There are numerous cases of patients presenting with both cancer and chronic lung disease who used to work in an environment where they were consistently exposed to plastic fibers. This prolonged exposure to microplastics was likely a contributing factor in their development of lung disease through years of damage caused by inflammation. Various studies have demonstrated that single-use plastics have also been the cause of several other health risks, such as hormonal disruptions, cardiovascular problems, and gastrointestinal issues.

In an effort to prevent serious risk factors that are presented by the chemicals found in single-use plastics, more stringent regulations should be put into place. These regulations aid in ensuring that safe, toxin-free products are provided to consumers and would also require a level of collaboration between health experts and policymakers to develop. In the process of developing these policies, these groups should prioritize an overall healthier population as their end goal. The implementation of these stricter regulations will no doubt result in a vast reduction of the associated health risks, and it will also act as a large step towards a healthier and safer environment for everyone to enjoy.

PERSPECTIVE 4 – AN EXCERPT FROM A REPORT BY A CONSUMER RIGHTS ADVOCATE

Consumers benefit from single-use plastics every day. Their food from the grocery store comes perfectly sealed in form-fitting bags and containers that prevent leakage and contamination. They choose plastic bandages that repel water, disposable masks that prevent disease, and single-use gloves that keep them safe from infection. Consumers consistently choose single-use plastics because they are more hygienic, safer, and more affordable than alternative products—and it is their right to experience these benefits.

Increasing regulations regarding single-use plastics will lead to lower product availability and higher costs that are forced onto consumers, which can be especially detrimental to those who already struggle economically. Instead of stringent regulation, we should push to educate consumers so that they can make informed choices for themselves. Most people want to do the right thing. If they learn of the potential risks of single-use plastics and are given ways to reduce their environmental impact through proper disposal and recycling, they will make the right choices. Investing in education and recycling infrastructure will allow for more sustainable use of these products while not infringing on the consumer's freedom of choice.

Answer Key for Test #1

SECTION I: LOGICAL REASONING

Question	Question	Question	Question
1. B	8. A	15. D	22. A
2. C	9. E	16. A	23. D
3. E	10. B	17. C	24. B
4. A	11. C	18. D	25. A
5. E	12. A	19. B	
6. D	13. E	20. E	
7. B	14. B	21. C	

SECTION II: READING COMPREHENSION

Question	Question	Question	Question
1. D	8. D	15. A	22. D
2. C	9. B	16. B	23. B
3. C	10. D	17. B	24. B
4. E	11. B	18. A	25. B
5. A	12. E	19. C	
6. D	13. D	20. D	
7. E	14. C	21. B	

SECTION III: READING COMPREHENSION

Question	Question	Question	Question
1. C	8. A	15. B	22. C
2. A	9. D	16. E	23. D
3. E	10. E	17. C	24. E
4. B	11. C	18. A	25. B
5. C	12. B	19. A	26. D
6. C	13. A	20. C	27. C
7. E	14. B	21. D	

SECTION IV: LOGICAL REASONING

Question	Question	Question	Question
1. B	8. E	15. D	22. C
2. A	9. B	16. A	23. D
3. A	10. D	17. C	24. B
4. C	11. A	18. E	25. C
5. A	12. E	19. D	
6. C	13. C	20. B	
7. D	14. B	21. E	

Answers and Explanations for Test #1

Section I: Logical Reasoning

QUESTION 1

<u>Overview</u>: This question asks students to select the statement that *most seriously* undermines the nutritionist's claims that his or her method of applying diet and exercise alone helped patients struggling with obesity to lose weight, and that this method of losing weight is the *best* method. The student must consider each answer choice in the context of what the nutritionist says in order to determine which answer is most correct.

THE CORRECT ANSWER:

B   The nutritionist's statement—that a healthy, balanced diet and the incorporation of daily exercise is the best weight-loss method—is strongly undermined by the information that significant factors in weight loss include physical makeup and metabolism, and that the nutritionist worked only with adults with very similar physical makeup and metabolism. This information throws into question whether the nutritionist's methods would work for adults with different physical makeup and metabolism, thereby undermining the claim that the nutritionist's method for weight loss is the best method.

THE INCORRECT ANSWERS:

A   Answer choice (A), although tempting, is ultimately irrelevant to the nutritionist's direct claims about the best method for weight loss; answer A is considered an *ad hominem* claim, that is, a claim directed about a person making an argument rather than about the merits of the argument itself. Simply because the nutritionist receives funding from the government does not mean that the nutritionist's study is biased. Nothing in the passage suggests that it is.

C   Like answer choice (A), answer choice (C) is interesting but does nothing to undermine the nutritionist's claims. It is not surprising to learn that another nutritionist disagrees with him or her, but disagreement with a colleague does not necessarily undermine the test results.

D   Far from undermining the test results and the nutritionist's claims, answer choice (D) actually supports them. This is because different methods of exercise might have different results regarding weight loss.

E   The statement about the number of patients provides further information on how the nutritionist carried out his or her test. However, it does not necessarily undermine the results. Eighty patients could conceivably provide the nutritionist with a large enough study group to derive useful results, so this choice does not necessarily undermine the claims.

QUESTION 2

<u>Overview</u>: Question 2 presents a scenario in which someone (Mike) is attempting to predict future events on the basis of his past experience. Three important factors must be considered: (1) the company for which Mike works is suffering due to the economic downturn, (2) the detail that Mike has had a strong sales record in the past but has struggled to maintain it in recent months because of the weak economy, and (3) the fact that Mike's boss has asked to see him. Mike concludes that his

boss will *not* fire him because of his time with the company, his excellent record, and his potential to succeed in spite of the crisis. The student is asked to consider how Mike's reasoning is flawed.

THE CORRECT ANSWER:

C   Answer choice (C) is the only selection that takes all of the elements into account and summarizes the substance of the problem with Mike's argument: He believes his success in the past will translate automatically to future success, despite his failure over the last few months to keep his sales high. He also believes that the company will look only at his past success and will not consider current factors, including his recent struggles and the economic situation as a whole.

THE INCORRECT ANSWERS:

A   Although answer choice (A) does address part of the problem with Mike's reasoning, it does not address all of it. Mike's belief in his loyalty to the company ("I've been working with the company for well over a decade") contributes to the flaw in his argument, but does not encompass it fully.

B   Answer choice (B) provides an interesting piece of information, but in terms of Mike's argument, it is largely irrelevant and does not address the flaw in Mike's reasoning in any way. It contributes a piece of information that might support the theory that the company will indeed fire Mike, but it fails to explain how Mike's own argument is problematic.

D   Answer (D), again, is interesting but irrelevant to Mike's argument and does not address the flaw in his reasoning. Mike being a close friend of his boss might make it more difficult for his boss to fire him, but since Mike does not mention this in his statement, it cannot be assumed that this contributes to his reasoning.

E   Answer (E) introduces potential competition for the sales job, which is not part of Mike's argument. Based on his past success, Mike may well believe that there is no one who would be better at the job, but this is not part of the argument presented.

QUESTIONS 3 AND 4

Overview: Questions 3 and 4 regard a passage about the history of medieval music manuscripts, noting specifically four important facts: (1) manuscripts were expensive to produce, (2) the Catholic Church was one of the few institutions able to take on this expense, as it had both the wealth and the scribes as human resources, (3) most extant music from the medieval period has been recorded on manuscripts, and (4) the majority of this music is sacred music. The passage includes the added suggestion that most popular music from that era is unknown today because very little was recorded on manuscripts.

QUESTION 3
THE CORRECT ANSWER:

E   In question 3, the student is asked to select a statement that is supported by the claims made in the passage. To do this, the student must infer from what is stated directly. Based on these claims, answer choice (E) is the only one that fulfills this requirement. The passage states: "Any medieval music not recorded on manuscripts has now been lost to history. Most of the medieval music still in existence is sacred music." If most extant medieval music is sacred music and any music not recorded on manuscripts has been lost to history, then it follows that most popular music was not recorded on manuscripts and thus has been lost to

125

history. It can safely be inferred from this fact that historians do not know much about popular medieval music because they have almost nothing to study.

THE INCORRECT ANSWERS:

A Answer choice (A) is incorrect because the passage does not offer an evaluative judgment on the music that is still extant, nor does it suggest anywhere that sacred music was recorded because it was the "greatest music" of the period. Historians might rightly debate this issue, but the passage neither discusses it nor implies anything about it.

B As with answer choice (A), the passage does not imply answer choice (B). The passage describes facts about the way medieval music was recorded and about what medieval music still exists, but it does not provide an answer to *why* most of the extant music from the Middle Ages is sacred music. Therefore, in no place in the passage does the author suggest that the Church recorded only medieval music because it did not value popular music. Answer (B) should be eliminated immediately.

C While answer choice (C) might very well be true, the substance of this statement is not discussed at all in the passage and cannot be inferred from any statement made within it. Answer (C) is thus irrelevant and should be eliminated immediately.

D The passage does indicate that the Church was not necessarily the *only* institution to have the means of affording manuscripts: "As a result, **few** people were able to produce or own them, and the Catholic Church, which had literate scribes as well as considerable wealth, produced and maintained **most** manuscripts during the Middle Ages." This suggests logically that other institutions, such as the aristocracy, might very well have been able to produce and maintain some of the manuscripts. However, nowhere does the passage discuss the contents of aristocratic households or that aristocrats might have held *large numbers* of manuscripts, so this statement cannot be inferred from the passage.

QUESTION 4

THE CORRECT ANSWER:

A The student is asked to consider which statement *cannot* be inferred from the passage. The passage makes a number of claims about manuscripts in the medieval period, but the only comment on the parchment from which the manuscripts were made is that it was expensive. It might seem logical to argue that if the parchment was expensive, it must also have been difficult to produce, but there is no statement in the passage that supports this claim, so the conclusion cannot be drawn safely. It is possible that the process of making parchment was not difficult, but that it required supplies or equipment that was expensive to obtain or use. This expense, if it existed, may also be due to difficulty in procuring or creating these supplies, but this does not affect the difficulty of making parchment once the elements are in place.

THE INCORRECT ANSWERS:

B The passage notes that the manuscripts were "painstakingly copied by hand" and that the only people qualified to do this work were the scribes (who were literate), suggesting that the work required a great deal of time and effort and that few people were able to copy manuscripts. From this, answer choice (B) may be inferred from the passage.

C   The passage claims that the Church produced most of the manuscripts. Due to the expense of the parchment and the painstaking work involved in creating manuscripts, it stands to reason that the Church selectively produced manuscripts that were important to them, which implies that sacred (religious) texts and music would be preferred over secular forms. Note that this does not necessarily suggest that the Church did not value popular music—see answer choice (B) from question 3—only that it was selective. The two qualities must be distinguished from one another.

D   The passage notes that the manuscripts were "copied by hand" and that the Church had "literate scribes" to do this job, suggesting that within the Church, they alone were qualified to copy down manuscripts. As a result, the passage does imply that only the literate (those who know how to read) were allowed to copy down manuscripts. Note that the question does not say that of all members of society, the scribes alone were allowed to copy down manuscripts. It is entirely possible that literate members of the aristocracy copied down manuscripts. What is significant with regard to this question is that scribes were *literate*, not that they were members of a certain class within society.

E   The passage comments, "Any medieval music not recorded on manuscripts has now been lost to history. Most of the medieval music still in existence is sacred music." From this, it may rightly be inferred that most non-sacred music from the medieval period has been lost to history, so the passage implies answer choice (E).

QUESTION 5

Overview: Question 5 records a conversation between Lito and Miteki, with Lito making an argument about an action he believes needs to be taken and Miteki responding to that argument. Specifically, Lito notes that the one-lane bridges on the island of Kauai have become dangerous due to the increase in tourist traffic and argues that the bridges should be widened. Miteki rebuts with a comment that Kauai is committed to protecting the plant and animal life on the island and that widening the bridges could endanger these plants and animals. The question asks the reader to identify the flaw in Miteki's response.

THE CORRECT ANSWER:

E   In her response, Miteki ignores the substance of Lito's argument—the potential danger from the one-lane bridges and the need to widen them—and instead tries to redirect the conversation toward a related but different topic, specifically the environmental impact of widening the bridges. Thus, **answer choice (E)** correctly evaluates the flaw in Miteki's response: She fails to address the core of Lito's comments and instead develops a secondary argument.

THE INCORRECT ANSWERS:

A   The conversation does not discuss the accuracy of the information in either Lito's argument or Miteki's, so there is no way to know whether Miteki is relying on faulty information. Answer choice (A) may be eliminated immediately.

B   Although Miteki's response does indeed fail to address the substance of Lito's argument, her mistake is not that of circular reasoning, so answer choice (B) may also be eliminated immediately.

C   There is no suggestion in the conversation that either topic is more important than the other, so the judgment that the substance of Miteki's response is less important than Lito's cannot be inferred from the conversation. Moreover, such a judgment does not address the flaw in Miteki's reasoning.

D   Miteki responds to Lito by picking up on one element of his argument—the one-lane bridges—and then developing an unrelated argument of her own. She does not, however, develop any of Lito's supporting claims (i.e., that the number of accidents has increased or that there are more tourists in Kauai).

QUESTION 6

<u>Overview</u>: Question 6 offers a quotation from an art scholar about the Impressionist artist Renoir in which Renoir is discussed within the context of two earlier artists. The passage offers details about these earlier artists, as well as information about Renoir's personal artistic style. The question asks for a statement that best summarizes the conclusion of the passage. Because the passage does not state its main point directly, the student must infer that statement of summary from the information within the passage.

THE CORRECT ANSWER:

D   In describing each of the three artists named—Rubens, Watteau, and Renoir—the passage offers very different details about each one. Rubens is remembered for "creative choice of subject matter," Watteau for his "ability to interweave themes from Italian theatre into his paintings," and Renoir for "his application of light and shading, his use of vibrant color, and his ability to create an intimate scene." None of these qualities is closely related, so the only answer that explains the purpose of each description is answer choice (D), which states that Renoir is noted for following a tradition of individual style. What is more, Read describes Renoir as the "final representative," so it is safe to say that Read believes there is no painter after Renoir who has this quality.

THE INCORRECT ANSWERS:

A   The only artist noted specifically for his subject matter is Rubens, and the passage does not indicate that this quality may be attributed either to Watteau or Renoir.

B   Herbert Read comments on Renoir carrying on the "artistic tradition that started at Rubens and ended at Watteau," but this statement does not indicate Read's personal opinion about whether or not all three men may be considered the greatest artists in Western history.

C   Read notes that Renoir is the "final painter" of a certain artistic quality, but he makes no comment about artists after Renoir, nor does he suggest that no great artists have arisen since Renoir. It is, of course, possible that he makes this claim elsewhere in his analysis, but the claim is not recorded in this particular passage.

E   Again, Read makes no comment on whether Rubens (Flemish), Watteau (French), or Renoir (French) had the greatest impact on painting between the 17th and 19th centuries. What is more, Read notes that Renoir carries on a tradition that "runs directly from Rubens to Watteau," so it is very possible that the unnamed painters who fell between Rubens and Watteau were neither Flemish nor French.

Answers and Explanations for Test #1

QUESTION 7

<u>Overview</u>: This question presents a statement by a school principal regarding how well students are doing in certain subject areas. The students recently completed some testing, and the principal notes that the students scored badly in the math tests compared to their performance on reading tests. The principal then notes that students spend more class time on reading than on math and concludes that students need to spend as much time on math as on reading in order to improve the math scores. The question asks the student to compare the flaw in the principal's reasoning to the flaw in the reasoning of the answer choices.

In order to find an answer choice with a comparable flaw, it is first necessary to identify how the principal's argument proceeds and then decide where the flaw develops. The principal first looks at the test results of two different subjects and sees that the students did badly on one and well on the other. Looking for a quality that distinguishes these two, the principal realizes that the students spend less time on math than on reading. Thus, the conclusion follows that students should spend as much time on math as on reading. The problem with this is that the argument assumes correlation = causation, where more time spent on a subject is assumed to be the cause of the improved test scores with no regard for other considerations, such as the skills of the math teachers at the school, the usefulness of the curriculum, and so forth. The correct answer choice will follow this pattern of correlation = causation, with one fact being assumed to be the cause of another without consideration of other factors.

THE CORRECT ANSWER:

B   Answer choice (B) states that families that stay at three- and four-star resorts have the most relaxing vacations and attributes this outcome to their staying at the resort. If true, this would be a causal relationship. However, there is nothing in the statement to support the conclusion that staying in a three- or four-star resort is the sole, or even primary, cause of the families' relaxation, nor is there any indication that no families will find any other kind of vacation just as relaxing. Therefore, (B) is an example of assuming that correlation = causation as in the principal's statement.

THE INCORRECT ANSWERS:

A, D   Answer choices (A) and (D) are incorrect because the conclusions reached in both arguments do not parallel the principal's conclusion. The argument in choice (A) is that parents should read in order to help improve their children's speech development skills. The argument in choice (D) is that students should take certain kinds of high school classes to be successful in college. Both answer choices suggest that a specific action should be taken to achieve results, but there is a causal link suggested, not just a correlation that is assumed to be causative.

C   Answer choice (C) mentions that more upfront money is required to invest in stocks, which are more successful than options. One might be tempted to think that this implies that a larger investment causes a greater return, a situation parallel with the classroom time and test scores in the scenario. However, (C) does not actually say this, only that options do not require a large investment, and it may well be that investing an equal amount in both options and stocks would have the same results (i.e., options lose money while stocks gain).

E   Answer choice (E) has no relevance to the principal's conclusion and can be eliminated immediately. There is neither correlation nor causation involved in the reasoning in this scenario.

129

QUESTION 8

Overview: Question 8 presents a scenario in which the CEO of a fast-food chain makes an announcement about upcoming revisions to the chain's menu. The company is completely overhauling its menu items so that all items offered will now be healthier. Specifically, the announcement notes that the company will be removing unhealthy fats and offering smaller portions. The question asks the student to consider which of the answer choices most undermines the effect of the CEO's announcement. To find the correct answer, it is necessary to focus on the details in the CEO's comments and on what, in particular, would call into question the validity of the CEO's remarks.

THE CORRECT ANSWER:

A **Answer choice (A)** states that although the fast-food chain is indeed making the announced changes in its menu, it is also retaining certain addictive additives that have, by implication, long been in its food. As a result, the continued inclusion of these additives calls into question the company's actual commitment to offering healthy foods and raises questions about the claim that the company's food will be a healthier option than that offered by other fast-food chains. Therefore, choice (A) most seriously undermines the CEO's statements.

THE INCORRECT ANSWERS:

B That the CEO is receiving a large bonus is potentially suspicious, but it does not by itself undermine the CEO's claim about providing healthier food options. In other words, nothing about the bonus suggests that the menu will not offer healthier items than before; answer choice (B) does not address evidence for or against the CEO's claim. There is no reason to be surprised that the company is rewarding the CEO in advance for a plan that will benefit the company.

C The response of the focus group calls into question the way that customers will respond to the food, but it does not call into question the CEO's comments about the healthy qualities of the food. Thus, answer choice (C) may be eliminated immediately.

D While the merits of advertising to young children might be arguable, the ads themselves seem to support the company's claim that it is offering healthier choices by encouraging children to request the better menu items when they visit the fast-food chains. As a result, this answer choice seems to bring some validity to the CEO's claims of a commitment to better health.

E The CEO makes no claim to having removed all items from the old menu. Instead, he claims that the ingredients have been improved and the menu revised. Answer choice (E) does more to support the CEO's claims than it does to undermine them.

QUESTION 9

Overview: The head of a regional psychiatric association makes a statement about a study that suggests the importance of spirituality in helping patients live longer, healthier lives. The head of the association also comments that depression has been noted, in some cases, to shorten the lives of patients. The speaker concludes that members of the psychiatric association should encourage patients to pursue spirituality in the expectation that it will provide them with longer and healthier lives. The question asks the student to consider on which assumption the speaker's conclusion is based.

THE CORRECT ANSWER:

E   In reaching his conclusion, the head of the psychiatric association does not distinguish between different forms of spirituality. While the cited study implies that some forms of spirituality may be better than others, the speaker does not make that distinction in making the recommendation to encourage patients to explore spirituality. As a result, the conclusion he reaches suggests that all forms of spirituality are equally healthy and that all will be equally beneficial to the patients.

THE INCORRECT ANSWERS:

A   While the head of the psychiatric association indicates that some of the patients being treated by members of the association have suffered from depression, he does not indicate that all of them have. Therefore, answer choice (A) may be eliminated, as the conclusion in the passage is not based on this assumption.

B   As the head of the psychiatric association only mentions the practice of spirituality as being healthy, it cannot be assumed from the passage that he bases his conclusions on the practice of a specific kind of spirituality or that the patients who experienced positive results from the practice of spirituality were practicing the same form.

C   The head of the psychiatric association indicates that the positive aspects of spirituality were observed among the patients, but he does not comment anywhere on whether members of the psychiatric association practice spirituality or whether they should. Rather, his conclusions relate directly to the patients practicing spirituality, and it cannot be assumed that his conclusion is based on the importance of spirituality to the association members. (It might be true that he also recommends the practice of spirituality to members, but this is an inference from his comments, not an assumption on which they are based.)

D   The head of the psychiatric association does say specifically that depression "can lead to an early death in some cases." He does not suggest, however, that the result of depression is inevitably death. Further, his conclusion that the members of the psychiatric association should encourage patients to practice spirituality is not based on the assumption that depression will always lead to death but rather that it can shorten the lives of some patients.

QUESTION 10

Overview: The student is asked to consider which of the answer choices most explains the disparity in price drop between the cost of crude oil per barrel and the cost of gasoline at the pump. In order to determine the difference, it is necessary to think about the specific statements made within the passage. This question asks for inferences only inasmuch as those inferences can be made directly from the information in the passage. Several of the answer choices provide distant possibilities, but only one sufficiently explains the discrepancy in price without deviating from the details of the passage. Question 10 presents a scenario involving cause and effect, and this is what students need to consider: What cause directly explains the effect of a drop in the price of crude oil that is not reflected in prices at the gasoline pump?

THE CORRECT ANSWER:

B   **Answer choice (B)** provides a logical explanation for the disparity in price while not deviating from the details in the passage. The cause suggested is that refineries have had to

131

absorb the higher price of crude oil in recent months; this has had the effect of those refineries delaying passing on the lower price of crude oil to customers at the gas pump.

The Incorrect Answers:

A, C Although answer choices (A) and (C) provide some explanation for the drop in the price of crude oil per barrel, they provide absolutely no explanation for the higher price at the gasoline pump, leaving open the question regarding the disparity in price. As a result, both may be eliminated immediately.

D Answer choice (D) also offers some indication about what might affect the price of crude oil per barrel, but it fails to address the discrepancy in price, that is, why the cost of crude oil has decreased without a corresponding drop in prices at the gasoline pump. If anything, answer choice (D) raises further questions, since if there are alternative energy options, the price of gasoline should naturally decrease according to the laws of supply and demand.

E Answer choice (E), although it reflects a potential result of continued low crude oil prices, does not address the question of why gasoline prices are still high in comparison to crude oil prices. While it might be inferred that the loss of oil production companies entails less competition (and therefore higher prices), there is not enough information in the passage to imply such a conclusion or to select (E) as the best answer.

Question 11

Overview: Question 11 presents a passage that considers how possible restrictions on freedom of thought or freedom of conscience could render these otherwise guaranteed freedoms impossible. The passage refers to the Universal Declaration of Human Rights, a document that establishes the need for all to have the freedom of thought, the freedom of conscience, and the freedom of religion; the passage points out that these freedoms might ultimately be nonexistent in the face of thought-controlling techniques. More specifically, the passage notes the potential for propaganda or educational manipulation that would train children to think a certain way from childhood, thus removing from them any real freedom of thought or conscience while still allowing them to believe that they have such freedoms. The question asks the student to summarize the argument implied in the passage. An implied argument is one that is not overtly stated, so the student must read between the lines, so to speak, to arrive at a conclusion about the point of the passage. That being said, the passage contains all information necessary for deriving such a conclusion, so the student does not require extraneous information.

The Correct Answer:

C The passage states, "If children are taught from an early age to think or believe a certain way, it might not be possible for them to have real freedom of thought or conscience as adults, as they may have no real ability to think for themselves." This suggests that the purpose of the passage is to explain the subtle restrictions that might exist on freedom of thought or conscience. Such restrictions are not explicit or codified in law but (according to the passage) could be used to control these freedoms while allowing the perception that they still exist.

The Incorrect Answers:

A Answer choice (A) seems very likely, but it is important to realize that although the passage suggests that freedom of thought or conscience *might not* be able to exist, it does not state anywhere that they absolutely *do not* or *cannot*. Instead, the passage makes a hypothetical

132

suggestion about what might occur in some, but not all, cases. Therefore, answer choice (A) assumes too much about the point of the passage.

B   Nowhere does the passage state that freedom of thought or conscience is controlled in the same way as freedom of speech or expression. In fact, the passage states that there are laws restricting freedom of speech or expression, but there are no laws restricting freedom of thought or conscience. Answer choice (B) may be eliminated immediately.

D   The passage cites the Universal Declaration of Human Rights to make a point about the perceived guarantee of freedom of thought or conscience, but it then goes on to undermine this Declaration with the information that these freedoms can still be restricted. There is no indication that the passage makes a statement on the need for the Declaration.

E   At no point does the passage suggest that the restrictions on freedom of speech or expression should be lifted, so answer choice (E) can be eliminated immediately.

QUESTION 12

Overview: Question 12 records a conversation between Conrad and Eloise as the two discuss an upcoming change in environmental standards for vehicles in the town of Ecoville. Conrad states that the town is making "excellent," beneficial changes, but Eloise points out that immediately implementing the new standards would place a financial burden on those in a lower income bracket. Since it is impossible to expect any town not to have some lower-income residents, Eloise suggests that Ecoville delay or revise the standards until the requirements can be better funded. The question asks the student to consider the method Eloise uses to counter Conrad's argument.

THE CORRECT ANSWER:

A   **Answer choice (A)** offers the best summary of Eloise's argument: She does acknowledge the reasonableness of Conrad's argument about the importance of new environmental standards, but she also offers evidence that indicates a potential problem in the implementation of these standards. If lower-income families cannot afford to purchase new vehicles or convert them according to the new standards, then the town will be unable to bring the standards into effect.

THE INCORRECT ANSWERS:

B   Eloise does agree with the substance of Conrad's argument (regarding the value of new environmental standards), but she does not offer any alternative reasons for that argument. She merely points out that the plans need to be delayed or revised, and the details she provides explain her reason for this claim; they do not constitute alternative reasons for Conrad's argument itself.

C   Eloise does not explicitly point out a flaw in Conrad's reasoning. Instead, she points out a weakness in the implementation of the new environmental standards. She does not provide a more logical perspective but offers evidence that undermines the claim that the standards should be implemented immediately.

D   Eloise begins by agreeing with Conrad about the importance of the new environmental standards, so we can see from her first sentence that she does not disagree with him entirely.

E   Eloise addresses Conrad's argument directly by agreeing with him in theory, if not in every detail, and she goes on to address very specific problems with the potential implementation of the standards for which he is arguing. So, she does not redirect the argument to a secondary point.

QUESTION 13

Overview: A large public health organization has recommended the banning of the herbal sweetener stevia on the grounds that stevia poses cancer risks, among other health concerns. The public health organization specifically requests that the FDA acknowledge the dangers and ban the sweetener for human consumption. The student is asked to select the answer choice that, if true, most undermines the public health organization's claim about the dangers of stevia.

THE CORRECT ANSWER:

E   **Answer choice (E)** claims that the public health organization has no tests to back up its claims about the dangers of the sweetener. If studies have shown no correlation between consumption of stevia and incidence of cancer or other health problems, this suggests that the public health organization has no evidence to support its claim that stevia is dangerous. Therefore, answer choice (E) most undermines the organization's argument.

THE INCORRECT ANSWERS:

A   Although the fact that the studies were funded by the head of the largest manufacturer of artificial sweetener raises questions about a conflict of interests, this in itself does not directly undermine the claims of the public health organization. That is, an apparent conflict of interest does not necessarily mean that the public health organization offers biased or unreliable results.

B   The use of stevia in Japan without reported negative side effects is interesting, but it does not prove that stevia is not dangerous. This answer choice does not suggest that formal studies, for example, indicate that there is no correlation between consumption of stevia and incidence of cancer or other health problems. Mere common knowledge that stevia is used commonly in Japan does not imply that stevia is safe.

C   Once more, this answer choice raises a question about a conflict of interests—is the head of the public health organization trying to get a job in the FDA by providing an important health warning and thus indicating his usefulness to the FDA? Perhaps, but the passage does not indicate this in any way, nor would this motivation necessarily mean that the organization's claims are incorrect or unreliable. Answer choice (C) does not clearly undermine the organization's claims.

D   The endorsement of a large diabetic association indicates that some believe in the health value of stevia, but this does not undermine the claims of the public health organization. As there is no indication that the diabetes association has conducted studies illustrating that stevia is safe, for example, the endorsement of stevia by the diabetes association is irrelevant to the public health organization's argument. Answer choice (D) can be eliminated at once.

QUESTION 14

Overview: Question 14 presents a scenario in which a large hospital in the town of Riverton has an established policy of turning away patients with no insurance or with insurance that is insufficient

to cover their medical needs. The mayor of Riverton has taken a stand against this practice and has asked the city council to pass an ordinance that requires hospitals to accept all patients, regardless of their insurance coverage. The city council has refused on the grounds that the hospital is a private business and should not have to serve those who cannot pay. The student is asked to consider which assumption among the answer choices can be inferred from the city council's argument.

THE CORRECT ANSWER:

B   Although the passage does not directly mention anti-discrimination laws, it does mention that the mayor perceives the hospital's policy to fall under these laws, explaining his reason for taking the matter before the city council. The city council's decision, then, indicates that they do not believe any laws forbidding discrimination apply to a hospital that is refusing service to uninsured or underinsured patients.

THE INCORRECT ANSWERS:

A   There is nothing in the city council's decision or in the passage to indicate that the majority of residents in Riverton already have sufficient coverage. In fact, the outcry raised against the hospital suggests otherwise.

C, D   There is no information in the passage to suggest that the city council bases its decision on the possibility of government funding or on another hospital accepting patients. The passage does mention that the hospital under discussion is the "primary" one, indicating that there might be others, but there is no suggestion regarding a hospital in a nearby town or about its policies concerning uninsured patients.

E   Although the city council might very well be composed mostly of members who support a different political party than that of the mayor, it is impossible to deduce from the passage that the council is so composed or that this contributes to the city council's decision regarding the hospital.

QUESTION 15

Overview: Question 15 recounts information about a test regarding the effects of drinking milk on calcium levels in women over the age of 40. The passage details what the participating women were asked to do, mentioning specifically that all followed the requirements closely. However, the passage also notes that the test results indicated a disparity between the rise in calcium levels in some women over others. The question asks the student to choose a statement that best explains the discrepancy in results. To select the correct answer, the student must pay close attention to the details in the passage and be careful not to assume details that are inconsistent with the information the passage presents.

THE CORRECT ANSWER:

D   The passage indicates that all of the women were required to drink the required two eight-ounce glasses of milk each day and that all did this faithfully. There is nothing, however, to indicate that the women were not allowed to take a multivitamin with calcium, so **answer choice (D)** provides the best explanation about why some women had higher levels of calcium than others when all were following the stipulations of the test carefully.

THE INCORRECT ANSWERS:

A   Although the difference between whole milk and low-fat milk might result in different calcium levels, it is impossible to deduce this from the passage; contrast this with correct answer choice (D), which specifically indicates that the vitamins some women took included calcium. Because one cannot infer from the passage that the fat content of milk affects its calcium levels, it also cannot be inferred with any certainty that the fat content of the milk contributed to the disparity in the test results.

B   A vitamin D deficiency does decrease the ability to absorb calcium from milk, but answer choice (B) indicates that the women were treated for this deficiency in the past, which implies that this effect is no longer relevant. In addition, the passage states that all of the participants in the test were "in similar states of health " at the time of the study. Therefore, the past treatment for vitamin D deficiency is not likely to be the cause of lower calcium absorption during the study.

C   As with answer choice (A), it is possible that an age difference affected the results, but there is no indication in the passage or in the statement itself that this explains the difference in calcium levels among the women. Had answer choice (C) made the additional claim that women over the age of 50 have more difficulty in absorbing calcium, this choice might be reasonable. As it is, though, it must be eliminated.

E   Answer choice (E) provides no explanation for why giving birth would affect calcium levels in women, so it cannot be correct within the context of the passage.

QUESTION 16

Overview: The passage presents an argument about the need for better standards to determine federal funding for the performing arts, and the student is asked to identify the way in which the argument proceeds. In order to do so, the student should consider the argument step by step: (1) a general claim about the importance of performing arts groups who offer traditional repertoire, (2) a claim about the value to small communities of such groups, including their close proximity to small communities, (3) the comment that federal funding favors groups with progressive material, even though these groups draw smaller audiences than traditional groups, and (4) the claim that federal funding should allot more money to traditional groups. With these steps of the argument in mind, the student can consider the answer choices.

THE CORRECT ANSWER:

A   Based on the outline presented above, **answer choice (A)** is the one that best describes the pattern of reasoning in the passage. The author of the passage begins by presenting a general statement about the importance of traditional groups, develops this view with supporting details, and then concludes with a suggestion for future action.

THE INCORRECT ANSWERS:

B   Although the author of the passage raises awareness about a problem, there is no indication that the author is demanding attention at any time, and based on the opening of the passage, it is clear that the author does not *begin* the argument with a demand; rather, the author begins by presenting a general claim.

C   Far from undermining the opposition, the author points out that *avant-garde* groups contribute something very important to the performing arts. And although the author does

136

raise questions about the way federal funding is allotted to the performing arts, the author does not draw a conclusion from this but rather offers a suggestion for an alternative action.

D   The author does not begin the passage with a call to action. Instead, the author opens with a general remark about the importance of traditional performing arts groups. What is more, the author does not at any point discuss problems with those who oppose the argument in the passage.

E   The author does publicize a concern within the passage and encourage action to be taken, but the author does not discuss alternatives for addressing the concern. Nor does this answer choice reflect the progression of the author's argument within the passage.

QUESTION 17

Overview: The student must consider an editorial in the Williamsburg newspaper in which the writer claims that all students in local schools should be required to attend the colonial center at Williamsburg because of its exceptional historical value. The question asks the student to consider which of the answer selections most undermines the writer's argument. To do this, the student must consider the substance of the argument—that "students are missing out on this opportunity," that "very few local schools take students on field trips" to the colonial center, and thus that "All local schools should be required to take the students to the colonial center, and funding should be provided to make this recommendation a reality"—and then consider what would most undermine the reasonableness of this argument.

THE CORRECT ANSWER:

C   **Answer choice (C)** claims that local schools have already polled families and have found that almost all the students in the local schools have already visited the colonial center with their families. Although this does not call into question the editorial writer's claim that the schools are not taking students to the colonial center, it does offer a reason for why schools do not do so, and it strongly undermines the claim that students are missing out on the opportunity to visit the center. Therefore, answer choice (C) undermines the argument that schools should be required to take students to the center and that extra funding should be made available.

THE INCORRECT ANSWERS:

A   If anything, answer choice (A) only validates the editorial writer's argument by indicating that the local schools in the Williamsburg area focus on the kind of field trips that the colonial center would offer. Answer choice (A) can be eliminated at once.

B   Although answer choice (B) suggests that the editorial writer is motivated by the writer's job (as head of marketing for the colonial center and being responsible for bringing more students there), the writer having this job does not necessarily undermine his argument itself. If the writer's claim that very few children from local schools have been to the colonial center is true, for example, then perhaps the argument is still strong.

D   Like answer choice (A), answer choice (D) provides support to the writer's argument by indicating that the school would receive a discount, so the funding itself would not create too much of a burden. Answer choice (D) can be eliminated immediately.

E   Answer choice (E) provides a reason for why the schools might have refrained from pursuing too many field trips in recent months, but the editorial indicates that the lack of

137

field trips to the colonial center is not a new concern but an ongoing one. Additionally, since the writer of the editorial is arguing for funding, the price of gasoline should not be as much of a concern, as that would be budgeted into the funding. Answer choice (E) does not sufficiently undermine the editorial.

QUESTION 18

Overview: Question 18 presents a scenario in which a large airport is planning to make changes that will benefit domestic passengers but create hassles for international passengers. The hassles are such that many international travelers who frequent the airport have signed a petition and have promised to take their business elsewhere if the airport proceeds with the proposed changes. Nevertheless, the airport has made the decision to go forward with the changes. The question asks the student to infer which answer choice contributed to the airport's decision to continue with the new plans.

THE CORRECT ANSWER:

D   The correct answer choice must indicate some kind of alternative benefit that would explain the airport's willingness to risk the loss of international travelers. Because the proposed changes to the airport will benefit the domestic passengers ("changes intended to improve the ease of flying for domestic passengers"), the airport must have decided that the changes will bring in more domestic passengers, who will more than offset any loss of international passengers.

THE INCORRECT ANSWERS:

A, B   Although the airport might very well be counting on the reasons given in answer choices (A) and (B), nothing in the passage suggests that the airport made a decision based on those reasons. Answer choices (A) and (B) are not supported by the passage.

C   Although answer choice (C) could be a valid reason, nothing in the passage leads the reader to assume that the airport has already spent a large amount of money on the proposed changes. Instead, it suggests that the airport expects to benefit monetarily by drawing new domestic travelers.

E   Answer choice (E) describes a plan the airport might very well use, but there is nothing in the passage to suggest it, so it cannot be inferred that the airport made its decision based on distant plans for improvements in international travel.

QUESTION 19

Overview: A conservative voter comments on a policy traditionally opposed by conservative voters in an attempt to prove to fellow conservatives that the policy is worth supporting. Specifically, the conservative voter argues that universal healthcare is not as costly to taxpayers as other conservative voters usually believe, and that the government should universalize healthcare because it would actually spend less money per person than it currently spends. The student is asked to locate a weakness in the voter's argument.

THE CORRECT ANSWER:

B   The weakness in the voter's argument rests on the fact that the voter seems to assume that the only way to reduce the cost of healthcare per person is to universalize healthcare (the voter argues for universal healthcare strictly on the grounds that it would save money relative to the current healthcare system). However, there might be other options for

reducing the cost of healthcare per person without universalizing healthcare. **Answer choice (B)** accurately states this problem.

THE INCORRECT ANSWERS:

A Answer choice (A) is incorrect because the voter does not explicitly define what he means by universal healthcare. Because he does not define what it would mean for healthcare to be universal in the first place, he does not offer an inconsistent definition of universal healthcare.

C There is no evidence that the voter's claims are unfounded. We cannot know from the passage alone whether his claims of government spending are based on fact or are inflated.

D The conservative voter does reject his usual partisan position in order to encourage other conservatives to support something that is not traditionally a part of the conservative platform. However, doing so does not necessarily weaken his argument. Rather, it shows that the voter has considered the position carefully before deciding to go against his party's usual stand.

E An *ad hominem* attack is a personal attack, and there is no indication of any personal criticisms in the conservative voter's argument. Therefore, answer choice (E) can be eliminated immediately.

QUESTION 20

<u>Overview</u>: Question 20 asks the student to consider an argument about language development in children before puberty and to summarize the main point of the passage. Specifically, the passage begins by pointing out that specialists in language development know that pre-pubescent children learn languages better than post-pubescent children, as the brains of pre-pubescent children are more adapted to absorbing languages. The passage then points out that funding is generally limited for incorporating second-language lessons to elementary children, so schools tend to delay the learning of second languages until high school, or after puberty. In order to discern the main point, the student must consider the purpose of these details, sorting out primary details and secondary details, and consider them in the context of the argument in the passage. It is important to remember that the student is not necessarily being asked to restate the argument itself (that schools should teach second languages to pre-pubescent children) but to summarize the entire point of the passage in the context of the argument.

THE CORRECT ANSWER:

E **Answer choice (E)** best combines all of the primary elements within the context of the argument to arrive at a main point: Because of children's ability to absorb new languages before puberty, schools should adopt second-language lessons for elementary-age children.

THE INCORRECT ANSWERS:

A Answer choice (A) summarizes the point of the details in the passage but does not place these details in the context of the argument being presented. The fact that children learn languages best before puberty is significant, but it needs to be placed alongside the argument about the importance of schools teaching second languages to pre-pubescent children. Answer choice (A) leaves out important elements of the passage.

B   The author of the passage does point out that there is not enough government funding for teaching second languages, but this point seems to be made within the context of *why* schools delay language classes until the high school years; it is not a primary detail.

C   Answer choice (C) offers a secondary detail but does not place this detail within the bigger picture offered by the passage. It does not summarize the main point of the passage and can be eliminated at once.

D   Although the author of the passage does indicate that children would greatly benefit from learning second languages in the elementary years, the author does not pass judgment on schools that do not offer these programs. Instead, the author provides an explanation for why these programs do not exist, suggesting that such hindrances should be overcome. Answer choice (D) fails to summarize the main point of the paragraph.

QUESTIONS 21 AND 22

Overview: Questions 21 and 22 are based on information contained within a passage about the English village of Eyam, widely known as the "plague village" because of the village's decision in 1665 to isolate itself during an outbreak of plague rather than risk infecting others. Over a year later, more than 75 percent of the people in the village had died from the plague. However, almost 25 percent had *not* died, and most of these survivors never caught the plague at all. The passage concludes by noting that researchers have discovered that descendants of plague survivors from Eyam carry a specific gene mutation known as delta 32. Question 21 asks the student to consider the purpose of the paragraph and infer a conclusion from it. Question 22 then asks the student to consider which answer choice would most undermine the conclusion implied in the passage.

QUESTION 21

THE CORRECT ANSWER:

C   The final sentence in the paragraph is not immediately linked to the previous sentences, but there is an implied connection: Some researchers believe the delta 32 mutation found in descendants of the plague survivors helped them resist infection. Since most of the survivors did not contract the disease at all ("Hancock's story is not unique; most of the survivors proved to be immune to the infection altogether"), the statement regarding the researchers' discovery suggests that they believe the gene contributed to survival.

THE INCORRECT ANSWERS:

A   Although answer choice (A)—that the delta 32 mutation is limited to the village of Eyam—could conceivably be accurate, the passage does not claim this anywhere. It claims only that descendants of survivors carry this gene, with the implication that their ancestors who survived the plague carried it as well. But the passage does not rule out the possibility that the gene appears in people in other parts of the world who also survived the plague.

B   Again, answer choice (B) might be true, but the passage does not claim or suggest this anywhere. The passage is focused instead on the possibility that the gene contributed to the survival of certain residents. By stating that it is "interesting" that 25 percent of the villagers survived the plague, it does imply that they did have a disproportionally high rate of the delta 32 mutation; in the immediate aftermath of the plague, all or nearly all of the survivors must have had the mutation. However, because more than 350 years have passed, this may not be true today because the survivors' descendants may have moved away and unrelated people may have moved in.

D The passage makes no suggestion that the delta 32 mutation developed in response to the plague. If anything, it seems to suggest that the gene might already have been carried by certain residents in Eyam and was thus responsible for the survivors' ability to resist the plague infection.

E The passage makes no evaluative statement regarding the decision by the residents of Eyam to isolate themselves; it merely presents the information as fact. Therefore, answer choice (E) can be eliminated immediately.

QUESTION 22

THE CORRECT ANSWER:

A **Answer choice (A)** presents a situation in which other researchers have discovered that the delta 32 mutation does *not* actually resist plague infection in lab rats, with the suggestion that the conclusion drawn by earlier researchers (about the gene's resistance to the plague) is false. If true, answer choice (A) would most clearly undermine the conclusion of the passage.

THE INCORRECT ANSWERS:

B As the passage does not imply that the delta 32 mutation was exclusive to the village of Eyam, answer choice (B) does not undermine the conclusion of the passage in any way. In fact, the presence of the delta 32 mutation in others suggests that the gene did contribute to plague resistance and might go toward supporting the conclusions of the passage.

C Answer choice (C) provides an interesting piece of information, but this information does not undermine the conclusions of the passage. That the delta 32 mutation might also appear to resist HIV infection merely suggests a possible connection between plague infection and HIV. This is, however, irrelevant to the conclusions made in the passage.

D, E Neither answer choice (D) nor answer choice (E) offers any information that undermines the conclusions implied in the passage. Both present details that add context to the passage but have no clear connection to its purpose or conclusion.

QUESTION 23

Overview: Question 23 provides information about the origins of the microwave oven, explaining Percy Spencer's role in its invention and its subsequent development by Raytheon. The passage gives details about Raytheon's original model and notes that the company was never able to attract a wide consumer audience to its Radarange microwave oven. However, in the 1960s, the Litton company began developing and marketing microwave ovens with immediate success. The question asks students to consider which of the answer choices best explains the reason for Litton's commercial success, in contrast to Raytheon's lack of success.

THE CORRECT ANSWER:

D In the middle of the passage, the author notes that Raytheon's Radarange model of the microwave oven was a large, heavy appliance for which general consumers had little interest. **Answer choice (D)** indicates that the Litton company developed a far more compact oven that is still familiar today. Given the size of the Radarange and the negative public response, it is reasonable that consumers were far more interested in a small oven that could fit easily into a kitchen.

141

THE INCORRECT ANSWERS:

A   The fact that Litton marketed its new oven at a trade show in Chicago might very well have contributed to the public awareness of the oven, but there is nothing within the passage to suggest that Raytheon did not do something similar. The best answer choice should indicate a reason for why consumers would clearly choose one over the other *within the context of the passage.*

B   The question specifically asks why Litton was more successful at selling microwave ovens *in the US*, so information about the response in Japan is irrelevant. Answer choice (B) can be eliminated at once.

C   That Litton's model made the microwave oven a popular appliance with American families, and the claim that more than 90 percent of American families own microwaves today, merely adds to the information in the paragraph and proves that Litton was very successful. It does not, however, explain why Litton was more successful than Raytheon.

E   Answer choice (E) is tempting because it indicates that Litton might have had better technology than Raytheon and that the public responded by purchasing Litton's oven instead of Raytheon's. There is nothing in the passage to suggest, however, that Raytheon's technology was flawed or inferior—only that Raytheon's model was large and cumbersome. Thus, answer choice (E) requires inferences that cannot reasonably be drawn from the passage.

QUESTION 24

Overview: The passage provides information about the origin of vaccines, describing conflicting details: The English scientist Edward Jenner usually receives credit for being the first to develop vaccinations in the late 18th century, but historical evidence suggests that the Ottoman Turks were inoculating people before that. Additional details indicate that the peoples of China and India have been using various forms of vaccination for centuries. The student is asked to select an answer choice that best summarizes the main point of the passage.

THE CORRECT ANSWER:

B   All the details in the passage lead to one central suggestion: Although the Englishman (and hence Westerner) Edward Jenner is usually credited with the discovery of vaccines in the late 18th century, historical evidence suggests that peoples in the East were using vaccines long before Jenner began using them. This most clearly summarizes the passage.

THE INCORRECT ANSWERS:

A   The information regarding Lady Montagu's experience with vaccines in Turkey is useful in establishing that inoculations were already familiar to some societies before Jenner's discovery, but it is not the main point of the passage. Therefore, answer choice (A) can be eliminated for having insufficient information.

C   Answer choice (C) summarizes important details in the paragraph, but it fails to summarize the larger point—that *because* there is evidence of vaccination during earlier centuries in China and India, Jenner cannot necessarily be credited with the discovery of vaccines. Answer choice (C) leaves important information out of the summary.

D   The information about inoculation use in China and India well before Jenner's work strongly suggests that the Ottoman Turks cannot claim the discovery of vaccines, but the passage makes no claim that the Ottoman Turks discovered vaccines (or that they are said to have discovered vaccines). Rather, the passage claims only that they were using them before Jenner.

E   The passage makes no claim that Jenner himself took credit for the discovery of vaccines, claiming only that Jenner is generally credited with this discovery. What is more, there is no indication in the passage that Lady Montagu's son was vaccinated for cowpox, the illness that Jenner treated with his vaccines.

QUESTION 25

<u>Overview</u>: Question 25 is one of the more difficult questions in this section of the test because it requires the student to pay very careful attention both to the information in the passage and to the question itself in order to deduce the flaw in the economist's reasoning. The economist makes a claim about traditional indicators during a weak economy: The value of the dollar falls and the price of gold rises. The economist then notes that all economic indicators point to a weak economy, but the expected low dollar/high gold movement is absent. The economist then concludes that the market can be expected to turn around. From a purely economic perspective, there are a number of problems with the economist's reasoning; however, the student does not need to know specific details about economics beyond the information contained in the passage. The most important consideration is that the economist notes a specific precedent: When there is a weak economy, the dollar should fall and gold should rise. Because gold is not rising, the economist concludes that the precedent still holds firm and that the market will be strong again. This conclusion raises the central question of whether the market precedent is still relevant, and this is an issue the economist fails to account for.

THE CORRECT ANSWER:

A   In deriving her conclusion, the economist discusses only the precedents that determine market movement. Her information, however, suggests that the movements in the market might be anomalous and thus that precedent alone cannot determine the conclusion that she reaches. Therefore, the economist's conclusion does not adequately consider the anomalies she indicates, as she draws an incorrect interpretation from them. **Answer choice (A)** most clearly states this.

THE INCORRECT ANSWERS:

B, C   Answer choices (B) and (C) require knowledge about economics in general (and the market in particular) that is not contained within the passage. Although both answer choices might very well be true, this cannot be determined from the information provided within the passage.

D   Answer choice (D) suggests that the economist should focus on the movement of market sectors over stock market indicators and the prices of the dollar and gold. But the passage does not suggest anywhere that an economist should focus on one element of market movement over another, so this answer choice makes assumptions that cannot be inferred from the passage.

E   Answer choice (E) is tempting because it suggests that the economist is overlooking key data in reaching her conclusion, but the passage offers no indication that certain data is

required to reach a conclusion—only that certain precedents are traditional in reaching a conclusion. Therefore, answer choice (E) makes assumptions that cannot be inferred.

Section II: Reading Comprehension

QUESTION 1

Overview: The student is asked to identify the primary purpose of the passage. The most effective approach to identifying the primary purpose is to read the entire passage and look for its core message and intent. All of the answer choices can be found within the passage, but they do not necessarily relate to the author's primary purpose for writing the passage. The student should consider what the author wants the reader to take away from the passage. The author begins by noting Dostoyevsky's profound impact on literature and then describes his themes and impacts. The passage closes by giving examples of his influences on other significant writers, suggesting a cohesive purpose throughout.

THE CORRECT ANSWER:

D The primary purpose of this passage is to highlight how Fyodor Dostoyevsky profoundly impacted literature through his exploration of deep psychological themes and moral dilemmas. The passage describes how Dostoyevsky's approach to character development shaped literary discourse by influencing writers such as Tolstoy, Kafka, and Camus. His intricate character portrayals made him a pivotal figure in literary history whose work continues to resonate with both writers and readers.

THE INCORRECT ANSWERS:

A The passage does describe Dostoyevsky's themes in writing, but they are mentioned to support the idea of the overarching significance of his impact on literature. The discussion of his themes plays a supporting role to illustrate a broader point, and the themes serve as examples to show his influence on literature and character development.

B The author describes Dostoyevsky's character development in the passage and compares his characters to those of other writers. However, the discussion of character development is part of the bigger picture; it is meant to demonstrate how Dostoyevsky's character development is part of his lasting impact on literature.

C There are two meanings for the word *contemporary*, both of which are used in the passage. Dostoyevsky's influence on contemporary, or modern, writers is described in the third paragraph. In the fourth paragraph, the author compares and contrasts Dostoyevsky with Tolstoy, who was a contemporary of Dostoyevsky. This means that they lived and produced work at the same time. However, while these comparisons are described, neither is the author's primary purpose of the passage; rather, they serve to show Dostoyevsky's broader influence on literature and character development.

E The author of this passage emphasizes Dostoyevsky's narrative style and thematic explorations. However, the passage goes on to describe how these elements have resonated with and influenced modern literature, which is the main purpose of the passage. His narrative style is shared to show how it has influenced and shaped modern literary discourse.

QUESTION 2

Overview: The student is asked to identify which character is reminiscent of a Dostoyevsky character. This requires understanding the themes explored by the author and transferring that knowledge to a modern character archetype. The passage states that Dostoyevsky's characters grappled with existential dilemmas and exhibited moral complexity and psychological depth.

THE CORRECT ANSWER:

C   This character questions the constant battle between the greater good and personal gain, echoing Dostoyevsky's character exploration of moral complexity and psychological depth. The character's navigation of moral ambiguity is similar to the inner turmoil and moral conflicts that define Dostoyevsky's characters.

THE INCORRECT ANSWERS:

A   This character's world revolves around appearance and superficial connections. This would be a lighter and more surface-level exploration of character because the emphasis is on external validation rather than deep moral and psychological explorations.

B   This character, defined by moral clarity and a proactive stance on societal issues, diverges from the morally ambiguous characters created by Dostoyevsky. The passage mentions moral incongruity and tumultuous inner conflicts, which are much different than this character's description.

D   This character, with her pragmatic outlook and focus on external achievements, differs from Dostoyevsky's characters. According to the passage, Dostoyevsky's characters experience deep inner turmoil and introspection rather than focusing on pragmatic and immediate concerns.

E   This character, driven by clear ethical values and a commitment to positive change, is a clear contrast to Dostoyevsky's characters. The passage describes Dostoyevsky's characters as grappling with existential dilemmas and suffering tumultuous inner conflicts. Dostoyevsky's characters are more introspective than community focused and more conflicted rather than having clear values.

QUESTION 3

Overview: The student is asked to identify the choice that does **not** show what the comparison of Dostoyevsky to the other authors is intended to do. The mentions of Tolstoy, Kafka, and Camus serve several purposes in this passage. Their approaches are compared, showing how they align with Dostoyevsky's literary approach. The fourth paragraph focuses on these comparisons, but this also serves as a part of the bigger picture, positioning Dostoyevsky in a broader literary context and showcasing his influence and timeless relevance.

THE CORRECT ANSWER:

C   Tolstoy, Kafka, and Camus all have their own distinct literary styles. While they were influenced in their own ways by Dostoyevsky's writing, they were not imitators of his style. The passage describes his influence and lasting relevance but does not suggest that they merely emulated his style without adding their own unique contributions to literature.

THE INCORRECT ANSWERS:

A   The comparison of Dostoyevsky to these other authors provides contextual contrast by showing the similarities and differences of their literary approaches. Tolstoy, in particular, approached similar themes within the same historical period, but he took a more structured approach as compared to Dostoyevsky's turbulent manner.

146

B   By comparing Dostoyevsky to these other authors, the author of this passage is able to showcase Dostoyevsky's influence on other literary movements and writers. While differences in each writer's approaches were also given, the comparison shows Dostoyevsky's lasting influence on subsequent writers.

D   The comparison of Dostoyevsky to Tolstoy, Kafka, and Camus helps to illustrate the evolution of literary themes. Dostoyevsky's writing laid the groundwork for future explorations of complex psychological and philosophical themes, and future writers built upon this approach.

E   Dostoyevsky's timeless relevance is highlighted by showing how his themes and narrative style resonate with other writers. He not only influenced contemporaries like Tolstoy, but he continued to influence later writers as well.

QUESTION 4

Overview: This question asks the student to identify the organization or categorization of the passage. The question requires the student to understand the different literary structures and styles and apply that knowledge to the passage to determine which one fits best. Since each answer choice includes *and*, both terms in the correct answer should hold true for the passage.

THE CORRECT ANSWER:

E   The passage is thematic because it relates to a particular subject. The passage explores Dostoyevsky's contributions to literature and then situates these contributions in a broader literary context. The passage is also comparative since his importance and contributions are established by comparing his works with other authors.

THE INCORRECT ANSWERS:

A   The passage is not chronological or biographical. A chronological passage would be organized in a time-based sequence. If the passage was biographical, it would focus on Dostoyevsky's personal life, background, and experiences.

B   The passage is not narrative, since a narrative passage would describe events in a storytelling format. While the passage does have descriptive elements, particularly when describing Dostoyevsky's writing style, the primary purpose is more to compare writing styles rather than to describe them.

C   This could be an expository passage, since expository writing is meant to explain or teach information. Expository writing can also set forth an argument by using comparisons. However, this is not an analytical passage. It lacks the critical analysis that would involve a deep examination of language use, themes, and narrative techniques in a more academic manner.

D   This is not an argumentative or persuasive passage. It is structured to provide information, not to persuade the reader of a particular point of view. It does not present arguments and counterpoints to attempt to convince the reader.

QUESTION 5

Overview: This question asks the student to make an inference about the answer choices and how they relate to the passage. An inference can be reached based on reasoning from the text evidence. After reading the passage, the student will be able to narrow down the choices based on which is

147

most likely. The answer choices focus on how literature, writers, and styles might have been different prior to Dostoyevsky's writing. The answer is based on his contributions to literature and his influence on subsequent authors.

THE CORRECT ANSWER:

A   This choice states that prior to Dostoyevsky, literature may not have delved as deeply into the human psyche. The passage highlights his contributions to literature, including his explorations of existential despair, moral dilemmas, and the human psyche, suggesting that before his time, literary works may not have focused as much on these themes.

THE INCORRECT ANSWERS:

B   While the passage does describe how Dostoyevsky wrote about complex characters, there is nothing to suggest that writers prior to his time did not include complex characters in their novels. A complex character would not necessarily have to explore the same themes at the same depth that Dostoyevsky delved into.

C   The passage explains how Dostoyevsky influenced Tolstoy, a contemporary of his. This does not suggest that prior to his time, other authors did not influence their contemporaries. The comparison serves to help illustrate his lasting impact on literature.

D   The passage describes Dostoyevsky's narrative style as offering "a stark view into the souls of his characters." This implies that he used a level of introspection and psychological depth that might not have been previously used by other authors. It does not, however, imply that prior narrative styles might not have been diverse in nature.

E   The passage describes how Dostoyevsky's characters faced difficult moral dilemmas. It does not suggest that characters in literature prior to this faced no dilemmas, moral or otherwise. Conflict, including internal conflict, is an important component of literature, and it can be shown in many forms.

QUESTION 6

Overview: This question asks the student to consider why the author mentioned Dostoyevsky's inclusion of faith and Christian themes in his writing. The passage describes several themes used by Dostoyevsky, but these themes in particular have significance in portraying the depth of his characterizations when presented along with contrasting themes. The student will need to consider all the themes mentioned in the passage to grasp the context of this particular reference.

THE CORRECT ANSWER:

D   According to the author, Dostoyevsky's integration of faith and Christian themes into his writing provides insight into the inner thoughts of his characters. Dostoyevsky's characters have profound moral complexity and psychological depth, and faith and Christian themes are part of these characters' spiritual agonies and quests for redemption.

THE INCORRECT ANSWERS:

A   There is no mention of Dostoyevsky's relationship with religion. The mention of faith and Christian themes is in relation to Dostoyevsky's writing and not indicative of his own beliefs.

B   While the passage does mention how Tolstoy approached spirituality and morality in his writing, the bigger picture is that faith and Christian themes in Dostoyevsky's writing serve to illustrate the depth of exploration of the human psyche in his work.

C   The author's mention of Dostoyevsky's integration of faith and Christian themes in his writing does not serve to contrast with the writing style of modern writers. His narrative style and character development helped to shape modern literature, and his exploration of faith and Christian themes to show the moral complexity of characters was a part of this influence.

E   While the inclusion of Dostoyevsky's integration of faith and Christian themes does help to show the author's understanding of Dostoyevsky's thematic approach, the author did not include them to highlight the breadth of Dostoyevsky's themes. Rather, the author describes the use of Christian themes as an example of the depth of Dostoyevsky's characters, along with existential questions and social critiques.

QUESTION 7

Overview: This question asks the student to consider the meaning of a term within the context of the passage. The word *existential*, as used in the fourth paragraph, describes how Dostoyevsky's characters grappled with existential dilemmas and then relates how Kafka followed Dostoyevsky in his existential exploration. Preceding this, the author describes how the characters experience tumultuous inner conflicts and existential despair. These clues point toward a meaning that relates to an introspective exploration of the human condition.

THE CORRECT ANSWER:

E   The term *existential* refers to an individual's subjective experience of being, or existence. When Dostoyevsky's characters experience tumultuous inner conflicts and existential despair, they are experiencing a deep, turbulent exploration of the subjective experience of existence.

THE INCORRECT ANSWERS:

A   The term *existential* does not refer to faith or a quest for spirituality. The word *existential* by itself simply means *existence*. It is usually used in a context involving contemplation of the meaning of that existence. One application of this is in existential philosophy, or *existentialism*. The emphasis of existentialism aligns more closely with the inherent meaninglessness of life and finding one's own purpose rather than meaning added by faith, spirituality, or anything beyond the physical realm. In addition, because the passage is not about existentialism, this answer would be incorrect even if it was an accurate description of the philosophy.

B   Individual freedom is a component of existentialism, but this does not fully encompass the meaning of the word as used in the context of the passage. Existential philosophy includes a need for people to construct their own meaning in life due to individual freedom and the inherent meaninglessness of life. As with answer choice (A), this choice is not an accurate description of existentialism, nor is it an accurate description of the term *existential* as used in the passage.

C   The passage primarily explores Dostoyevsky's characters' psychological depth, spiritual angst, and moral dilemmas. His writing concerns the inner conflicts and moral ambiguities faced by humans. There is no mention of the biological aspects of human survival.

D   While Dostoyevsky does comment on social structures within his writing, this passage is primarily concerned with the individual's introspective journey, not how an individual fits into the bigger picture of society.

QUESTION 8

<u>Overview:</u> This question asks the student to select the choice that best characterizes the author's attitude toward nuclear energy. The student should begin by reading the entire passage, paying close attention to what information the author includes and any signal words that can help to show the author's attitude. The choices include information about the risks and benefits of using nuclear energy and the use of other forms of energy, so the student should find that information in the passage as well to understand how it relates to the overall attitude toward nuclear power. The author might use positive terms to characterize the use of nuclear power or might warn against the dangers of its use. They might describe the risks as insurmountable or might mention them briefly before dismissing any safety concerns. These clues will help guide the student to the author's overall attitude toward the subject.

THE CORRECT ANSWER:

D   The author believes that there are many benefits to using nuclear energy, and its use should be increased. The author does mention risks of its usage, but then continues to extol the many benefits of nuclear power. The passage begins by describing nuclear energy as reliable and emission-free, and it repeats this in the last paragraph, where nuclear energy is also described as affordable and safe. The author states that an increase in reliance on this power source will benefit future generations.

THE INCORRECT ANSWERS:

A   While the author does describe the large nuclear power plant disasters at Three Mile Island, Chernobyl, and Fukushima, this is done in a way that shows them as mere bumps in the road while advancing our reliance on nuclear energy. The author is not cautioning against the risks but describing how they were overcome.

B   The author does describe some risks of the use of nuclear power, but the passage mostly describes the benefits of its usage. The author does not advise caution but instead advises that the use of nuclear power should be increased to benefit future generations.

C   The passage describes nuclear energy as replacing the use of fossil fuels, not as something to use in conjunction with fossil fuels. The author recommends the use of nuclear power in conjunction with renewable energy sources to lessen dependence on fossil fuels.

E   While the author does mention safety issues with nuclear power, they are described as historical issues that have largely been resolved. The author also states that it is the second safest source of energy after solar power and pushes for an increase in usage.

QUESTION 9

<u>Overview:</u> The student is asked to determine what information could help them make a more informed opinion about nuclear energy. This suggests that the passage is biased or presenting

information in an incomplete manner and the addition of certain information could add to the student's understanding of nuclear power, creating a more balanced passage. The student should check to see if any of the choices are already included as part of the passage so that those choices can be eliminated. They will then need to decide which choice will best add to the information presented in the passage to create a more well-rounded picture of the use of nuclear power.

THE CORRECT ANSWER:

B   The passage mostly discusses the advantages of using nuclear power, and the author aims to persuade the reader that nuclear power is a safe, reliable, clean, and affordable source of energy. To help the reader develop a more informed opinion, the author should include an unbiased rundown of the drawbacks of using nuclear power. While some safety issues were discussed, they were quickly dismissed as historical issues that would not occur now due to improvements in safety. The author also mentions nuclear waste storage but does not go into detail and glosses over the cost issues.

THE INCORRECT ANSWERS:

A   The author already described some advantages of nuclear power over fossil fuels in the passage. The passage mostly describes the benefits of nuclear power but leaves off many of the arguments against it. A description of the drawbacks or disadvantages of nuclear power could help the reader develop a more informed opinion.

C   While adding more information about the issues that caused the Chernobyl disaster would illustrate historical safety concerns, the subsequent changes in power plant design might render some of those points moot and would not be useful in forming an opinion today. Instead, the passage could use a rundown of the current potential issues with and drawbacks to using nuclear power.

D   The passage is already about advantages of nuclear power, and adding more information about its benefits would not lead the reader to a more informed opinion. The reader needs more information about any drawbacks to the use of nuclear power.

E   Nuclear energy's carbon impact is mentioned a couple times in the passage as a benefit of using the power source. Rather than a more-detailed description of the carbon benefits, a rundown of the drawbacks would help the reader develop a more informed opinion about the power source.

QUESTION 10

Overview: This question asks the reader to find the best choice that lines up with the reasons that nuclear energy might be cautioned against. The author described the benefits of nuclear energy in detail and listed the benefits clearly, especially in the last paragraph. The potential disadvantages to using nuclear energy are more spread out throughout the passage and not as clearly listed, so the reader will need to find them and distinguish which ones are actually potential disadvantages.

THE CORRECT ANSWER:

D   The passage mentions concerns with safety, costs, and the storage or disposal of nuclear waste. The final paragraph clearly mentions safety and cost concerns, but the third part is not as clearly described. The passage states that nuclear waste is stored until the radiation is no longer dangerous, but this means places must be designated to store radioactive waste for long periods of time.

151

THE INCORRECT ANSWERS:

A   This choice includes carbon output, which is only described in the passage as an advantage of nuclear power, not a disadvantage. Safety and cost efficiency are correct within this choice, but the inclusion of carbon output in this choice makes it incorrect.

B   Safety is a concern, but carbon output is only described as an advantage to using nuclear power.

C   Safety and costs are described as potential concerns, but the frequency of building new plants is explained as something positive. The author recommends that new plants should be built to help ensure that future generations benefit from this power source.

E   Nuclear chain reactions are described as a part of the process for creating nuclear bombs, but this is not described as a danger in using nuclear power.

QUESTION 11

Overview: The student is asked to determine the meaning of the word *renaissance* in the context of the passage. A word can have multiple meanings on its own but will mean something in particular when used in context. The student should locate the word in the passage and decide which choice most closely conveys the meaning of the word as it is used in the passage. The student will likely be able to eliminate choices that are obviously incorrect or that do not convey the correct meaning.

THE CORRECT ANSWER:

B   The line including this word is as follows: "And as a response to the incident, a major reduction in the number of nuclear reactors occurred until a renaissance of nuclear energy in the 2000s." This suggests that the building of new power plants experienced a decline until a "renaissance" of some sort. The wording and the clue word *until* suggest that the decline in building nuclear plants changed course. The word *renaissance*, in this case, refers to a renewed interest in building nuclear plants.

THE INCORRECT ANSWERS:

A   While the word *renaissance* means an increase in focus on the creation of artwork and sculpture when it refers to the Renaissance period, it does not have this meaning in the context of the passage.

C   The sentence refers to a decline in the building of nuclear power plants "until a renaissance of nuclear energy." This wording suggests that the renaissance is a departure from this decline and is an increase in building plants.

D   The sentence refers to a decline in the building of nuclear power plants and then signals that the opposite happened with the word *until*. This refers to more power plants being built, not just a decision to consider using more nuclear energy.

E   This choice refers to newer ways to supply energy, but the sentence refers specifically to a "renaissance" of nuclear energy.

QUESTION 12

Overview: The student needs to determine which choice best characterizes the author's treatment of the topic of nuclear power plant disasters. These disasters were mentioned in the third paragraph, but the author does not go into great detail about them. The student needs to determine

152

Answers and Explanations for Test #1

how these descriptions fit into the passage and how they add to the author's treatment of the topic as a whole. Some of the choices may include information that the author did not disclose, eliminating them as options. Others might mischaracterize the author's attitude toward the information, eliminating them as options as well.

THE CORRECT ANSWER:

E The disasters were mentioned in the passage, but the author does not dwell on this information. Instead, the author goes on to describe the safety issues as historical and explains that improvements in power plant construction have essentially eliminated any future safety concerns.

THE INCORRECT ANSWERS:

A The author does not describe the disasters in much detail and does not warn the reader of potential future disasters. Instead, the author describes these accidents as historical, positioning them as things that are unlikely to happen again.

B The author describes the disasters but does not caution against the building of new plants. Instead, in the final paragraph, the author advocates for the continued usage of nuclear power to help future generations.

C The author describes what led to the disasters but does not express a preference for ending the use of nuclear power. The author strongly advocates for the continued use of nuclear power throughout the passage.

D The author does position these disasters as unusual but does not say that the occurrences will likely increase. Instead, the author explains the issues as historical and relays how improvements to safety measures have made repeats of these disasters unlikely.

QUESTION 13

Overview: This question asks the student to determine the author's purpose for writing the passage. An author might intend to persuade, entertain, or inform the reader. To find the author's purpose, the student will need to read the passage to get a sense of what the passage is about and what information is being shared by the author. If the author is trying to persuade the reader, he or she would likely present an argument to convince the reader of a point of view or encourage the reader to take action about something. If the author is entertaining the reader, he or she might include a plot, dialogue, or other elements to keep the reader engaged. If the author is informing the reader, he or she will educate the reader about a topic by presenting information in a certain way. The author may make comparisons, contrast items or topics, or describe a concept. The student should determine how the author is presenting the information in the passage as well as what information they are presenting.

THE CORRECT ANSWER:

D The author begins by introducing the topic of color field painting. In the thesis sentence, the author explains that the color field painting movement fits in among other art movements and describes how knowing the background of the movement can lead to a greater understanding and appreciation.

153

THE INCORRECT ANSWERS:

A   The author does not describe color field painting as superior to abstract expressionism. Instead, the author describes abstract expressionism to give context to the color field painting movement.

B   While the motivations of the action painters and color field painters are described in the passage, the purpose of this inclusion is to describe color field painting's place in art history.

C   This seems like a strong choice, because abstract expressionism and two of its subsets (color field painting and action painting) are described in the passage. But given the passage's overall focus on color field painting, the description of abstract expressionism seems like context for understanding color field painting rather than the main purpose in itself.

E   The focus of the passage is color field painting, not abstract expressionism. The author does explain how the movements are different from each other, but the focus is to relay color field painting's background and its place in art history.

QUESTION 14

Overview: The student must find the relationship between the art movements described within the passage. Several movements are described or mentioned, including abstract expressionism, Fauvism, and action painting, and their influence on each other is explained. To complicate the relationship, some concurrent movements overlap. The student needs to identify the different movements within the passage and then use the text to determine which ones happened before, after, or at the same time as others.

THE CORRECT ANSWER:

C   Both color field painting and action painting are described as subsets of abstract expressionism happening concurrently within the larger abstract expressionist movement. The term *abstract expressionism* was first used to describe the works of Wassily Kandinsky, who was influenced by Art Nouveau and Fauvism. Therefore, Fauvism and Art Nouveau came first, then abstract expressionism, then color field painting and action painting.

THE INCORRECT ANSWERS:

A   The passage describes action painting and color field painting as subsets of abstract expressionism, which means they were parts of the larger movement. It also describes Fauvism as influencing abstract expressionism, so Fauvism occurred prior to those.

B   Answer choice (B) is technically a correct representation of the timeline, but it is not the best answer. The passage explains that color field painting and action painting were contemporary subsets of abstract expressionism, which means that they occurred at the same time after abstract expressionism began. However, this is not the best answer choice because it equates abstract expressionism and Fauvism, but Fauvism actually preceded abstract expressionism.

D   The passage explains that abstract expressionism began in the 1920s, color field painting and action painting emerged as subsets of abstract expressionism in the 1940s, and the second wave of abstract expressionism occurred in the 1960s.

E   The abstract expressionist movement did not happen after action painting since action painting was a subset of abstract expressionism.

QUESTION 15

<u>Overview</u>: The student must choose what best distinguishes action painting from color field painting. Action painting is described in the third paragraph as another subset of the abstract expressionism movement. The description compares and contrasts some of the techniques and motivations behind action painting with those of color field painting. The student will need to read this carefully to understand how the two movements differed, including their approaches, techniques, and motivations.

THE CORRECT ANSWER:

A   Action painters prioritized the use of movement to create their art. The process was more important than the end result. Color field painters used flat fields of color on large canvases to fill the viewer's field of vision with color.

THE INCORRECT ANSWERS:

B   This choice states that color field painters were heavily influenced by Fauvism and Art Nouveau. The passage describes abstract expressionism as being influenced by these movements, not color field painting.

C   Action painters did try to connect with the viewer's subconscious. However, color field painters did not use subject matter in their art. Instead, they used large, flat fields of color.

D   Both action painters and color field painters, like all abstract expressionists, expressed emotion through aesthetics, albeit in different ways. Color field painters tried to provoke the viewer's emotions and to convey spirituality and transcendence to the viewer through their use of color, while action painters sought to connect with the viewer's subconscious.

E   Action painters did not use representational subject matter in their work. Instead of portraying objects, they focused on expressing emotions.

QUESTION 16

<u>Overview</u>: This question asks the student to choose the closest meaning for the word *eschewed* from the passage. This word is used in the first sentence of the second paragraph: "A subset of abstract expressionism, color field painting eschewed subject matter and instead focused on both color relationships and people's optical responses to them." Reading the word in context and locating similar relevant information within the passage will help the student discover the correct meaning.

THE CORRECT ANSWER:

B   When color field painters eschewed subject matter, they deliberately avoided using subject matter in their art. The word *instead* helps to provide a clue because instead of using subject matter, they focused on color relationships and optical responses to them. This is further reinforced in the fourth paragraph, when the passage describes color field painting as using large fields of color and avoiding any sense of an image versus a background.

THE INCORRECT ANSWERS:

A   The color field painters did not include a lot of subject matter within their art. Instead, they focused on color relationships, creating large fields of color.

155

C   This word does not refer to a transition of one period of art to another. It is describing color field painters' action toward subject matter, and it means that they avoided using it.

D   Since the passage explains that color field painters focused on color relationships and optical responses instead of subject matter, the word refers to their avoidance of using subject matter in their artwork. They did not focus on including a particular subject matter.

E   The passage states that instead of subject matter, color field painters focused on color relationships. This describes how they avoided using subject matter, not that they understood the significance of it.

QUESTION 17

Overview: The student is asked to determine the organizational pattern of the passage. The organizational pattern is how the author arranges the information to best present it to the student. There are several ways information can be presented. A problem-and-solution structure begins with describing a problem and then presenting one or more solutions to that problem. A compare-and-contrast style involves comparing and contrasting two or more items. A claim-and-counterclaim format presents a claim and then gives the counterargument to that claim. A chronological organization structure gives information in the order that it happened. A cause-and-effect format will describe a cause and then give the effects that it had.

B   The passage describes the color field painting movement by comparing it to and contrasting it with other art movements. The primary comparisons are to the contemporary movement of action painting and the broader movement of abstract expressionism that both color field painting and action painting belonged to.

THE INCORRECT ANSWERS:

A   The passage does not present a problem and solution. The passage is about color field painting, and it describes art movements.

C   The passage does claim that the color field movement is best understood within the context of other art movements, but this is not set up as a claim and counterclaim.

D   The passage begins with the art of the 1940s, goes back to the 1920s, returns to the 1940s, then moves to the 1960s, so it is not chronological.

E   The passage does not give a cause and its effect. Instead, it describes the significance of color field painting and how it fits in with other art movements.

QUESTION 18

Overview: The student is asked to determine the tones used by the authors in the two passages. The tone of a passage is the author's attitude toward the subject, and it can be found in the author's word choice, imagery, and sentence structure. The descriptive words used by the author help to create a mood within the writing. Passages such as these, with the same topic, can be presented with very different tones depending on how each author treats the subject. Authors might use positive or negative descriptive words or might stay fairly neutral. They might project enthusiasm, compassion, or urgency through their word choice.

THE CORRECT ANSWER:

A The author of Passage A uses an informative and neutral tone. He or she presents factual information about genetically modified crops and acknowledges concerns about them as well. Passage B is critical and cautionary, focusing on the possible drawbacks of GMOs while highlighting risks and negative consequences.

THE INCORRECT ANSWERS:

B Passage A is neutral and informative rather than enthusiastic or intense. The author presents the information factually and evenly. Passage B is not dismissive or scornful. It is critical of the use of GMOs and cautionary of the risks and negative consequences.

C Passage A is optimistic about the future of GMOs but not nostalgic. Nostalgia would show a fondness for the past. Passage B is not persuasive or sarcastic. A persuasive tone would attempt to sway the reader to the author's point of view, while a sarcastic tone would use irony to mock the subject of the passage.

D Passage A is not sympathetic since it is not showing pity or sorrow toward a misfortune. Passage B does not have an anxious or urgent tone. An anxious tone would show worry or unease, and an urgent tone would express a need for immediate action.

E Passage A is not colloquial since it is not written in an informal tone. It has a more formal and informational tone. Passage B is not argumentative or defensive. An argumentative tone would show disagreement, while a defensive tone would be anxious to avoid criticism.

QUESTION 19

Overview: This question asks the student to choose the option that best characterizes the difference between the main ideas of the passages. To determine this, the student must find the main idea of each passage and then determine the difference between the two. The main idea is the overall message that the author is trying to express. It can often be found in the first and last paragraph of a passage, but not always. Research or informational writing will often include the main idea in the final paragraph, while persuasive writing may include it at the beginning. The student should consider what message the author is attempting to share with the reader and how the passage supports that message.

THE CORRECT ANSWER:

C The main idea of Passage A is to present a positive view of genetically modified crops, stating that GMOs have the potential to benefit society. This is shared at the end of the last paragraph, and a list of the benefits of GMOs is included at the end of the first paragraph. Passage B presents a critical view of GMO use, emphasizing the risks and consequences of including GMO crops in our food supply.

THE INCORRECT ANSWERS:

A Passage A does mention concerns about GMO use, but the concerns are not the focus or main idea. This passage presents a positive view of GMO use. Passage B mentions the inequities between large farms and small-scale farmers due to the cost of GMOs and pesticides, but this is not the focus of the passage.

B Passage A does relay nutritional advantages of GMO use, but this is not the main idea of the passage. Passage B does criticize the environmental consequences, but the overall idea

157

expressed in this passage is the risks and consequences of including GMOs in our food supply.

D Passage A does mention the financial benefits for farmers when using GMOs, but this is not the main idea of the passage. The passage overall explains the potential of GMOs to benefit society. Passage B touches on the issues raised by intellectual rights when using GMOs, but the overall message of this passage is the risks and consequences of genetically modifying food.

E Passage A does emphasize that certain crops, including corn and soybeans, are heavily available in GMO form. The overall main idea of this passage, though, is the potential benefits to society that GMOs can create. Passage B does warn about ill effects that are possible due to the consumption of GMOs, but the main idea is the overall risks and consequences of GMO use.

QUESTION 20

<u>Overview</u>: The student must determine which idea is best supported by both passages. This necessitates a close reading of both passages to find which choice the authors of both Passage A and Passage B would agree with. While the passages have different tones, different main ideas, and share a lot of different information, the student will be able to find a similarity within both passages that is expressed by one of these choices. The student can eliminate choices by dismissing any that is expressed in only one passage, or in neither.

THE CORRECT ANSWER:

D Both passages cite the safety standards that are applied to GMOs. They also both refer to concerns expressed about their safety, although Passage A mentions it briefly and Passage B focuses on the concerns and risks.

THE INCORRECT ANSWERS:

A Passage A focuses on the advantages that GMOs pose for society, but Passage B does not characterize them as advantageous. Both passages do mention the potential risks that some express about their use.

B Passage A expresses that there are a large number of GMOs already present in our food supply. Passage B mainly expresses the risks of GMO use and does not express that the positives should be focused upon.

C Both passages mention concerns over GMO use, but Passage B focuses mostly on the risks of including GMOs in our food supply. While Passage B recommends caution about their use, neither passage recommends pausing their use entirely.

E Passage A describes the effectiveness of GMOs against certain pests but does not state that their costs are too high to justify their use.

QUESTION 21

<u>Overview</u>: The student is asked to decide which choice the authors of these passages would likely disagree over. The student will need to closely read each passage and find the points of agreement or disagreement. The incorrect options will be points that the authors would agree over, so if the student finds these points of agreement, those choices can be eliminated. The two passages express

different tones and include different information, but there are a few similarities. The different points of view will lead to the choice in which the authors disagree.

THE CORRECT ANSWER:

B The authors would disagree on whether GMO foods should be used to address nutritional deficiencies. While the author of Passage A expresses that this is a positive use of GMOs, the author of Passage B describes potential adverse health effects and warns that caution should be used when proceeding with GMO use.

THE INCORRECT ANSWERS:

A Both passages express that GMO practices benefit owners of farms. Passage A describes the benefits of GMOs to farming, and the student can assume this includes large and small farms. Passage B describes how GMO practices benefit large agribusinesses more than small-scale farms.

C Both passages express that the term "GMO" is most frequently associated with crops. Passage A describes this association outright, and Passage B explains GMO use but only refers to its association with crops.

D Passage A describes the criticism of GMO use briefly. Passage B expresses criticism and concern with GMO use throughout the passage.

E Passage A explains how GMOs have benefited farmers in multiple ways, including greater resistance to pests and droughts. Passage B explains that GMO use has benefited large agribusinesses more than small-scale farmers.

QUESTION 22

Overview: This question asks the student to choose the statement that is supported by one or both of the passages. This means that the correct choice might only be supported by the information in one of the passages, or it might be supported by information shared by both. The student can eliminate any choice that is supported by neither passage, and this will narrow down the options. Close reading of the details in both passages and comparison with each option will help the student arrive at the correct answer.

THE CORRECT ANSWER:

D While Passage B is critical of the use of GMOs with regard to our food supply, Passage A expresses the benefits of GMO use on farming practices and foods. Passage A states that our foods can be nutritionally enhanced with GMOs.

THE INCORRECT ANSWERS:

A Passage A refers to corn and soybeans, not meat or fish, when describing GMOs. While animals can be genetically modified, neither passage expresses that most GMOs found in stores are meat and fish.

B Passage B describes how the use of antibiotic-resistant genes is limited when modifying foods. Passage A does not mention antibiotic-resistant genes.

C Passage B describes how GMOs create an uneven playing field with regard to different sizes of farms due to the costs of seeds and pesticides.

E   Passage A states that genetic modification reduces the need to use pesticides on crops, not that it eliminates the need. Passage B refers to pesticide use, stating that those who cannot afford GMO seeds must use a high amount of pesticides. It does not say that the need is eliminated when using the GMOs, though.

QUESTION 23

Overview: The student must determine what aspect of GMOs is discussed positively in Passage A but not in Passage B. This requires a close comparison of the information in the passages. The student will need to find information in Passage A that is not discussed as a benefit of GMOs in Passage B. The answer choices might contain benefits that were not introduced in either passages, benefits that were only discussed in Passage B, or even aspects that are not benefits of using GMOs. The student can eliminate choices that are negative features and those that were not covered in either passage.

THE CORRECT ANSWER:

B   Passage A mentions that GMOs can be made with proteins that are toxic to pests, which is described as positive in decreasing the need for externally applied chemical pesticides. Passage B, on the other hand, discusses concerns about these genetic changes, including a possible increase in "superbugs" and "superweeds," which are pests that have evolved resistance to pesticides/herbicides.

THE INCORRECT ANSWERS:

A   Passage B describes benefits to large farms, not to small-scale farmers. Passage A does not describe any benefits of GMOs to small-scale farmers.

C   Passage B explains that the intellectual rights surrounding GMOs can be an issue. Passage A does not discuss this aspect.

D   Neither passage discusses GMOs' impact on the reduction of greenhouse gas emissions.

E   Passage A describes the increased nutritional profile of GMO foods, but Passage B does not discuss nutritional quality at all.

QUESTION 24

Overview: The student will need to decide how the author of Passage A would most likely respond to the comment in Passage B about the potential adverse health effects of consuming GMOs. Passage B mostly warns of the negative effects of GMOs, while Passage A mostly shares the positive benefits of GMO use. Using the information shared in the passages, the student will choose the answer that best aligns with the author's attitude from Passage A and the information shared in the passage. This will require close reading and making inferences about how the author feels about the topic.

THE CORRECT ANSWER:

B   The author would likely cite the strict safety standards that GMOs are subjected to and remind the author of Passage B that the benefits far outweigh the risks. This is alluded to when the author mentions the concerns but then lists the benefits of GMO use.

THE INCORRECT ANSWERS:

A   The author of Passage A would not recommend pausing the use of GMOs. The author describes the many benefits of their use and describes how those benefits outweigh any concerns about the potential health risks.

C   The author of Passage A would not recommend finding safer options than GMOs. The passage is about the benefits of using GMOs, and the author recommends their continued use.

D   While the author of Passage A cites food security as a benefit of using GMOs, he or she does not advise that adverse health effects would be a reasonable tradeoff. Instead, the author mentions the concerns that some have about GMO use but quickly dismisses those concerns by listing the benefits.

E   Passage A describes how pervasive GMOs are in our current food supply. Avoiding them entirely would be possible but difficult due to their pervasiveness.

QUESTION 25

<u>Overview</u>: This question asks for a potential drawback of GMO use according to both passages. The student will need to closely compare the passages to find what they have in common. Some choices will be present in one passage or the other, but only one will be mentioned in both passages. The student can narrow down the options by eliminating any that is not mentioned in both passages.

THE CORRECT ANSWER:

B   Both passages mention the potential implications of GMOs on human health. Passage A describes concerns over the safety of including modified produce in our food supply. Passage B states this more directly, citing concerns over risks to human health.

THE INCORRECT ANSWERS:

A   Passage B mentions the costs associated with farming GMO crops and how those costs unfairly affect small farms. Passage A does not describe the effects of these costs.

C   Passage B describes the possibility of creating "superbugs" as a negative aspect of GMO use. Passage A talks about increased resistance to pests but does not mention the "superbug" aspect.

D   Passage B describes the risk of introducing toxins into the food supply through genetic modifications. Passage A does not mention this risk.

E   Passage B talks about the use of antibiotic-resistant genes in GMOs and the risk of their transfer into the human digestive tract. This is not discussed in Passage A.

Section III: Reading Comprehension

QUESTIONS 1–7

<u>Synopsis</u>: This passage discusses the significance of Federalist No. 10, one of the 85 Federalist Papers written by James Madison, Alexander Hamilton, and John Jay. The author begins by noting that Federalist No. 10 was not traditionally viewed as one of the most important Federalist essays but that it received more attention in the 20th century due to its subject matter: the issue of dealing with factions. Given the rise in the importance and power of political parties, as well as various partisan groups, the author points out that it is hardly surprising for No. 10 to seem increasingly relevant. But the author is quick to note that it is erroneous to assume No. 10 had no relevance for its own era.

In the second paragraph, the author introduces the topic of the Anti-Federalists, the group that opposed the Federalists (of which Madison, Hamilton, and Jay were members) on the grounds that the Constitution would give too much power to a central government. More specifically, the Anti-Federalists believed that the United States could never truly be united and that the only way to unite in one sense would be by forcing some to abandon their beliefs. After the ratification of the Constitution, the Anti-Federalists were overruled and their group disbanded.

In the final paragraph, the author examines the reception to Federalist No. 10 in the late 18th century and beyond, after the demise of the Anti-Federalists. No. 10 received very little attention until the 20th century, when scholars began considering the relevance and significance of Madison's arguments and applying them to the modern day. The author cites two historians with differing viewpoints and concludes that although many historians—by questioning the historical relevance of Federalist No. 10 versus its contemporary relevance—have missed the point altogether, No. 10 addresses issues that have plagued every government and society throughout history and thus is not limited in relevance to one era. As a final word, the author refocuses briefly on the Anti-Federalists, claiming that although they did not win the argument about the Constitution, history has suggested that their arguments were sound.

QUESTION 1

<u>Overview</u>: Question 1 asks the student what the passage is doing in a broad sense. The student needs to consider the main point of the passage and how the author goes about arriving at his or her conclusions, reflecting on the overall goal of the passage. Is it comparative? Persuasive? Narrative? Or something else altogether? In reviewing the answer choices, the student must think clearly about the author's methods, so as not to confuse informational details with the broader purpose of the passage.

THE CORRECT ANSWER:

C   The author mentions in the first paragraph that Federalist No. 10 was not traditionally viewed as being a significant essay but has gained in scholarly importance over time. This establishes a time-honored view of the essay. But the author then takes a new approach to considering this essay by pointing out that it is not only relevant to the current era but is also relevant to the era in which it was written. The author notes that no historian has made this argument, so the author is essentially offering a new perspective on a scholarly argument that has been going on for some time.

THE INCORRECT ANSWERS:

A   Although the author hints at contrasting viewpoints along the way—the traditional viewpoint that No. 10 is irrelevant versus the current viewpoint that it is significant, the viewpoint of Charles Beard versus the viewpoint of Douglass Adair—the overall format of the passage is not mainly one of contrast. The author's purpose is not to consider in detail the differences between these various contrasting views and the reasons behind them; rather, the author intends to offer a new perspective, as described above.

B   The "traditional argument" is the argument that Federalist No. 10 had little relevance to the 18th century but is far more relevant in the modern era. The author notes in the second paragraph the presence of factions during the 18th century and then states in the second-to-last sentence that Federalist No. 10 addresses issues that are relevant to every era. Therefore, the author cannot be said to be defending the traditional argument.

D   At no point does the author define any terms, other than to explain who the Anti-Federalists were, and this is not the main point of the passage. Nor does this answer choice explain the author's format for developing the main point.

E   Although the author does consider the "popular" academic position (of the modern relevance of Federalist No. 10, but not the 18th-century relevance), the author does not necessarily challenge its validity. Although the author refers to Douglass Adair's opinion, there is no reason to believe that Adair's view is the popular one: indeed, considering the author's statements in the first paragraph about the current applicability of No. 10, it would seem that Adair's perspective does not necessarily mesh with the popular position.

QUESTION 2

<u>Overview</u>: The student must consider the author's main point (as opposed to the author's method, from question 1). This means that the student must combine all of the various pieces of information within the paragraph and formulate a statement of summary. The student should take a few seconds to mentally prepare a brief summary, as this will help determine the correct answer. Simply put, the author is making two statements: (1) Federalist No. 10 contains arguments that are relevant to any time period, and (2) the Anti-Federalists were essentially right in their belief that factions would always exist. With these two points in mind, the student can find the correct answer quickly.

THE CORRECT ANSWER:

A   **Answer choice (A)** restates the summary sentences from above, noting that Federalist No. 10 has a universal application for all eras and that the Anti-Federalists understood the reality of factions.

THE INCORRECT ANSWERS:

B   Answer choice (B), although stating information that can be derived from the passage, fails to offer a complete summary of the author's purpose in the passage. The student should watch for answer choices that provide correct information but that do not provide *enough* correct information. Just because the statement is true according to the passage does not mean that it offers a complete summary of the passage.

C   Answer choice (C) summarizes the traditional argument regarding Federalist No. 10, as well as Douglass Adair's position. However, the author indicates disagreement with this

163

viewpoint in all three paragraphs, so this answer choice must also be incorrect. Answer choice (C) can be eliminated immediately.

D   Answer choice (D) is slightly difficult because the author *could* be suggesting that Federalist No. 10 (and thus the Federalists) did not appreciate the inevitability of factions. However, the passage makes no clear comment about this at any point. The author suggests that Madison believed factions had to be quelled but does not mention the opinion of the Federalists on whether factions would always exist. The author states only that Anti-Federalists believed factions would always exist and would interfere with a nation's unity. Answer choice (D) has no unambiguous support in the passage.

E   The author does suggest that the Anti-Federalists were right on one account (that factions were inevitable), but there is no mention at any point of human nature, nor can it be assumed that the author is referring to human nature when discussing the arguments of the Anti-Federalists. Answer choice (E), therefore, makes unsupported inferences. In addition, this answer choice makes no mention of Federalist No. 10, which is the subject of the passage.

QUESTION 3

Overview: Question 3 asks the student to consider Douglass Adair's quotation about Federalist No. 10 being a "a document that was exclusive in application and in relevance to the time of its composition" and then infer one of the answer choices from it. The student should bear in mind that the question does not ask for the meaning of the quotation within the context of the passage or even what the author's opinion of the quotation seems to be. This is not a trick question; it is a fairly simple one, and that in itself might seem to be tricky.

THE CORRECT ANSWER:

E   Given the simple meaning of the quotation—that Federalist No. 10 is limited in relevance to the 18th century, when it was written—it can be inferred that Douglass Adair did not believe No. 10 to have relevance in any time period outside the 18th century.

THE INCORRECT ANSWERS:

A   Although it is entirely possible that Douglass Adair believed all of the Federalist Papers to be limited in relevance to the 18th century, the quotation does not suggest this. Such a claim cannot be assumed from the quotation alone.

B   Again, it is entirely possible that Douglass Adair disagreed with Charles Beard's position about the role of the Constitution in class exploitation, but the quotation under discussion makes no reference to that, nor does it suggest any commentary on Beard's own views. In fact, Adair's connection to Beard is only noted in that Adair paraphrases Beard's beliefs about the Constitution. No mention is made of Beard's own words on No. 10 or of Adair's opinion about Beard's thoughts on No. 10.

C   Adair's comment about Federalist No. 10 is specifically related to the relevance of that essay to its own era. Clearly, Adair believes that the information within No. 10 relates to factions during the 18th century, and the Anti-Federalists were a faction and believed that factions were inevitable. But there is no evidence in the quotation to claim that Adair is agreeing with the Anti-Federalists in any way. He is simply remarking on the way that No. 10 should be applied historically.

D   Adair makes no comment on current political situations, and there is nothing in his quotation to suggest that he would apply Federalist No. 10 to the modern era if problems like those of the 18th century reappeared. Answer choice (D) makes inferences that have no support in the passage.

QUESTION 4

<u>Overview</u>: The student is asked to select an answer choice that is suggested by the passage. This means that the student is not looking for the main point of the passage but a statement that can be inferred from it (not a statement necessarily made explicitly in the passage). The student needs to keep the main point in mind, however (see question 2). In locating the correct answer choice, it is necessary to avoid any choices that step too far outside of the claims specifically given in the passage. (That is, a reasonable inference does not make assumptions that have no support in the passage.)

THE CORRECT ANSWER:

B   The passage notes in the second paragraph that the Federalists did win the primary argument for the Constitution and states at the end of the final paragraph that the Anti-Federalists had the last word, suggesting that they were correct about factions. As stated by "Cato," the Anti-Federalist position indicates that this group believed it would be impossible for people of such varying differences to live comfortably together in the long term, suggesting that unity could be achieved only by force, and that such unity would not be real. **Answer choice (B)** encompasses this by stating that the Federalists succeeded in ratifying the Constitution but that the Anti-Federalists were right about the impossibility of real long-term unity.

THE INCORRECT ANSWERS:

A   The author does state in the first paragraph that the Federalist Papers were "highly influential," and the author also says in the second paragraph that in writing them the Federalists contributed to the successful ratification of the Constitution. But the passage does not imply that the essays were an *essential* contribution, which would suggest that the Constitution could not have been ratified without them. Although this might be true, the passage makes no statement to support it clearly.

C   Although the author might very well believe that more Americans needed to listen to the Anti-Federalists, there is no such clear statement in the passage. What is more, the passage does not mention free speech at all, and although free speech is a freedom guaranteed by the Bill of Rights, the passage provides no reason to single out one freedom over others.

D   The author states that upon the ratification of the Constitution, the Anti-Federalists "more or less ceased to exist, its members left with little choice but to accept the system that had been adopted," and that they were silenced. But the author does not comment on irony or even suggest it, nor does the author imply that this was a *great* irony of the 18th century.

E   Answer choice (E) contradicts the statement in the first paragraph that Federalist No. 10 is now viewed in importance alongside those that are traditionally considered to be the most significant essays. In addition, the answer choice is too vague in its phrase "some of the others," offering little information about the essays to which No. 10 is being compared.

QUESTION 5

<u>Overview</u>: The student must consider which of the answer choices the author would most likely agree with, based on the statements made within the passage. As in question 4, the student needs to think carefully about what the passage says and what can be inferred from this, without straying too far from the actual statements made in the passage.

THE CORRECT ANSWER:

C   The author states that after the ratification of the Constitution, the Anti-Federalists "more or less ceased to exist, its members left with little choice but to accept the system that had been adopted"; the author also begins the last paragraph with the phrase, "With the silencing of the Anti-Federalist faction." These statements suggest that the Federalists were silenced, that is, that they were forced to be quiet about some of their ideas after the Constitution was ratified.

THE INCORRECT ANSWERS:

A   Far from agreeing with the statement that Federalist No. 51, No. 78, and No. 84 remain the most important, the author states in the first paragraph that many now see No. 10 as being of equal importance. Because the author does not contradict this statement anywhere in the passage, it can be assumed that the author agrees with the new importance afforded to No. 10.

B   The author mentions Charles Beard's theories and explains why they were well received but makes no evaluative statement about them, either explicitly or implicitly. Answer choice (B) can be eliminated immediately.

D   Although the author clearly disagrees with Douglass Adair's argument, there is no indication that the author thinks it is "intentionally misleading."

E   The passage implies that the author agrees with the Anti-Federalists on at least one issue (that of factions), but the claim that the Anti-Federalists had a "more realistic appreciation of social and political challenges than the Federalists did" is a much broader, stronger claim. There is no evidence that the author would endorse that claim.

QUESTION 6

<u>Overview</u>: Question 6 asks the student to provide a definition for a word in the passage, considering the word within the context of the sentence in which it is located. A question that requires the student to select a definition usually means that the word will not be used as expected: in this case, the word *unkindred*, which usually signifies a non-relationship, is being employed differently, so the student must consider which of the answer choices best replaces the word in the sentence.

THE CORRECT ANSWER:

C   The context in which the word *unkindred* can be found is as follows: "… the '<u>unkindred legislature</u>' recommended by the Constitution would lead to the biblical example of the house collapsing because it had been divided against itself" (emphasis added). In other words, "Cato" is describing the legislature as "unkindred," noting that the differing interests of diverse Americans will create too much division. The correct answer choice, therefore, will need to provide a meaning that indicates variance or distinction that leads to division, and *disparate* is such a word.

THE INCORRECT ANSWERS:

A   Of the remaining answer choices, choice (A) is the most tempting because it encompasses the suggestion of many differences to which "Cato" is referring. In this case, however, *diverse* does not suggest a *negative* difference, so *diverse* would not replace *unkindred* as well as *disparate*, the word in answer choice (C).

B   Although disorganization seems to be a secondary effect of the various differences that lead to disunity, the quotation does not suggest that the legislature itself is disorganized or that it is disorganization that causes factions. The word *disorganization*, therefore, implies more than can be inferred from the quotation.

D   The quotation does not indicate that the legislature is unique but rather that it is filled with differences.

E   Although one of the results of disunity seems to be antagonism that creates factions, the quotation does not necessarily suggest that the legislature starts out as antagonistic. The correct synonym needs to indicate a cause (*disparity*) that creates an effect (*disunity and factions*), so *antagonism* is approaching the quotation from the wrong direction.

QUESTION 7

<u>Overview</u>: The final question asks the student to consider the organization of the passage (i.e., the way the author organizes and presents the information in order to make the argument). To answer this question, the student should review each paragraph quickly. Sentences to target include the first and last sentences of each paragraph. This question does not require any inferring; it is simply a matter of considering the arrangement of the information within the passage and comparing this arrangement to the answer choices. In several cases, the student might be able to eliminate answer choices by looking at the first item in the choice.

THE CORRECT ANSWER:

E   The layout of the passage is fairly simple: the author begins by considering an idea, follows this idea with some historical information, and then uses the historical information to argue in favor of a main point. **Answer choice (E)** describes this organization.

THE INCORRECT ANSWERS:

A   Although the author does mention several theories in the final paragraph, the author does not begin the passage with these theories. And although the author does narrow the focus in the final paragraph, there is no sense that the focus is on one of the theories presented; in fact, the author presents an entirely new take on the topic. Answer choice (A) can be eliminated immediately.

B   The author does begin the passage with the hint of a main point, but the historical information contained within the second paragraph is not a diversion. Instead, it offers the historical context for the author's primary argument in the final paragraph.

C   The author does not begin the passage with a wide historical focus and then narrow to a contemporary one. In fact, the historical and contemporary focuses play off one another throughout the passage, with the author concluding that both are of equal relevance to a discussion of Federalist No. 10.

D   Answer choice (D) seems briefly promising, but it does not correctly describe the organization of the paragraph. Although the author hints at a thesis in the first paragraph, there is no statement of a clear thesis. Additionally, the author does not use the historical information to defend a thesis from the first paragraph; instead, the author uses it to make the primary argument in the final paragraph. The statements in the passage place the opinions about Federalist No. 10 in the context of contemporary opinions, but the author does not suggest that these quotations come from leading authorities.

Questions 8–14

Synopsis: This passage discusses the linguistic issue of why there are not more Celtic influences in the English language. The author begins by discussing the linguistic influences that scholars already recognize and have identified—Old English (or the language of the Anglo-Saxons), Old Norse, French, and Latin—and then proceeds to explain that scholars consider the lack of Celtic words to be a mystery. When the Anglo-Saxons arrived in Britain, a considerable population of Celts lived there already. Yet there are very few Celtic words in the English language, leading scholars to wonder why the Celts appeared to make no linguistic impact on the Anglo-Saxons. The author notes that scholars have offered several theories. Some argue that the Anglo-Saxons did not need the Celtic words because they had enough of their own; a problem with this view is that the Anglo-Saxons borrowed plenty of words from other languages. Some scholars have suggested, then, that the Anglo-Saxons viewed the Celts as inferior people and thus avoided their language. The fact that the Celts ultimately migrated north and west—away from the Anglo-Saxons—seems to support this theory.

In the second paragraph, the author considers this theory and raises questions about it, citing linguistic scholar David Crystal, who points out that there is considerable evidence that the Anglo-Saxons gave their children Welsh (or Celtic) names. For example, there is a record of an Anglo-Saxon king and a renowned religious poet bearing Welsh names. It is unlikely that the Anglo-Saxons would deliberately choose names from the language of a group of people believed to be inferior, so Crystal points out that this theory does not bear up under scrutiny.

In the third paragraph, the author again cites Crystal with his suggestion that the English word *cross* might derive from Celtic sources. Again, it is unlikely that the Anglo-Saxons would adopt a word with such religious significance from a despised language. The author concludes by noting that the mystery of why there are so few Celtic words in the English language might never be solved, but that the theory that the Anglo-Saxons ignored Celtic words because the Celts were viewed as inferior ultimately does not have much historical or linguistic support.

Question 8

Overview: Question 8 asks the student to consider the main idea of the passage. This question does not ask for any inferences, so the student just needs to consider the author's argument and summarize it. Each paragraph contains a topic, and these topics ultimately contribute to a primary point. What the student needs to watch for in the answer choices are options that mention a supporting idea but that do not reflect the main point of the passage. The correct answer choice must encompass the evidence in the passage with a single statement.

The Correct Answer:

A   Although the first paragraph seems to provide a great deal of information about the background of the English language, as well as theories about the lack of Celtic words, it is the final sentence of the first paragraph and the first sentence of the second paragraph that indicate the direction the passage will be taking. The author notes that one theory in particular seems to have support, but then goes on to say that a leading linguistic scholar disagrees with it. The rest of the passage explains Crystal's evidence that weakens the initial theory, and the final sentence of the third paragraph provides the main point: "It is unlikely that the mystery of the missing Celtic words will ever be solved satisfactorily, but what little evidence remains suggests that the mystery can no longer be written off as a case of a conquered people becoming linguistically obsolete." **Answer choice (A)** most closely summarizes this.

THE INCORRECT ANSWERS:

B   Answer choice (B) focuses on a supporting piece of evidence Crystal has provided to undermine a theory, but that is not, in itself, the main point of the passage.

C   Although the author does suggest that there might be considerable significance to the few Celtic words that are in the English language, the author does *not* claim or suggest anywhere that these words render other linguistic sources less significant. Additionally, the author does not indicate that there is any evidence contradicting the traditionally recognized influences.

D, E   As in answer choice (B), the example of the English changing German names during World War I, as well as the example of the occurrence of Welsh names among the Anglo-Saxons, is intended to give supporting evidence; such examples are not meant to represent the primary argument. In addition, answer choice (E) states, "of all the Celtic peoples, the Welsh had the greatest linguistic impact on Anglo-Saxon daily life," an idea unsupported by the passage.

QUESTION 9

Overview: The student is asked to select a synonymous phrase for a word that is used in the passage. The student will need to consider the word itself, with its dictionary definitions, and then place the word within the context of the sentence and consider how it is being used. (If the student does not know the meaning of the word, the student should infer what basic idea is intended by considering the context in which the word appears.) In question 9, the word to be examined is *connotation*, which is defined as a connection, association, or secondary meaning. In the passage, the word is being used to convey the English concern that their names were connected to German names or assumed to be German. With this in mind, the student needs to consider the answer choices.

THE CORRECT ANSWER:

D   Of all the answer choices, **answer choice (D)** best conveys the idea of "connection" and "assumption" with the phrase *potential association*. As the passage notes, the English changed their names "to avoid sounding too Germanic." In other words, they feared the potential of their names being associated with German names.

THE INCORRECT ANSWERS:

A   Answer choice (A) offers a good option, but the passage does not suggest that the English knew there would be a *clear relationship*, nor does the word *connotation* in the context of the passage suggest a clear relationship. Instead, it suggests the possibility of a connection between English names and German names, a connection that answer choice (A) does not indicate.

169

B   Although the fears of the English were about a linguistic matter (they were concerned that their names might be connected with German names), the phrase *linguistic origin* cannot replace the word *connotation* in meaning. The linguistic origin of the name is what creates the association of the family with their German background, but is not itself the association.

C   Although the word *connotation* can, in some cases, indicate a definition that is more theoretical than it is concrete, there is nothing in the use of the word *connotation* in the passage to suggest that the English were concerned about a *theoretical definition*.

E   Although the decision by some English people to change their names might have been based on emotion, the passage does not suggest this. There is no clear suggestion of emotion in the passage.

QUESTION 10

Overview: Question 10 asks the student to consider the purpose of the discussion of *cross* in the third paragraph. It was noted in the explanation for question 8 that the possible origin of the word *cross* represents supporting evidence for the main point of the passage. Therefore, the student should immediately recognize that the correct answer will indicate the way in which this discussion supports or points to the main argument. Recall that the main argument of the passage is that, despite the rarity of Celtic words in English, linguistic evidence suggests an influence on the English language from some Celtic words, so it is no longer possible to claim that the Anglo-Saxons deliberately avoided the people or the language in the belief that the Celts were inferior.

THE CORRECT ANSWER:

E   Bearing the main point of the passage in mind, **answer choice (E)** is the only answer choice to place the *cross* discussion within the context of this main point. Choice (E) notes that the information about the word *cross* offers evidence that the few Celtic words that exist in the English language are quite significant; this indicates that the Celtic influence might have been more important than was previously thought. This point supports the main argument.

THE INCORRECT ANSWERS:

A   The passage does not claim that many Celtic words influenced English; rather, the passage notes that there are few such Celtic words.

B   The discussion of the word *cross* does suggest that an Old Irish (Celtic) word might have influenced an Old Norse word, but the passage does not indicate at any point that there were other Old Irish words that influenced Old Norse words. Answer choice (B) makes assumptions that are not supported by the passage, so it can be eliminated immediately.

C   The discussion of the word *cross* does not illustrate the fallacy of assuming that the Celtic language had a great influence on English. Rather, the author simply takes it for granted that no one will assume that the Celtic language had a very great influence on English.

D   David Crystal's contribution to the passage is to show that there are signs of Celtic influence on the English language. The passage does not make any claim, however, that Crystal believes that Celtic words make up an *important part* of the English language.

QUESTION 11

Overview: As with question 10, question 11 asks the student to consider the role of a certain example—this time, the one about English actions toward German names during World War I. And

as with the discussion of the word *cross*, this particular information offers secondary details that support the main point of the passage. The student needs to consider the English/German names discussion within the context of the main point as well as within the context of the statements immediately around it. The correct answer might or might not specifically mention the main point of the passage, but it will show that the example fits well with that main point.

THE CORRECT ANSWER:

C   The discussion of the English decision to change German or German-sounding names during World War I follows a point by David Crystal about how the Anglo-Saxons would probably not have given their children Welsh names if those names were associated with something or someone negative. Since there is no immediate connection to Welsh names and German names, the student can assume that the author is intending to use this particular example to show how perceptions of peoples (whether they are Germans or Celts) influence the use of names associated with those peoples. **Answer choice (C)** expresses this idea.

THE INCORRECT ANSWERS:

A   The passage makes no reference to human nature, and although it might be thought that associating names from certain linguistic backgrounds with either positive or negative qualities is a facet of human nature, there is not enough information in the passage to support this point. More specifically, the question of human nature is not related to the question of the impact of certain Celtic words in the English language.

B   If the discussion of the English response to German names were being used to support the traditional theory about Anglo-Saxons viewing the Celts as inferior, this argument might indeed undermine the theory of Welsh influence. But in the context of the second paragraph, it actually supports the point about Anglo-Saxons embracing certain Welsh influences because it indicates clearly that the Anglo-Saxons did *not* avoid Welsh names.

D   Answer choice (D) seems briefly promising, as the example of the English immediately follows this statement by the author: "it is unlikely that Anglo-Saxon parents would bestow Celtic names on their children if those names were closely associated with a despised language or a group of people deemed inferior." This seems to suggest that if the English during World War I did to the Germans what the much earlier Anglo-Saxons did *not* do to the Welsh, then the English might have viewed the Germans as inferior. But once again, this is not the main point of the illustration.

E   The passage does not indicate at any point that English names might really be German. In fact, it seems to suggest just the opposite—if many English people changed their previously German names, then their names are now English. More to the point, however, this inference does not have a strong connection to the main point of the passage.

QUESTION 12

<u>Overview</u>: Question 12 asks the student to consider the author's tone toward the traditional argument that the Anglo-Saxons might have deliberately avoided Celtic words because they viewed the Celts as inferior. Certain key words in the passage will help discern whether the author's tone is one of vitriolic disagreement, patronization, or something else altogether. Such phrases include "Other scholars have **suggested the theory**...," "leading linguistic scholar David Crystal **disagrees**...," "the mystery **can no longer be written off**..." All of these phrases suggest a polite

171

scholarly discussion in which one scholar (the author) disagrees with other scholars—firmly but not rudely. The student should select an answer choice that best reflects this.

THE CORRECT ANSWER:

B   **Answer choice (B)** is the only answer choice to present the best description of the author's tone: *scholarly disagreement*. The author is polite but holds to a certain view and defends that view.

THE INCORRECT ANSWERS:

A   The author might hold firmly to an opinion, but there is no tone of *insistence*, nor is the author *self-righteous* at any point.

C   The author disagrees with the traditional viewpoint, but disagreement alone does not mean a patronizing attitude, and this passage does not suggest a patronizing tone at any point. Had the author mentioned the differing viewpoint in a condescending way in order to belittle those who held it, the tone might be described as patronizing. As it is, however, the author never "talks down" to those with opposing viewpoints, allowing the rest of the discussion to focus on evidence that supports his own perspective.

D   The author's concern about the traditional viewpoint might be justifiable in his or her own mind, but the passage does not necessarily convey this tone. Instead, the tone is a scholarly one that leaves emotion at the door and relies on evidence.

E   Although the author does disagree with the traditional viewpoint, there is nothing in the passage to indicate vitriol (bitterly harsh language). Answer choice (E) can be eliminated immediately.

QUESTION 13

Overview: The student is asked to consider the primary purpose of the passage.

This is slightly different from considering the main point of the passage in that the student is looking from an even broader perspective without necessarily paraphrasing and summarizing details. However, knowing the main point is helpful in that the main point shapes the primary purpose of the passage. In this case, the author's final statement provides some indication of this: "what little evidence remains suggests that the mystery can no longer be written off as a case of a conquered people becoming linguistically obsolete." The author suggests that there is evidence to counter a specific viewpoint and discourages embracing this viewpoint without considering the evidence.

THE CORRECT ANSWER:

A   **Answer choice (A)** reflects the intention of the passage, as displayed in the final sentence: The author's purpose is to caution against making a historical judgment (the traditional viewpoint about the Anglo-Saxons deliberately avoiding Celtic words) without considering the further linguistic evidence (the Welsh names and the word *cross*).

THE INCORRECT ANSWERS:

B   The author does not necessarily indicate that the theory advocated is a new one; in fact, the author suggests that the leading authority David Crystal holds this theory, so the author is

doing more to summarize Crystal's theory than to produce a new one. Answer choice (B) does not have enough support within the passage.

C The author is indeed discussing Crystal's opinion, but the purpose of the passage is not so much to defend his position as to caution against holding the traditional theory with respect to the linguistic evidence.

D The author does attempt to disprove a traditional theory, but there is no real focus on the linguistic evidence that supports this theory. (In fact, the author does not even mention the linguistic evidence that supports it and mentions only historical evidence of the relocation of the Celts.)

E The author discusses two of the opposing theories, but there is no comparison in the passage.

QUESTION 14

<u>Overview</u>: The final question for the second Reading Comprehension passage asks which answer choice the author would likely agree with. As with all questions like this, the student needs to consider what is stated directly in the passage and what can be inferred from these statements. The student should also take qualities such as tone into account.

THE CORRECT ANSWER:

B The author notes in the first paragraph that there are few Celtic words in the English language and then implies in the second and third paragraphs that *although* there are few words, these words suggest a significant linguistic role (significant because the word *cross* itself, for example, has religious significance).

THE INCORRECT ANSWERS:

A Although the author suggests that *one word* in the English language might have a Celtic origin as opposed to an Old Norse origin, it cannot be inferred that the author believes there are more words (in English) of Celtic origin than of Latin or Old Norse origin. In fact, the author states several times that there are not many Celtic words in the English language, so the passage does not support the inference that one word is indicative of a much broader trend.

C The author uses the example of the word *cross* to indicate the potential for significant Celtic influences on English. Although this is related to the issue of how the English viewed the Celts (favorably or unfavorably), the passage does not indicate that the author believes that the origin of the word *cross* is enough by itself to indicate how the English viewed the Celts. The author also cites David Crystal's mention of the Welsh names, so it cannot be inferred that the author believes that the origin of *cross* by itself is sufficient regarding the issue of how the English viewed the Celts.

D The author cites the information in answer choice (D) as one reason why some scholars believe that Anglo-Saxons did not absorb many Celtic words. However, the author also points out that this theory "is inconsistent with evidence that the Anglo-Saxons borrowed everyday words from other languages, such as Old Norse and French."

E The author notes that it is unlikely that the Anglo-Saxons would have given their children Welsh names if they believed the Celts to be inferior, but it cannot necessarily be inferred from this alone that the Anglo-Saxons *unquestionably* had a high opinion of the Celts. This strong claim goes well beyond anything stated or implied in the passage.

QUESTIONS 15–21

Synopsis: Questions 15–21 are based on a reading passage that discusses beauty and whether it can be objectively quantified. The author begins by presenting the general point that beauty has always fascinated people and then mentions that scientists in the modern era have begun considering beauty from a forensic perspective, asking whether beauty can be measured and quantified scientifically. The author writes that scientists believe that they *can* measure and quantify beauty, and their tests—based on the results from volunteers of many social and cultural backgrounds— indicate that there are some people who are definitely, consistently perceived as beautiful and some who are not. The author states that even infants are not immune to beauty and that studies indicate that babies are drawn to beautiful faces.

The author begins the second paragraph with a hint of caution, however. Although beauty might be quantifiable and objective, the response to beauty has potentially serious consequences. The author cites the research of psychologist Nancy Etcoff to show that beauty is often confused with goodness and that beautiful people are, in many cases, assumed to be good in some sense. Teachers tend to score attractive students higher; employers tend to award jobs to the attractive applicants; even voters tend to place their support behind the attractive candidate. The author's tone suggests that this is a concern worth looking into more closely.

In the third paragraph, the author discusses the question of whether people are looking at the beauty and character relation the wrong way around. Perhaps beauty and character (or personality) *are* related, but it is character or personality that affects beauty. Once again, the author cites Etcoff, this time with an anecdote about the notoriously unattractive writer George Eliot. Although author Henry James thought her ugly at first, he revised this view significantly after he had spoken with her and had come to know her better. The author concludes by suggesting that scientists look more closely at the way that character affects beauty, or the perception of it, because character might play a much larger role in beauty than previously thought.

QUESTION 15

Overview: Question 15 asks the student to summarize the main point of the passage by considering the author's central idea. The student should recognize that the primary point of the passage lies in the last part of the final paragraph, when the author recommends studying how character or other such personal qualities affect beauty: "Scientists studying the phenomenon of beauty would do well to turn their attention to the more intangible qualities that define beauty and to consider what lies beneath the skin in addition to what lies on it." The answer choice that best paraphrases this sentence will be the correct answer.

THE CORRECT ANSWER:

B   **Answer choice (B)** best summarizes the final sentence of the third paragraph by stating that scientists need to consider qualities other than those on the face in order to study beauty as accurately as possible.

THE INCORRECT ANSWERS:

A   Answer choice (A) is incorrect because the passage makes no mention of society's claims about beauty or that society believes everyone to be uniquely beautiful. The passage does

mention that scientists are testing beauty to see "whether beauty is simply a subjective perception," but this perception is not attributed to society.

C   Although the passage makes the suggestion that beauty *might* be related to character or personality, the author's main point is not to argue this but rather to suggest that scientists reconsider the way they study beauty.

D   The author notes that scientists believe some people will always be perceived as beautiful, observing that beautiful people often receive privileges on the basis of their outward appearance. But this is not the author's main argument.

E   At no point does the author indicate that scientists will be unable to quantify beauty; in fact, the author suggests that scientists have already been fairly successful in quantifying beauty (lines 27–35), so answer choice (E) contradicts statements that the author makes in the passage.

QUESTION 16

<u>Overview</u>: Question 16 asks the student to select a belief of the author that can be inferred from the passage. The student should keep the passage closely in mind and use only the direct statements of the passage to determine the correct answer. In many cases, wrong answer choices will contain bits of information that *seem* correct. But the question is not asking what the author seems to believe; the question is asking the student to infer a correct answer from what the author *does* say.

THE CORRECT ANSWER:

E   In the third paragraph, the author makes the following statements: "Character might affect beauty, and not the other way around," and "It may be that although physical features are indeed important in determining beauty, beauty itself is not simply 'skin deep' and can be defined by more than an arrangement of eyes, nose, and lips." From this, the student may deduce that the author is suggesting that personality might affect the perception of beauty. **Answer choice (E)** correctly summarizes the author's implied belief.

THE INCORRECT ANSWERS:

A   The author does note that "Today, scientists are beginning to consider the question of beauty." However, this does not in itself imply that scientists have long ignored beauty (this is a stronger claim than what the author suggests), but only that today's scientific community has begun studying beauty.

B   Although the author opens the third paragraph with the statement, "Scientists claim that a certain combination of features is universally considered beautiful," the author does not suggest anywhere that this is a view he or she supports. Answer choice (B) cannot be inferred as the author's belief.

C   The author's comments that beauty is often associated with character suggest a tone of caution toward this issue, but the passage does not offer any indication that the author believes it should *never* be the case that beauty is associated with character. Answer choice (C) infers too much from the author's statements in the passage.

D   The author does not claim that beauty is relative to cultural standards. Answer choice (D) can be eliminated immediately.

QUESTION 17

Overview: Question 17 asks the student to determine which answer choice best expresses the reasoning behind the author's argument. This question essentially requires the student to identify the main argument and then identify the reasons the author gives for that argument. All information necessary for identifying the correct answer is contained within the passage. The main point is that scientists, in their studies of beauty, should consider studying character or personality alongside their study of physical beauty. This suggests that the author's reasoning is that there must be something more than outward appearance that determines beauty. The answer choice that best expresses this idea will be correct.

THE CORRECT ANSWER:

C **Answer choice (C)** best summarizes the reasoning that inner qualities might affect outward appearance. This answer choice includes the author's statement from the first paragraph that beauty often seems mysterious, as well as alluding to the statements from the last paragraph about Henry James perceiving George Eliot as more beautiful after he had come to know her better.

THE INCORRECT ANSWERS:

A Although the author does encourage scientists to expand their approach to studying beauty, the author does not mention the idea of "definitive results" anywhere in the passage, nor is the author's focus on whether or not such results can be achieved.

B Although the author mentions the scientific study about infants recognizing beauty, there is no indication in the passage that this is due to infants also recognizing character. What is more, this answer choice does not express the reasoning behind the author's main point.

D The author does not seem to support beautiful people receiving privileges just on the basis of their beauty, but the author makes no mention of long-term consequences in society (mentioning only "interesting consequences"), so answer choice (D) has no support in the passage. In addition, answer choice (D) does not describe the reasoning behind the author's main point, so it can be eliminated immediately.

E Although the author does indicate the reasoning described in answer choice (E), this answer choice does not clearly express the reasoning behind the author's *main* point, relating instead to a secondary point.

QUESTION 18

Overview: Question 18 asks the student to consider the discussion of how teachers respond to attractive students in classroom situations and then place this discussion within the context of the passage; in particular, the student is to identify the purpose of this information in the passage. First the student should place the discussion within the context of the main point, and then examine it in relation to the surrounding sentences. The main point states that scientists should consider character along with physical features in studying beauty. The sentence immediately before the beginning of the teacher and student discussion is, "Beautiful people are often assumed to be better than unattractive people in terms of character or other traits." Therefore, the correct answer will reflect the idea that attractive people are often assumed to have better character (or other superior traits) than unattractive people.

THE CORRECT ANSWER:

A   **Answer choice (A)** best reflects the idea that character is often associated with appearance. Additionally, answer choice (A) is suggestive of the information that teachers scored attractive students higher, judging their qualities on the basis of their looks.

THE INCORRECT ANSWERS:

B   Although the author does not indicate approval of the idea that beauty can determine character in the eyes of some, the author also does not explicitly discuss disapproval or express the view that beautiful people receive "unnecessary privileges." The information about teachers and attractive students in classroom situations is not intended to illustrate that there is a problem with unnecessary privileges; rather, it functions as evidence for the statement that perceptions of beauty influence perceptions of character.

C   The author does not indicate anything about the character of the students except to say that it was perceived to be good based on the how the students appeared. This is not the same as the claim that character affects how people appear (rather, it is the reverse).

D   There is no discussion in the passage about youth affecting beauty. (In the discussion of the school children, there is no claim that children are perceived as beautiful *because* they are young; in fact, the discussion explicitly mentions that some children are seen as less attractive, rather than as uniformly beautiful.) The author does cite research showing that employers hire applicants based in part on the beauty of applicants and that voters choose candidates based in part on the beauty of candidates. However, there is no support in the passage for the idea that youth is associated with beauty.

E   Although the author does mention that there are some features universally deemed beautiful, there is no mention of the way teachers respond to beauty in students around the world. Nor does the author indicate that the studies cited (regarding how teachers respond to attractive students) can be described as universal. Answer choice (E) infers more than the passage supports.

QUESTION 19

<u>Overview</u>: Question 19 asks the student to review the information about Henry James's meeting with George Eliot and to identify the purpose of this particular discussion, that is, what the author is trying to indicate by including it. To select the correct answer, the student needs to place the Henry James and George Eliot discussion within the context of the main point as well as the surrounding sentences. The main point is that scientists should consider studying character or personality when studying beauty. In the sentence immediately before the anecdote about James and Eliot, the author notes, "Etcoff hints at the effect of character or personality in determining beauty." From this, the student can determine that the purpose of this particular section in the passage is to indicate that beauty is not always determined exclusively by outward appearance and that qualities of personality or character can be a significant part of the perception of beauty. The answer choice that best expresses this will be correct.

THE CORRECT ANSWER:

A   **Answer choice (A)** is the only answer choice that effectively conveys the idea that personality or character can affect the perception of beauty.

177

THE INCORRECT ANSWERS:

B   Although the author does say that George Eliot was "a woman who was generally considered to be very unattractive," the author does not make any suggestion that George Eliot would be judged differently today, even by the "scientific" tests referred to in the passage. In fact, the author notes that scientific studies show that perceptions of beauty based on outward appearance alone are universal, so there is no reason to think that Eliot would be judged differently today.

C   Although the author does tell the anecdote to indicate that Eliot's personality or character played a significant role in James's perception of her beauty, there is no clear suggestion that the *only* way to perceive her as beautiful was by interacting with her. Answer choice (C) makes inferences that are unsupported by the passage.

D   The author makes no comment on James's standards of beauty. In fact, the placement of the story within the passage suggests that James is intended to represent the average person with a standard appreciation for certain physical features, so it is inaccurate to claim from the passage alone that James's standards were different than the standards of others.

E   Although answer choice (E) is essentially correct in its statement, this statement does not, in and of itself, contribute to the author's reason for including the anecdote. The George Eliot and Henry James story contributes to the author's main point as well as supporting the statements immediately surrounding it. Answer choice (E) does not explain how the story does this.

QUESTION 20

Overview: The student must consider the meaning of the word *phenomenon* within the context of the passage and select a synonymous phrase that best replaces it. As always with word replacement questions, the student must consider not only the word itself but the way that it is being used in the passage. It is entirely possible that several of the answer choices *could* be correct, but only one of them will be the best choice. In the passage, the word *phenomenon* as a description of beauty is being used to suggest something that is not unique to one person but is remarkable and worthy of being studied. The correct answer choice will reflect this.

THE CORRECT ANSWER:

C   The author notes that beauty is often mysterious, and notes the strong responses that people may have to beauty or a lack thereof. This indicates that the *phenomenon of beauty* is that beauty is a remarkable and interesting quality.

THE INCORRECT ANSWERS:

A   The passage does indicate that beauty is a *reality*, but it does not suggest anywhere that this reality is *unexpected*. Answer choice (A) has no support within the passage.

B   The phrase *intriguing occurrence* may replace the word *phenomenon* in some contexts because a phenomenon can be something that does happen (*occurrence*) and that is worthy of study (*intriguing*). However, this is not the meaning of *phenomenon* as used in this sentence.

D   Although some might see beauty as abstract, the passage does not make any indication of this. What is more, the passage does not indicate that beauty is an *experience*.

E   *Subjective analysis* does not make sense as a replacement for *phenomenon* in the sentence ("scientists studying the subjective analysis of beauty"), so it can be eliminated immediately.

QUESTION 21

<u>Overview</u>: The last question of the third reading comprehension passage asks the student to consider the author's tone toward the issue of beautiful people receiving privileges or being judged as better on the basis of their beauty. The student should note that although the author indicates disapproval of this, there is no clear statement of anger toward it. Rather, the author's tone is largely one of giving information. Using expressions such as "interesting consequences," the author is not demanding that the reader believe one thing over another or suggesting anger or combativeness. The correct answer choice will reflect the author's intention to provide information without strong emotion.

THE CORRECT ANSWER:

D   The phrase *informative interest* best expresses the author's tone because it conveys the attitude that the author takes: one of providing information and suggesting mild interest but not a strong emotion such as insistence or anger.

THE INCORRECT ANSWERS:

A   The author's tone is not one of combativeness; on this basis alone, answer choice (A) can be rejected. In addition, rather than sounding skeptical, the author indicates that the information cited about the issue is accurate.

B   The author does not mock the issue at any point, nor is there a tone of amusement, since the author takes the issue seriously. Answer choice (B) can be eliminated immediately.

C   The author does not seem to give in and assume the problem is inevitable, so there is no sense of *quiet resignation*.

E   The author might very well be angry, but this tone is not apparent in the passage. And although the author's concern might be righteous, this does not suggest in itself that the author's tone is one of *righteous anger*.

QUESTIONS 22–27

<u>Synopsis</u>: Questions 22–27 derive from two passages, which offer slightly different perspectives on the issue of free trade. The author of the first passage begins by quoting 18th-century economist Adam Smith and noting that Smith's arguments about the need for free trade remain relevant in the modern day. The author goes on to claim that most Americans support free trade (as well as outsourcing) and that the majority of economists recognize that free trade is necessary for economic growth because it allows a society to import the items that it cannot make as cheaply, thereby focusing its resources on what it can produce in a cost-effective way. What is more, the author claims that in terms of trade and the United States, free trade also benefits its trading partners, particularly when those partners have smaller or weaker economies than the US. By importing the items produced in these countries, the US is helping to improve the standard of living there by paying workers more than they might receive from traditional work in these economies. The author does note a downside, however. Citing Harvard economist Gregory Mankiw, the author points out that free trade often receives bad press during a weak economy, but suggests it is not an abundance of foreign imports that causes economic problems so much as a scarcity of exports. The author concludes by noting that a strong economy will have a healthy balance of imports and

179

exports, and that the US should increase its manufacturing and export output in a weak economy in order to create stability.

The second passage takes a rather different approach to the question of free trade. The author begins by acknowledging that free trade is a good thing (it is a sound economic practice) and that most economists affirm its contribution to economic strength, particularly in a global economic system. At the same time, the author points out that *unrestricted* free trade has negative qualities. Citing the economist Ha-Joon Chang, the author notes that unrestricted free trade can create problems not so much for the US but for its trading partners when they are smaller and weaker. Economies are always changing, and many times a small-business owner will find that the demand for their product is no longer enough to support their business. The US has a strong welfare system, as well as plenty of government assistance for struggling business owners to get back on their feet; however, smaller and weaker economies seldom have any such programs or available assistance. As a result, small-business owners in many of these economies simply become poorer rather than wealthier, and their standard of living decreases rather than improves. The author also cites Swedish economist Peter Soderbaum, who points out that few economists take secondary factors into account when considering the value of free trade; these include factors such as environmental consequences, the changes to a culture, and even the disappearance of traditional lifestyles in some societies that can come as a result of free trade. These factors are seldom calculated into the free trade equation. The author of Passage B concludes by encouraging economists to create a new system for analyzing benefits and detriments of free trade, a system that would include these factors and thus illustrate a far more accurate picture of the cost and value of free trade.

QUESTION 22

<u>Overview</u>: Question 22 asks the student to consider which answer choice both authors would likely agree on. Considering the differences in conclusion between the two authors, there are few similarities in the passages, except that both authors begin by claiming that free trade is a good thing and both note somewhere in their respective passages that at times free trade can raise questions and controversy. The correct answer choice will reflect this.

THE CORRECT ANSWER:

C   The author of Passage A states the following: "Harvard economics professor Gregory Mankiw argues that the majority of economists also recognize the importance of free trade" and "Mankiw also cautions against faulting the free movement of imports into the US during a time of economic weakness." The author of Passage B notes the following: "As most economists agree, free trade is a sound economic practice and necessary for the US to function effectively in a global economy, but unrestricted free trade is fraught with potential dangers that few economists seem willing to acknowledge or address." Both authors agree that free trade (1) is an important element of economic strength and (2) is sometimes controversial. **Answer choice (C)** best expresses this.

THE INCORRECT ANSWERS:

A   Although the author of Passage A suggests that free trade is *entirely* beneficial to trading partners and particularly beneficial to the smaller and weaker economies, the author of Passage B argues that free trade can be problematic for smaller and weaker economies. The two authors do not agree on the statement in answer choice (A).

B   The author of Passage A argues that in a weak economy, the US should increase manufacturing. This does perhaps suggest that the US will thereby increase jobs. However,

the author of Passage B makes no statement suggesting the government should create jobs, focusing only on the need for government assistance when business owners lose their businesses. It cannot be inferred that the author of Passage B is advocating job creation.

D   The author of Passage B suggests that free trade can be beneficial for a larger and stronger economy but not necessarily for a smaller and weaker one. In contrast, the author of Passage A indicates that free trade benefits both trading partners, as long as the economies balance their imports and exports. It cannot be inferred that the author of Passage A believes free trade to be damaging to one economy and beneficial to another.

E   The author of Passage A makes the argument in answer choice (E), but the author of Passage B makes no mention of exports, focusing instead on the idea that economists should create a new system for analyzing the peripheral dangers that free trade can cause.

QUESTION 23

Overview: Question 23 asks the student to select the answer choice that best summarizes Passage A. The author of Passage A focuses on the benefits of unrestricted free trade and notes toward the end that economies must balance imports and exports: "A balance of imports and exports is required to maintain a stable economy, and an increase in manufacturing for exports during economic weakness can actually bolster a struggling economy." The correct answer choice thus will reflect the author's focus on three areas: (1) free trade strengthens an economy, (2) free trade itself does not need to be restricted, but (3) economies need to balance imports and exports.

THE CORRECT ANSWER:

D   **Answer choice (D)** provides the best statement of summary for Passage A by including the three factors discussed in the Overview. The author notes that unrestricted free trade is broadly supported by the American public, then cites economists who support the view that free trade is a positive for the US economy and that importation can be balanced by exports rather than restrictions on trade.

THE INCORRECT ANSWERS:

A   The author of Passage A *does* mention Adam Smith and argues that his claims in *The Wealth of Nations* were sound; but this is not necessarily the *main point* of Passage A. As the Overview indicates, the author's main point is a combined focus on the importance of free trade, the need to avoid restrictions, and the need to balance imports and exports. Answer choice (A) focuses on a secondary detail in the passage.

B   The author of Passage A definitely concludes with a focus on the importance of balancing imports and exports, but this is the final statement that rounds out the author's three-part focus. Answer choice (B) fails to include the other two parts of this focus.

C   The author of Passage A does claim that economic weakness is not a result of unrestricted free trade, suggesting that it is instead a domestic problem (that is, related to a decrease of exports). However, answer choice (C) does not fully explain the author's main point. The author also states that free trade *is* a good thing and that what is specifically needed is a balance between imports and exports. Answer choice (C) does not convey this.

E   Answer choice (E) reflects secondary details the author discusses: that the majority of Americans support outsourcing, and the view that outsourcing can be good for economic growth. This, however, is not the main point of Passage A.

181

QUESTION 24

<u>Overview</u>: The student is asked to select the answer choice that best reflects the main point of Passage B. The author of Passage B acknowledges immediately that free trade is a good thing but qualifies the statement fairly early by raising questions about the problems with *unrestricted* free trade. Additionally, the author concludes by recommending that economists begin to consider the various effects of free trade, most of which they currently overlook. The correct answer choice will thus reflect this two-part focus: (1) unrestricted free trade can cause problems, and (2) economists need a different approach to free trade, an approach that considers the various effects of free trade.

THE CORRECT ANSWER:

E   By including details about the problems with unrestricted free trade and discussing the need for a new approach, **answer choice (E)** best expresses the two-part focus that is discussed in the Overview.

THE INCORRECT ANSWERS:

A   The author mentions in the first sentence that most economists will concede the value of free trade, especially in a global economy. But this is not the main point of the passage, and the author goes on to qualify the benefits of free trade very quickly. Answer choice (A), therefore, overlooks the main point of the passage.

B   Answer choice (B) reflects the position of Swedish economics professor Peter Soderbaum. The author uses Soderbaum's views to *support* the main point but not necessarily to express the main point itself. Answer choice (B) focuses on a supporting detail and fails to state the author's primary argument.

C, D   Again, answer choices (C) and (D) reflect supporting details that the author uses to lead up to the main point but are not themselves the main point. The author claims that one of the problems with unrestricted free trade is that it can leave business owners with no recourse when their governments lack assistance programs; the author argues that these programs—welfare programs and financial assistance opportunities—are an important part of helping small-business owners survive in an evolving economy. However, the author goes on to say that economists need to take these details into account for a new approach to free trade.

QUESTION 25

<u>Overview</u>: Question 25 asks the student to consider how Passage B responds to Passage A. The student must consider how Passage B essentially *replies* to Passage A. Based on question 22, the student should recall that both authors agree on the fundamental importance of free trade, but the author of Passage B offers some qualifications on the benefits of free trade. So, Passage B responds by agreeing with Passage A in part but by then providing a different perspective. The correct answer choice will reflect this.

THE CORRECT ANSWER:

B   **Answer choice (B)** best expresses the statements made in the Overview: that Passage B concedes the importance of free trade but then goes on to offer a qualification and thus an alternative thesis.

THE INCORRECT ANSWERS:

A   Although Passage B does provide a different argument than Passage A, Passage B does not point out a specific flaw in the reasoning of Passage A. Rather, the two passages (though both begin with a focus on free trade) are essentially discussing related but different topics. Passage B would point out a flaw in the reasoning of Passage A if Passage B gave evidence that, for example, global free trade *is* a contributing factor to a weak economy, but it does no such thing. Passage B simply has a different focus.

C   The authors of Passage A and Passage B ultimately address different concerns that arise with the issue of free trade; as a result, it cannot be said that the author's arguments in Passage A negate the claims that are made in Passage B. The author of Passage B is encouraging a new approach to studying the cost-value ratio of free trade, while the author of Passage A argues that the US should increase exports during a weak economy to get the greatest benefit from free trade. The connection between these two ideas is not strong enough to support the statement made in answer choice (C).

D   Both authors discuss free trade in the same way; they are simply addressing two different areas that free trade affects. What is more, the author of Passage B calls for a new approach to analyzing free trade but not necessarily a new definition of *free trade*. Therefore, it cannot be said from the information in either passage that the details about the secondary problems in Passage B undermine the definition of *free trade* in Passage A.

E   Again, the two authors address entirely different sides of the issue, and there is no information in Passage A to indicate that it assumes the truth of the argument in Passage B. Both authors basically start at the same point but go in very different directions, drawing conclusions that do not necessarily relate immediately to one another.

QUESTION 26

Overview: Question 26 asks the student to consider the following statement by the author of Passage B: "It is historically significant that the US was heavily protectionist until it became a world leader in the economy." The student must then define the word *protectionist* according to the immediate context of this statement as well as the context of all of Passage B. What the author is essentially claiming is that the US did not allow unrestricted free trade until it had built up a strong economy that could protect business owners from the very problems that the author of Passage B describes. In other words, the US did *not* support unrestricted free trade until it could sustain it. The correct answer choice will reflect this in some way.

THE CORRECT ANSWER:

D   Answer choice (D) best expresses the meaning of *protectionist* in the context of the sentence and of Passage B: "Protecting a domestic economy through government intervention." The passage explains that protectionist policies were in place until the domestic economy was strong enough to operate without government controls on trade, which indicates that these policies consisted of government interventions to restrict free trade and thus protect the domestic economy.

THE INCORRECT ANSWERS:

A, E   The author of Passage B does mention the need for government programs to assist in the case of failing small businesses. However, consider the statement containing the word *protectionist*: "It is historically significant that the US was heavily protectionist until it became a world leader in the economy." There is no indication that protectionist policies were specific to protecting small businesses from unrestricted free trade or that these policies consisted of welfare programs and federal loans.

B   Far from suggesting support for unrestricted free trade, the word *protectionist* suggests a strong opposition to unrestricted free trade. So, answer choice (B) can be eliminated immediately.

C   The author of Passage B acknowledges the reality of a global economy, but within the context of the passage, the sentence containing the word *protectionist* follows a discussion of smaller and weaker economies, not globalism. Answer choice (C) offers an incorrect definition in the context of the passage.

QUESTION 27

Overview: The final question in the Reading Comprehension section asks the student to identify the author's tone regarding free trade in Passage B as compared to Passage A. To answer this question correctly, the student should first identify the author's tone toward free trade in Passage A. It is enthusiastic and very supportive. As has already been established, Passage B offers a qualification of the benefits of free trade, so the author's tone does not have the same note of enthusiasm or support. Instead, the author's support seems more tentative. The correct answer choice will reflect this in some way.

THE CORRECT ANSWER:

C   The author's tone in Passage B could accurately be described as being more *cautious* toward the issue of free trade. The author does not take a stance on whether free trade should be unrestricted, but rather points out some concerns that should be addressed.

THE INCORRECT ANSWERS:

A, B, D, E   In answering a question like this one, the process of elimination becomes an important part of the strategy. To consider each incorrect answer choice in turn:

Answer choice (A) reflects an evaluative judgment the student should refrain from making for the purposes of the exam. Moreover, given the different focuses of the passages, it is not obvious that one is more *sophisticated* regarding free trade than the other.

Speculation suggests the lack of a clear conclusion, but since the author of Passage B offers a clear, specific recommendation to study the issue of free trade from other angles, the author's tone cannot be described as *speculative*. Answer choice (B) must be incorrect.

The author of Passage B might very well be happy to debate someone on the merits of his or her claims, but his or her tone toward free trade is less about debating than about caution. (The author does not, for example, argue at length about an opposing viewpoint's claims, as might be expected in a debating tone.) Answer choice (D) has no immediate application to the author's tone, so it is incorrect.

As with *sophisticated*, the choice of *pragmatic* indicates an evaluative judgment but much less obviously an objective description of tone. A pragmatic tone would be more definitive in stating what the most sensible trade policy would be, whereas the author is urging a new approach without specific policy recommendations. Answer choice (E), therefore, is incorrect.

Section IV: Logical Reasoning

QUESTION 1

Overview: Question 1 presents a passage in which the student must consider the contrast between criticism and opinion. The passage begins by noting that a distinction must be made between criticism and opinion and then continues with an explanation of this distinction, concluding that criticism is not necessarily everyone's right to have or share but that opinion cannot be denied. The question then asks for the answer choice that can be inferred from the passage. An inference from a passage is not an outright statement of the passage, but an inference does *rely* on direct statements; therefore, the correct answer choice will be derived from specific comments made in the passage.

THE CORRECT ANSWER:

B   **Answer choice (B)** makes the following statement: "Criticism and opinion are often confused with one another because some mistake a negative opinion for criticism." The passage begins by noting that criticism and opinion need to be distinguished from one another, implying immediately that the distinction is *not* always made. Thus, the first part of answer choice (B) can be inferred from the passage. Additionally, the passage notes that people who criticize others are "hoping to effect a modification" in behavior and that criticism generally has a negative connotation. Although the author of the passage notes that opinion does not always have a negative connotation, if the opinion is itself negative, such a connotation may be derived. From this, the student can correctly assume that a negative opinion is often confused for criticism, thus explaining the confusion that was stated in the first sentence of the passage.

THE INCORRECT ANSWERS:

A   Although the passage begins with the implication that criticism and opinion are often confused with one another, there is no mention in the passage of *wording criticism as an opinion*, nor can this inference be derived from any of the statements made in the passage. The author does note the difference between the *purpose* behind criticism versus opinion, but the author makes no recommendation about offering criticism in such a way that it would be welcome. Answer choice (A) has no support in the passage.

C   The passage implies that people make the mistake of confusing opinion with criticism, but it does not mention phases of thought at any point, nor does the passage indicate that opinion is a simply a phase that precedes criticism. In fact, the author notes that opinion is itself an endpoint that can be distinguished from criticism.

D   The author makes no mention of *different kinds of criticism*, instead discussing criticism as a whole rather than in separate forms. Answer choice (D) assumes information that is not in the passage.

E   Although the passage might very well go on to discuss the right to opinion as a component of freedom of speech, there is no such implication in the passage at this point, nor can such an idea be assumed merely from the information the passage provides. The author mentions only that "everyone should be entitled to *opinion*," but within the context of the passage, this relates more to the purpose behind opinion than to abstract freedoms.

QUESTION 2

Overview: Question 2 describes a scenario about a department store that has hired a new person to represent its brand. According to the passage, the company held certain standards for the new representative on the basis of the very positive public response to the previous representative. The company auditioned a number of applicants, and one applicant in particular was very interested in the job, explaining to the company how well she fit the image the company desired. The company agreed and hired her; the passage notes that this occurred without market research. Shortly afterward, the company featured her much less and then rehired the former representative for the job. The question asks the student which answer choice best explains this action, based on the information provided in the passage. The student needs to consider two key points noted in the passage: (1) the popularity of the previous representative and (2) the company's decision that, at the time of hiring the new representative, no market research was required. These factors play an important role in what would affect the department store's decision, and the correct answer choice will indicate clearly that a situation involving one (or both) of these factors would change the company's view about the new representative.

THE CORRECT ANSWER:

A   **Answer choice (A)** states that the department store chose to do market research after the fact and discovered that the new representative was not popular among customers. Instead of losing customers in order to keep an unpopular representative, the store apparently pushed her aside and rehired the former—and very popular—representative. All of this fits two key pieces of information provided in the passage: first, that the former representative was very popular, and second, that when the company hired the new representative, it decided that "no market research was *then* required." The latter statement suggests that the company might well have decided that market research was required after the fact. Answer choice (A) takes into account both pieces of information and offers a solid explanation for the department store's decision.

THE INCORRECT ANSWERS:

B   Answer choice (B) states that a tabloid magazine published an article questioning the new representative's character. Since the department store had a clear image requirement, this could very well affect its decision. But nothing in the passage suggests that there was such a tabloid magazine article, and it seems unlikely that the store would fire the new representative based solely on such an article or, more particularly, that the store would slowly replace her, especially since the store had evidently hired the new representative in the belief that she had a good image. Answer choice (B) does not offer enough information to justify the company's decision.

C   The actions of a competitor store and the popularity of their new representative could affect the department store's decision. But the passage does not say specifically that the new representative is unpopular, and the answer choice does not clarify among whom either representative is popular (or unpopular). If it turns out that the new representative of the other department store is more popular among customers of the first store, this might be a reason to question the long-term potential for their own representative. Answer choice (C) is unclear, however, and has no support in the passage.

D   Answer choice (D) essentially sums up what the passage tells us—that the department store believed it had made a mistake and decided to hire the former representative again—but it

186

does nothing to provide a *reason* behind the belief about a mistake. Because answer choice (D) offers no clear indication of the company's motivation, it cannot be the correct answer.

E   The passage indicates that the new representative was very interested in the position and believed that she would be good for it. This suggests that she would enjoy the job, rather than the opposite, and indeed nothing in the passage suggests she would *not* enjoy the job.

QUESTION 3

Overview: Question 3 asks the student to identify the flawed reasoning in the passage by considering which of the answer choices offers similarly flawed reasoning. The passage presents the scenario of a snowstorm in Denver, with the added information that all of the news outlets in Denver have cautioned drivers to be careful on their way to work, noting that getting to work will take extra time. The passage concludes with the statement that because of these factors, all the employees at First Community Bank of Denver will be late to work. To determine the correct answer, the student needs to determine the structure of the reasoning in the passage. The passage follows this line of thought: (1) A condition or problem is established and (2) thus everyone will be affected by the condition. The problem with this reasoning is that it does not allow for any anomalies. Suppose, for instance, several of the employees at First Community Bank of Denver decide to leave for work much earlier than normal in order to arrive at work on time. Suppose that the snowstorm affects certain parts of the city worse than others, so some employees will be able to get to work without as much trouble and can arrive on time. Suppose an employee lives in an apartment complex near the bank and can walk to work. None of these factors is considered; because the passage uses the inclusive word "all," the passage's conclusion leaves no room for anomalies. The correct answer choice will reflect this.

THE CORRECT ANSWER:

A   **Answer choice (A)** follows the pattern of reasoning given in the passage. First the answer choice claims that MSG can cause migraines; it then concludes that *everyone* who eats food with MSG should expect to develop a migraine. As with the passage regarding the snowstorm, the answer choice draws a conclusion about *everyone* from a general statement without allowing for the possibility of variation (perhaps not everyone metabolizes MSG in the same way, for example).

THE INCORRECT ANSWERS:

B   Answer choice (B) does contain a flaw in the reasoning—that Theodore *must* be taller than Ferdinand because he is two years older—but this flaw does not match the flaw in the reasoning of the passage. If answer choice (B) stated that all people are taller than those two years younger, it would have approached the same flaw, but it does not.

C   Answer choice (C) does not contain a flaw in the reasoning. It states that a power outage in Chicago occurred in an area with 300,000 customers, so the majority of these people were without power. This would seem to be true. Additionally, it does not use the "all" argument.

D   As with answer choice (B), answer choice (D) presents a scenario that involves only two people and in which the reasoning—although flawed—does not follow the pattern given in the passage. In addition to the fact that there is nothing to suggest that Nina *must* be angry with Edward, there is no suggestion that because of a general condition or statement of fact, *all* people must react or be affected in a particular way.

E Answer choice (E) is incorrect. Although the statement does indicate a general statement of fact (that lunch is served at noon) and draws a conclusion from that fact (some students must be hungry at noon), it does not claim that *all* students will be hungry.

QUESTION 4

Overview: Question 4 describes a situation in which the CEO of an automobile manufacturer announces plans to increase vehicle production due to an unexpectedly strong period in the economy. The passage adds that supplies for building vehicles currently have low prices and that the auto manufacturer hopes to use this time to produce vehicles in a cost-effective way. The implication is that this period of economic strength will not last and that the supplies will go up in price. This would make the vehicles *more* expensive for the manufacturer to build in the future, so by building them now, the manufacturer will have the freedom to reduce production or even lower the selling price of the vehicles when an economic downturn strikes. To select the correct answer, the student needs to consider these details as the prevailing justification for the CEO's decision to increase vehicle production.

THE CORRECT ANSWER:

C If a recent study indicates that the steel used by the auto manufacturer is expected to increase in cost over the next few months, it would justify the auto manufacturer's decision to build cars while the economy is good and the cost of supplies is low.

THE INCORRECT ANSWERS:

A An increase in the price of the auto manufacturer's stock should do nothing to hinder or contribute to its decision to increase automobile production. In fact, the rise in the stock price is likely to occur as a result of the CEO's announcement, so this is likely an effect and not a cause of the decision to increase production. It is possible that the CEO is making the announcement to increase production in order to bolster a failing stock price, but as there is nothing in the passage to suggest specifically that the company is hoping to improve its stock price, this cannot reasonably be inferred as a cause of the decision.

B Although answer choice (B) would be a good reason to increase production, it would not be as good of a reason as a sharp increase in the cost of steel. Other battery suppliers could increase production, and new suppliers could open up. In addition, batteries are a relatively small component of cars, so even if the cost of batteries were to go up due to the loss of one supplier, it would likely have much less of an impact on the total cost of manufacturing cars than a considerable increase in the cost of steel would.

D The decision to merge with another auto manufacturer has no clear connection to the company's decision to produce more cars, based on the information within the passage. The fact that the second auto manufacturer has a surplus of vehicles would more likely motivate the original auto manufacturer to put an increase in production on hold. Therefore, answer choice (D) provides no justification for the CEO's announcement.

E As in answer choice (D), the expected rise in the price of oil—with the accompanying decrease in the expected purchase of new vehicles—is far more likely to motivate the CEO to put a hold on production and not to increase it immediately. It might be argued that a reduced incentive to buy new cars in the future would motivate the company to increase production now in the hopes that customers would buy them now. However, this line of

reasoning does not address the CEO's explicitly stated concern to build cars while the necessary supplies are low in cost.

QUESTION 5

<u>Overview</u>: Question 5 describes a situation in which an IT company is planning to open a new office in the city of Nizhny Novgorod, Russia, where IT is a major industry. The passage notes, however, that the economy has been in a state of weakness and that many residents are out of work. The IT industry is also weak, and a number of IT businesses that have been in the city for some time are now closing. However, the company opening the new office is confident of its success. The question asks the student to consider an explanation for why this is. To select the correct answer, the student needs to consider the details in the passage, reflecting what might set this particular IT company above the rest, even during an economic downturn.

THE CORRECT ANSWER:

A   **Answer choice (A)** is the only answer choice that provides a sufficient explanation for why the IT company can be so confident of its success in spite of a struggling economy: Its technology is up to date (and thus will be in demand) and it is able to keep its costs low (thus offsetting the economic weakness). Answer choice (A) also notes that the other IT businesses in Nizhny Novgorod have not kept their technology up to date, so this places the company with the new office at a distinct competitive advantage.

THE INCORRECT ANSWERS:

B   Although purchasing an existing building instead of building a new one creates an immediate financial advantage, it does not explain why the IT company with the new office can succeed where its competitors cannot. Answer choice (B) gives insufficient details to explain the discrepancy.

C   The employment opportunities offered by the IT company with the new office have some potential to explain its expected success. However, it is not clear from the answer choice how the company will ensure its success in an industry and location where other IT companies have failed. This answer choice alone does not provide a sufficient reason for the company's confidence in its financial success.

D   The presence of industrial scenery does not clearly contribute to a lack of business success, so answer choice (D) does not explain why the IT company with the new office can be confident of its success. Were the answer choice to include some information about *why* the industrial scenery has hurt other IT businesses and *how* it has added to their failure, this might be a good possibility. As it is, though, answer choice (D) cannot be correct.

E   Far from explaining the reason for the IT company's confidence, answer choice (E) raises questions about the potential for its success by claiming that the company will immediately have large debts to pay off. Answer choice (E) can be eliminated immediately.

QUESTION 6

<u>Overview</u>: Question 6 presents a statement from a member of a local school board, arguing that there should be computers in every classroom in the school district. The school board member claims that the city is one of few cities in the state that do not have computers in every classroom, and as a result, the "schools are suffering." The speaker goes on to say that parents are moving out of the school district and that research indicates that students who attend schools with computers

in every classroom have the highest rates of graduation and receive better-paying jobs than students who did not have computers in their classrooms. The question asks for the answer choice that best explains the flaw in the school board member's reasoning; specifically, what does the school board member *not* establish in reaching the conclusion that computers should be available in every classroom in this particular school district? The student must consider each point of evidence the school board member offers. These points are: (1) There has been a loss in student body in the school district because parents are relocating to another school district, and (2) schools that have computers in the classroom have the highest graduation rates and acquire higher-paying jobs. Because the school board member cites research to support the claim about graduation rates and higher-paying jobs, the problem clearly lies in the claim about parents moving out of the school district. The correct answer choice will address this.

THE CORRECT ANSWER:

C   As noted in the Overview, the correct answer choice must note that the school board member fails to explain that parents move out of the district *as a result of* the lack of computers in the school district classrooms. That is, there is a correlation between classrooms with computers and student success, but there is nothing to indicate that the presence of computers is the sole or primary reason for this success, or that parents are relocating because they believe that schools with classroom computers are better because of the computers rather than other factors such as overall funding. Further, parents may be choosing to locate for reasons other than those stated in the passage, such as safety, available student activities, or school culture. Because there could be many reasons for parents relocating, the school board member must explain the connection between the lack of computers and the fact that some parents relocate.

THE INCORRECT ANSWERS:

A   Although funding is essential to the addition of computers to every classroom (and the reduced student body might suggest that the school district is losing funds instead of gaining them), the question of funding is not a part of the school board member's argument and thus does not contribute to the flaw in the reasoning.

B   Answer choice (B) is related to answer choice (A) in the sense that it suggests a problem with adding computers to a school district that has a reduced student body. This in itself is a reasonable issue to raise. However, it is a secondary issue given the passage, because the school board member's argument relies on the issue of parents relocating to new school districts (in addition to the claim about graduation rates and higher-paying jobs). Answer choice (B) does not address the immediate flaw in the member of the school board's reasoning.

D   Although the school board member should ultimately provide specific documentation for the claim about graduation rates and higher-paying jobs, the school board member does make the general claim that "research" supports this allegation. What the member of the school board does not establish, however, is that there is any research that shows that parents relocate due to a lack of computers in the classroom. Answer choice (D) does not address this.

E   Answer choice (E) has no connection to the school board member's claims, so it can be eliminated immediately. The school board member does say that the schools are suffering, but the evidence used to support this relates to parents relocating and research about

academic and employment improvements for students who had studied with computers in the classroom.

QUESTIONS 7 AND 8

<u>Overview</u>: Questions 7 and 8 are based on a passage about the presence of eating disorders in the fashion industry, particularly among models. The author notes that the fashion industry cannot ignore the reality of eating disorders but that there are a variety of objections to restrictions on the fashion industry, objections from both models and designers. Models often complain that they are naturally thin, while designers point out that eating disorders are not unique to the fashion industry; they claim that eating disorders are connected to personal concerns that cannot be addressed with rules regarding weight or BMI requirements. The passage concludes by noting that the industry is inclined to accept "awareness about eating disorders but not extra rules," that resources for dealing with eating disorders will be available, and that models should seek help when they realize they have a problem. Question 7 asks the student to determine the main point of the passage, while question 8 asks for the answer choice that best expresses the flaw in the fashion industry's reasoning.

QUESTION 7

THE CORRECT ANSWER:

D   There are several important details in the passage that contribute to the main point: (1) the fashion industry is not happy with the idea of further restrictions about weight and eating disorders, (2) the industry wants to provide awareness about eating disorders, and (3) the industry wants the models to initiate seeking help, though they will provide support. The correct answer will pull these three details into a summary statement. **Answer choice (D)** is the only answer choice to combine all three and thus restate the main point of the passage.

THE INCORRECT ANSWERS:

A   Although the response from designers suggests that they believe eating disorders are related to factors other than fashion and thus cannot simply be eliminated by changing weight requirements among models, there is nothing in the passage to suggest that the industry as a whole believes eating disorders are "inevitable" and impossible to eliminate.

B   Answer choice (B) expresses one part of the discussion in the passage: the viewpoint of models and designers on the source of eating disorders. It does not, however, express the main point of the passage, which notes that the industry is open to providing awareness but wants models to initiate seeking help. Answer choice (B) focuses on a secondary detail instead of the main point.

C   As with answer choice (B), answer choice (C) expresses a supporting detail of the main point: that the industry tends to seek out models who are naturally thin and that they are not necessarily thin in an unhealthy way. However, answer choice (C) does not go one step further to apply this to the bigger issue at hand: how the industry would prefer eating disorders to be treated. Answer choice (C) focuses on a secondary detail.

E   There is nothing in the passage to suggest that rules for BMI will be ignored; in fact, the passage notes, "Some countries have gone so far as to establish rules that require models to maintain a certain BMI if they expect to walk the runways." This indicates that the rules for BMI *are* being observed and that this is a source of frustration for designers and models in the fashion industry because they believe that BMI is not a sufficient indicator of healthy weight.

QUESTION 8

THE CORRECT ANSWER:

E   Question 8 asks the student to consider *why* the reasoning in the fashion industry is vulnerable to criticism. This requires the student to consider three details carefully: (1) Several countries have put BMI restrictions on models because they believe they are too thin to be healthy, (2) the industry admits that eating disorders exist but claims that they are based on *personal issues*, and (3) the industry wants to provide awareness but let the models seek help themselves. However, if an eating disorder is based on a personal issue, that very personal issue might prevent a person from seeking help; in putting the burden for seeking help on models themselves, the industry assumes that models are in fact able to do so. **Answer choice (E)** best expresses this idea.

THE INCORRECT ANSWERS:

A   The actions taken by several countries to establish BMI requirements indicate that public awareness might be involved in the issue, but the public is not actually mentioned in the passage, and the focus is almost entirely on the internal mood of the fashion industry toward eating disorders. Answer choice (A) infers details that cannot be supported by the passage.

B   Although the designers note that the fashion industry tends to gravitate toward thin models—suggesting that thinness is part of the desired look or trend—there is no clear mention of thin models being part of a short-term trend in the fashion industry. Answer choice (B) infers details that are not supported within the passage.

C, D   The details in answer choices (C) and (D) are implied in the passage: that the fashion industry does not create eating disorders, that they exist elsewhere in society, that models are naturally thin, and that most are not necessarily struggling with eating disorders. However, these details in particular do not represent the flaw in the industry's reasoning (in fact, they do more to support the reasoning than undermine it).

QUESTION 9

Overview: Question 9 presents the scenario of a warehouse company that has promised to pay its employees a 3 percent bonus each Christmas. In fact, this promise is treated as a guarantee and is included in the employee handbook. The company's new financial officer, however, claims that the company's budget will not support the Christmas bonus this year unless employees are willing to help out: The financial officer sends a memo to all employees, letting them know that the company *will* be able to pay the Christmas bonuses *if* the employees contribute by helping to generate advertising revenues. The question asks the student to decide which of the answer choices is true if the information in the passage is true. This is essentially a question about inference; the student must consider what the passage is saying and what can be inferred from it. Most important to note is the fact that the financial officer is more or less telling the employees that if they work harder to get the advertising revenues, they will get their bonuses. In essence, the financial officer is saying that the employees will receive the bonuses if they do something to bring the bonus money into the company—in other words, to work for their own bonuses.

Answers and Explanations for
Test #1

THE CORRECT ANSWER:

B   **Answer choice (B)** correctly deduces the implication of the financial officer's memo: that the employees will essentially be contributing to their own bonuses, making the bonus something less of a bonus. Because the bonuses come out of company revenues, it is true that the employees always indirectly fund their own bonuses, but this is the result of a year-long group effort; individual employees who do not directly contribute to company revenues are given bonuses as well. In answer choice (B), the employees are all individually tasked with raising revenues specifically to fund the bonuses.

THE INCORRECT ANSWERS:

A   The company's employee handbook guarantees a 3 percent Christmas bonus to its employees, and there is nothing in the passage to suggest that there is a codicil attached to this guarantee regarding whether the company's budget supports the bonus. By promising the bonus to employees, the company makes itself responsible to find a way to pay it, so answer choice (A) cannot be inferred from the passage.

C   Given the information about the financial officer's memo, it may be inferred that the company has not had any trouble paying the Christmas bonus in the past. However, this in itself does not necessarily mean that the company will not have trouble paying it this year. What is more, nothing in the passage suggests that the company's current financial state is a result of corruption on the financial officer's part. Answer choice (C) does not have sufficient support within the passage.

D   Although the financial officer might believe that downsizing would also benefit the company, there is no mention of this in the passage, nor can it be deduced from the information that is provided. Answer choice (D) is incorrect due to insufficient support.

E   Although the employees might very well be planning to strike, there is nothing in the passage to suggest that this is the likely response or that a strike is imminent if the employees do not receive their Christmas bonus. Answer choice (E) cannot be supported by details in the passage.

QUESTION 10

Overview: Question 10 presents a statement from a philatelist (a stamp collector) who is discussing a very rare stamp, "the rarest stamp in the world," according to the philatelist: the Swedish Treskilling Yellow. The philatelist notes that the stamp is so rare because it was originally printed in error and only one remains. In 1996, the Treskilling Yellow was sold for $2.06 million and is now the most expensive stamp in the world. The philatelist concludes that it is thus the most valuable stamp in the world. The student must consider which of the answer choices represents the assumption on which the philatelist's conclusion depends. The first factor to consider is the conclusion itself—that the Treskilling Yellow is the most valuable stamp in the world. The second factor is the detail that supports the conclusion: (1) that the stamp is the only one of its kind to have been found and (2) that it has sold for the highest price. According to the statements made by the philatelist, these details make the stamp the most valuable in the world, so the correct answer choice will reflect this.

THE CORRECT ANSWER:

D   **Answer choice (D)** best summarizes the details noted in the overview—that the philatelist considers the stamp to be the most valuable because it is unique and because it has sold for the most money.

THE INCORRECT ANSWERS:

A   The information in the passage suggests that the philatelist's belief in the stamp's value is based in part on the fact that there is only one stamp known to be in existence. Therefore, answer choice (A) cannot be correct, because the philatelist's comments cannot be said to assume that a second stamp would sell for as much.

B   Answer choice (B) is partially correct insofar as it expresses some of the information that supports the philatelist's claim: The original error that printed the stamp in a different color has contributed to its rarity and its desirability among stamp collectors. However, this is a supporting detail and does not necessarily indicate the primary assumptions on which the philatelist's argument depends.

C   Answer choice (C) offers a contrary assumption to answer choice (A): that the Treskilling Yellow would actually be *worthless* if a second stamp were found. However, there is nothing in the passage to suggest that the philatelist believes this, so answer choice (C) can be eliminated due to insufficient support.

E   The assumption that "the finest and costliest stamps in the world have originated from printing errors in Sweden" is utterly insupportable based on information in the passage. The philatelist notes only that *one stamp* is the costliest in the world, and this just happens to be because it is rare and because it is the result of a printing error. There is no further information about other rare and costly stamps, so answer choice (E) can be eliminated immediately.

QUESTION 11

Overview: Question 11 presents a passage that explains the early history of Karl Marx's *Das Kapital*. According to the passage, the book received very little attention upon its first publication, but in its later history became one of the most influential writings of the 20th century. The student is asked to consider—within the context of the statements in the passage—which answer choice best explains the reason for the *eventual popularity* of the book. The student should note that the question does *not* ask for the reasons behind the initial unpopularity of the book but rather what might have changed to make the book popular after Marx's death in 1883. This might seem like a question that requires a blind guess, but it is not. The necessary details for a correct inference are in the paragraph; the student must look closely and take them into account. The key sentence here is the last sentence of the passage: "After his death in 1883, however, there were growing changes in the international political climate, and *Das Kapital* grew in popularity, ultimately becoming one of the most influential political treatises of the 20th century." This sentence suggests that the book's popularity did not occur until there was a change in the general attitude toward politics. Additionally, the sentence immediately before this suggests that Marx wrote his book before the public was ready to read it. Therefore, the correct answer will reflect the idea that Marx's book became popular after a change in political views in the world.

THE CORRECT ANSWER:

A   **Answer choice (A)** best expresses the idea that Marx's book could not be popular until there was a significant change in the public political attitude.

THE INCORRECT ANSWERS:

B, E   Answer choices (B) and (E) provide a reason for why *Das Kapital* might not have been available to many readers, thus limiting the opportunities for its popularity. There is nothing in the passage, however, to suggest that *Das Kapital* was immediately popular with those who *could* read it, so neither answer choice (B) nor (E) offers a sufficient explanation of the book's eventual popularity.

C   Answer choice (C) offers a possible reason for why few readers would be unwilling to take on such a massive tome, but it does not offer an explanation for the book's *eventual popularity*. What is more, it does not infer a reason from information contained within the paragraph, so it cannot be correct.

D   The reception from academics might very well have limited the opportunities early on for *Das Kapital* to be taught at the university level, but once again, this does not explain the reason for the book's *eventual popularity*.

QUESTION 12

<u>Overview</u>: Question 12 offers historical information on the Black Death, noting that although it destroyed up to 60 percent of Europe's population, the plague might also have provided some positive contributions to European society. The author of the passage cites scholars who argue that the Black Death, by decimating those who had traditionally ruled Europe, opened the door of opportunity for the development of a European middle class. The question asks students to consider which of the answer choices, if true, most clearly undermines this claim. To select the correct answer, the student must focus on the main point: Some scholars argue that the Black Death contributed to the development of a middle class in Europe. The correct answer choice will provide a reason that calls this claim into question.

THE CORRECT ANSWER:

E   **Answer choice (E)** makes the claim that a "thriving middle class was already in development when the Black Death first struck Europe in the 1340s." If this is true, it strongly undermines the claim that the Black Death created an opportunity for the development of the middle class in Europe (because, presumably, such an opportunity was already there and had been taken advantage of).

THE INCORRECT ANSWERS:

A   The passage states that it was the peasantry, freed from serfdom, who began building businesses and forming a middle class in Europe. Answer choice (A) claims that the Black Death struck down very few of the peasantry (in contrast to the many members of the aristocracy who died). Far from undermining the passage, it offers secondary information that could be used to support it.

B   The demographic information of male deaths versus female deaths is not clearly connected to the information in the passage, so it does not undermine the argument made in the passage; it is simply not clearly relevant. Nothing in the passage suggests that it was men

195

only who built the middle class in Europe, and even if this were a safe historical assumption, it cannot be assumed from the passage alone.

C   Like answer choice (A), answer choice (C) offers information to support the argument presented in the passage. If after the Black Death there was an increase in pre-industrial productivity, indicating a rise in new trades, it would follow that the argument has at least some evidence.

D   Again, answer choice (D) presents information that strengthens the argument made in the passage by indicating that the aristocracy were weakened and lost the value of their lands during the ravages of the Black Death. This would have provided freedom for many serfs and given them the opportunity to purchase land at a low price. Answer choice (D) can be eliminated immediately.

QUESTION 13

Overview: A politician argues for ending trade with a major trading partner on the grounds that the trading partner engages in serious human rights violations. The politician notes that her country has always set a clear standard on the issue of human rights and that the only consistent path to take is one of ending trade with the trading partner. The question then asks for the answer choice that best expresses the assumption on which the politician's argument depends. To select the correct answer, the student first needs to identify the politician's primary claim: that despite the financial benefits of trade, the politician's country must end trade with a partner that is committing human rights violations because the politician's country opposes any kind of human rights violations. It is important to note that the human rights violations are coming from a *chief* trading partner, so ending trade with that partner could create a void in the economy of the politician's country. Because the politician does not address this void, it is safe to assume that she believes the economic void will not compare with the moral void that would follow continued trade with the trading partner. The correct answer choice will reflect this assumption.

THE CORRECT ANSWER:

C   **Answer choice (C)** best expresses the assumption on which the politician's argument depends: Upholding the standard of human rights is more important than the economic loss that would occur from ending trade with the trading partner.

THE INCORRECT ANSWERS:

A   The politician might very well hope that ending trade with the major trading partner will lead to an end in the human rights violations. She does mention that her country should "set the standard and encourage respect for human rights around the world." However, this does not in itself suggest that the assumption for her conclusion is based on an expected end to human rights violations. The politician's statement indicates instead that she believes her country should be willing to end trade with the trading partner because it is the right thing to do and because her country "cannot risk practicing a double standard." It might be that the trading partner will end its human rights violations in order to resume trade with the politician's country. However, nothing in the passage suggests that this is the primary assumption on which the politician's argument depends.

B   The products currently being traded might very well be closely connected to the human rights violations, but there is nothing in the politician's statement that implies this. Answer choice (B) is incorrect due to insufficient information to support the assumption.

D   The nature of the politician's responsibilities might contribute to her information about the trading partner that is committing human rights violations. However, her responsibilities do not, in and of themselves, contribute to the assumption on which her argument depends. If anything, the politician is simply doing her job. Answer choice (D) is not immediately relevant to the assumption of the argument.

E   Answer choice (E) describes more of a result than a cause; that is to say, it indicates a desired effect of ending trade with the trading partner but does not necessarily indicate the assumption on which the politician's argument depends. The politician notes, "We must instead set the standard and encourage respect for human rights around the world." So, she is encouraging her country to set an international standard that should be adopted internationally. But again, this is not the *assumption* on which her argument depends.

QUESTION 14

Overview: Question 14 presents a letter to the editor of a Dublin-based newspaper, in which the writer claims that the Irish government should stop funding the teaching of the Gaeilge (or traditional Irish) language in Irish schools because this language has historically been used as the language of Irish revolutionaries. The letter writer posits that, because of this history, the language will divide rather than unite and thus should not be funded by the government. The question asks the student to identify the flaw in the letter writer's reasoning. The primary point to note is that the letter writer makes sweeping assumptions about the role of the language in contributing to events in Ireland's history. There is a comment in the beginning that this is the "traditional" language, indicating that this is the language of Ireland's past and an inherent part of its culture. But the letter writer then goes on to say that this traditional language is connected primarily to revolution and will thus create "unrest" and "division" in Ireland. Given that the letter writer offers no real historical data to support this or an explanation about why or how the language itself contributed to unrest and division, the correct answer choice will reflect the letter writer's failure to explain how past events will *inevitably* become current problems simply by teaching the language.

THE CORRECT ANSWER:

B   **Answer choice (B)** correctly explains the flaw in the letter writer's reasoning: that the historical events will occur again simply through the teaching of a language and that the language itself will contribute to unrest and division in Ireland.

THE INCORRECT ANSWERS:

A, E   Although the letter writer certainly fails to explain that language is an important part of a culture and offers people a link to their past, these options do not address the specific claims made by the author. In other words, they do not point out a specific flaw in the author's own explicit reasoning.

C   Rather than relying on obsolete sociological data, the letter writer fails to provide *any* data, making a claim about the role of the language in Irish revolutions without offering any historical information to support this claim.

D   Answer choice (D) is incorrect because the author does not focus on an *isolated historical event*, claiming instead that the language is "the language of revolution among the Irish and has done more throughout history to contribute to unrest and even open conflict in Ireland than it has done to bring about peace." This indicates a series of historical events rather than just one.

197

Question 15

Overview: Question 15 asks the student to consider a passage about a local farmer's interest in establishing a certified organic farm, with a particular focus on the farmer's concerns about the cost of set-up. Since the passage notes that the certified organic farm requires fewer and less expensive supplies than a non-organic farm and that the maintenance cost is relatively low, the student is asked to select an answer choice that best explains the farmer's concerns about cost. The correct answer choice will supply a clear explanation for where the cost is involved—some outside expense that is related directly to the *set-up* of the farm.

The Correct Answer:

D   **Answer choice (D)** most clearly explains the reason for the farmer's concerns about cost. Although the cost of supplies and maintenance might be lower than that of a non-organic farm, the cost of the certification itself is very high, creating a financial burden for the farmer as he tries to establish the certified organic farm.

The Incorrect Answers:

A, C   Although the demand in the community for organic food and the presence of three other large organic farms might affect the farmer's success in the long run, these factors do not affect the cost of set-up, which is the farmer's concern. Answer choices (A) and (C) provide irrelevant information.

B   A need to hire expert consultants would increase the cost of setting up a certified organic farm just as certification fees would. However, there is no indication in the passage that setting up and running a certified organic farm requires hiring any personnel who would not be employed at a non-organic farm, including consultants. Therefore, answer choice (B) can be eliminated.

E   The passage notes that the certified organic farm requires fewer supplies and that these supplies are less costly when compared to the supplies required on a non-organic farm. As a result, even if the supplies are unique and must be special-ordered, as answer choice (E) claims, they still should not contribute to the cost about which the farmer is concerned.

Question 16

Overview: The student is asked to consider statements made in a commercial and to select an answer choice that exhibits similarly flawed reasoning. The commercial specifically states that the product being touted, Extra-Strength Spray-On Hair Growth, will enable men to regrow the hair that they've lost, claiming that if men *do not* try the product, they will have *no chance* of regrowing their hair. The flaw in this reasoning is that the commercial assumes that there is no way a person will be able to regrow his hair without using this product. However, there could be other options that will allow a person to regrow hair (for instance, surgical implants or another commercial hair growth product). The correct answer will mirror the structure of the argument given in the commercial. The structure is as follows: Given one condition (use of this hair product), there is a positive result (hair regrowth); given the absence of the first condition (use of this product), there will be *no* chance for the positive result (hair regrowth).

The Correct Answer:

A   **Answer choice (A)** offers the best comparison for similarly flawed reasoning. The answer choice claims that students who attend universities are more successful, so all students should attend universities in order to be successful and avoid failure. However, this

assumes that there is no way a student can be successful and avoid failure except by attending a university. The flaw in this is that there might be other ways a student could be successful (for instance, by attending a trade school, becoming an apprentice, or getting a job). Answer choice (A) most closely mirrors the structure of the reasoning given in the commercial.

THE INCORRECT ANSWERS:

B Answer choice (B) does not follow the structure of the commercial; it does not first state that a positive result will follow from a certain action and then go on to claim that the only way to achieve that result is by following that action.

C Answer choice (C) states that ovens develop a buildup of food residue over time and thus should be cleaned annually. But this answer does not explicitly indicate that a positive result will follow from a given action in the way that the passage does. Answer choice (C) is not immediately parallel to the argument in the passage.

D Answer choice (D) does not indicate that the only way to lessen toxicity is to buy green cleaning products, so the argument is not immediately parallel.

E Answer choice (E) bears no similarity to the passage. This answer choice states that Stan is unpopular because of his temper, so he will be removed from the team; the structure here is nothing like the structure of the argument given in the commercial, so answer choice (E) can be eliminated.

QUESTIONS 17 AND 18

Overview: Questions 17 and 18 discuss plans by the state of Hawaii to build a nuclear power plant in a town on the leeward coast of Oahu. The townspeople are not happy with this plan and have hired a spokesperson to explain their concerns about the intended facility. According to the spokesperson, the town's primary fear is that the new nuclear power plant will create another incident like the Chernobyl disaster; the spokesperson cites details of that disaster, including its long-term effects. Question 17 asks for the answer choice that most undermines the spokesperson's claims; question 18 asks for the problem that most undermines the state's plans to build the facility. To answer question 17, the student should begin by noting the main point of the spokesperson's argument: The people of the town are opposed to the building of the nuclear power plant because they fear an explosion like the one that happened at Chernobyl. To answer question 18, the student needs to consider which answer choice has the greatest effect on the state's plans by taking into account the options among the answer choices—the answer choice that provides a clear problem with the construction or running of the plant will be correct.

QUESTION 17

THE CORRECT ANSWER:

C **Answer choice (C)** explains the problem with the spokesperson's argument. In a discussion of an event that occurred over two decades before, the spokesperson fails to consider whether technology has improved since then (particularly in light of the reasonable assumption that since the events at Chernobyl, nuclear engineers would be motivated to ensure that such an accident would not happen again). Answer choice (C) states specifically that current nuclear power plants are designed to prevent similar accidents.

THE INCORRECT ANSWERS:

A   Answer choice (A) approaches a part of the problem in the spokesperson's argument, but it does not undermine it completely. This answer choice suggests that the fears of the people in the town are not justified but offers only a vague claim that they *cannot be applied*. Without further information to explain *why* they cannot be applied (such as the correct answer choice provides), this is simply not enough to undermine the argument effectively.

B   The role of the spokesperson as a paid lobbyist against nuclear power might motivate him to speak on the town's behalf, but this does not necessarily undermine his argument in any way. If anything, it simply explains why he was hired.

D, E   Although answer choices (D) and (E) offer explanations for why there should be support for the intended nuclear power plant, they both fail to offer a clear statement that *undermines the argument* of the spokesperson. In fact, both answer choices (D) and (E) essentially create red herrings (that is, change the subject) by diverting the spokesperson's argument in a different direction and thus fail to address the substance of the argument.

QUESTION 18

THE CORRECT ANSWER:

E   **Answer choice (E)** indicates the most serious problem that could undermine the state's plans to build the new nuclear power plant. If the facility needs cold water to cool the reactor core, the large amount of extra energy required to cool the reactor would add significant expense to the construction, operation, and maintenance of the facility, potentially damaging its chances of being a financially viable energy alternative.

THE INCORRECT ANSWERS:

A   The opinion of the community regarding the budget is a legitimate issue. The community's fears alone, however, do not necessarily indicate the most serious problem that could undermine the construction of the plant. Regardless of how well founded (or not) those fears are, these fears can be allayed, or the project might proceed in spite of them. (This contrasts with answer choice (E): If the statement that answer choice describes were true, it is very unlikely that the plant would be built.)

B   Although the value of the jobs that the plant will bring into the community is a worthwhile consideration, answer choice (B) offers too little detail to present a problem that is as serious as the problem indicated in the correct answer choice.

C   Answer choice (C) does raise questions about the connection between the state official and the manager of the nuclear power plant, but this alone does not necessarily mean that there is corruption involved. Answer choice (C) does not contain enough information to undermine the state's plans.

D   The plans of the local builder do not by themselves necessarily present a problem as serious as the problem described in the correct answer choice; again, the latter would almost certainly prevent the building of the plant, while this is not true of answer choice (D).

QUESTION 19

Overview: The student is given information about the female earless seal and the events surrounding gestation and breeding. According to the passage, the female earless seal gestates for

9–11 months (depending on the species of earless seal) and gives birth to and nurses only one pup at a time. The passage notes that during a bad season, up to three female earless seals in a colony will die three months after giving birth, although all of the pups usually survive. Considering that other female seals cannot nurse orphaned pups—since each lactating female can nurse only a single pup—a natural expectation is that the pups would die with their mothers since they have no one to nurse them. However, the pups all survive. The question asks the student to select an answer choice that best explains this discrepancy.

THE CORRECT ANSWER:

D **Answer choice (D)** indicates that the mother seals nurse the pups only up to a month at the longest, suggesting that after a month, the pups are capable of locating food for themselves. This answer choice thus provides a sufficient explanation for why the mother seals might die three months after giving birth while the pups survive: The pups are finished nursing by this point and can find their own food.

THE INCORRECT ANSWERS:

A The passage states that earless seals give birth to a single pup, then explains that the mother seals use most of their energy to nurse that single pup, fasting while lactating. This implies that a mother would not be able to nurse two pups well enough to ensure that both, or even one, would survive.

B Answer choice (B), although interesting, is irrelevant to explaining the discrepancy. The question asks for a reason that the pups survive although the mothers do not; answer choice (B) simply diverts from this point to say that very often the mothers do not die. Moreover, answer choice (B) ignores the statement in the question about the reason for mothers dying *during a bad season*. Answer choice (B) can be eliminated immediately.

C Answer choice (C) does not explain why seal pups survive even when their mothers die. It is not surprising that some female seals do not give birth (for instance, because they are not sexually mature). The existence of such seals alone does not explain why more pups survive (nothing in the passage suggests they would nurse the orphaned pups, for example).

E As with answer choice (B), answer choice (E) ignores the central question by offering interesting but irrelevant information. The question asks for a reason for the discrepancy between mother seals dying three months after giving birth and the pups surviving. Answer choice (E) merely provides information about some of the mothers living up to six months. This is unrelated to why pups live when mothers die.

QUESTION 20

Overview: Question 20 presents information about William Paley, a Christian apologist remembered for developing the watchmaker analogy: If a person came upon a watch and knew nothing about watches, would that person believe the watch to have simply appeared or to have no designer behind it? Paley thought not. Paley argued that a watch contains such complex mechanisms that a person would naturally assume the watch to have an intelligent designer. Similarly, the universe displays a vast complexity, and according to Paley, we can assume that it has an intelligent designer as well. The passage notes that Paley's argument is often thought to be flawed. The question asks the student to identify the flaw in the reasoning by selecting an answer choice that best expresses the nature of the logical fallacy. (The student does not need to know

201

specific details about logical fallacies; within the answer choices, there are enough details to help the student select the correct answer.)

THE CORRECT ANSWER:

B   Paley's analogy is weak because it relies on a logical fallacy known as *begging the question*, or circular reasoning. The argument is based on the premise that anything complex must have been intentionally designed by an intelligent being, and the conclusion is also that anything complex must have been intentionally designed by an intelligent being. However, that an object like a watch is known to be the result of intentional design does not necessarily imply that other complex objects, such as the universe, must have come about in the same way. By assuming that a designer is required, Paley fails to consider any alternative explanations.

THE INCORRECT ANSWERS:

A   There is nothing within Paley's analogy to suggest he is creating a distraction; rather, he is making a specific comparison between two items.

C   Nothing in the passage suggests that Paley is attacking any person on personal grounds.

D   Paley uses a comparison between a watch and the universe, but at no point does his argument clearly appeal to the sympathies of others. In this particular example, an appeal to sympathy might consist of an attempt to win over supporters by appealing to religious views. The passage does not indicate that Paley does this.

E   Paley does not at any point appeal to any specific authority. An appeal to authority involves a clear appeal to an outside source, such as religious figures or biblical claims. Paley does not do this in the passage.

QUESTION 21

<u>Overview</u>: Question 21 presents information about the condition of plant growth in Iceland. According to the passage, the Icelandic climate forbids much new plant growth and delays normal plant growth considerably. Apparently, only one species of tree exists in Iceland because previous residents in past centuries cut down most of the trees, and few have been able to grow back. Additionally, the passage notes that the plant life is exceedingly delicate and that off-road vehicles are not allowed in certain places, and hikers are expected to avoid stepping on certain plants. The question asks the student to identify which of the answer choices is most correct given the statements made in the passage. The student is essentially being asked to make an inference. Note that this question does *not* ask for the main point of the passage, so the statement that is correctly inferred will not necessarily be the primary focus of the passage; it will simply be something that can be deduced from what is stated in the passage.

THE CORRECT ANSWER:

E   Of all the answer choices, **answer choice (E)** is the only one that can correctly be inferred from the information in the passage. The author states that "little plant growth will be able to survive" in Iceland, that "plants require a long period of time to grow in Iceland," and that "plant life in Iceland is also notoriously delicate." This suggests that off-road vehicles have the potential to destroy plant life, leaving plants unable to grow back for long periods of time or, in some cases, unable to grow back at all.

THE INCORRECT ANSWERS:

A   The passage notes explicitly, "Because of both the severe cold and the severe heat, plants require a long period of time to grow in Iceland." This indicates that the extreme heat of the volcanoes would not encourage plants to grow any better than the extreme cold of other parts of Iceland.

B   The passage states that the plant life is "notoriously delicate" and that it takes years for plants to grow back. Answer choice (B) contradicts this, so it can be eliminated immediately.

C   The passage does state that one species of tree survives in Iceland, but it does not identify that species or imply what it might be.

D   Although the information in answer choice (D) might be accurate, there is nothing in the passage to suggest that it is. The passage notes only that Iceland's climate forbids extensive plant growth and that plants can take a very long time to grow. Therefore, the details in answer choice (D) cannot be inferred from the passage.

QUESTION 22

Overview: Question 22 presents details about the Highland Cattle, the shaggy breed of cattle iconic to the Scottish landscape. The author mentions that the Highland Cattle are strong and "resilient" and that they have lived in Scotland for an extensive period of time. The author also notes that the Highland Cattle have traditionally lived in the wild, are well-used to the harsh Highland climate, and might live up to 20 years and give birth 15 times. The question asks what inference can be drawn from the statements in the passage. Note that this question does *not* ask for the main point, so the student must look at each answer choice carefully to decide which is most likely to be correct.

THE CORRECT ANSWER:

C   The author states specifically, "The Highland Cattle are most common in the remote areas of the Highlands, where they live and breed in the wild. They are known for their hardy ability to withstand the elements." The author also states in the previous sentence that the Highland Cattle have lived in the Scottish Highlands for "unknown centuries." This suggests that the cattle have found a way to adapt to the harsh northern climate of Scotland during the centuries that they have lived there and have thus learned to survive in that climate.

THE INCORRECT ANSWERS:

A   The author of the passage notes that the Highland Cattle have traditionally lived wild in the Scottish Highlands, but there is nothing in the passage to suggest that the cattle are not good for human consumption and can be used only for grazing. Answer choice (A), then, cannot be inferred from the passage.

B   Although the passage indicates that the Highland Cattle are native to Scotland and have adapted to the climate of Scotland, the passage does not necessarily suggest that this is the *only* breed that can survive in Scotland. Answer choice (B) states details that are not supported by the information in the passage.

D   The author of the passage makes no mention of the interaction between Highland Cattle and human residents of the Highlands, so answer choice (D) cannot be inferred from the information in the passage. It can be eliminated immediately.

E   The passage does not make claims on the availability of food for the Highland Cattle, so this answer choice cannot reasonably be inferred. (Rather, as the author notes that Highland Cattle have lived wild in the Highlands for "unknown centuries," it stands to reason that the availability of food has been adequate.)

QUESTION 23

Overview: Question 23 gives information about the vision deficiency known as colorblindness, wherein sufferers have varying degrees of an inability to distinguish color. The author explains that colorblindness is believed to originate from a mutation of the X chromosome. The author also states that men have an XY chromosome makeup, while women have an XX chromosome makeup. The question asks for a statement that may be inferred from the passage based on the information contained within it.

THE CORRECT ANSWER:

D   At the end of the passage, the author notes, "Men carry a single X chromosome, possessing an XY-chromosome makeup, while women carry two X chromosomes, giving them the potential to combat colorblindness with an extra X chromosome." This suggests that men are more likely to be colorblind than women because men have only a single X chromosome. Of all the answer choices, **answer choice (D)** can best be inferred from the passage.

THE INCORRECT ANSWERS:

A   The author makes no comment on the percentage of colorblindness sufferers in the population, so it is impossible to infer safely that colorblindness is a rare condition. The student might know from prior knowledge that colorblindness *is* a fairly rare condition, but the question asks what can be inferred from the passage, not what the student already knows to be true. Answer choice (A) cannot be inferred.

B   Again, the information in answer choice (B) might well be true, but it cannot be inferred from the passage. The author notes only that colorblindness "limits the ability of the sufferer to see certain colors clearly. The condition may affect a person in varying degrees, ranging from mild colorblindness with a red or green color deficiency to complete colorblindness with no ability to distinguish any colors beside dim shades of brown." This in itself does not suggest clearly that colorblindness sufferers would be able to see camouflage well.

C   The author does not discuss the way that colorblindness is passed on, much less the idea that colorblindness is a hereditary condition. Although the author does imply that women are less likely to be colorblind than men, the author does *not* necessarily imply that women alone pass the condition on. Answer choice (C) cannot be inferred from the passage.

E   As with answer choice (C), the author does not discuss whether colorblindness is an inherited condition. So, it is impossible to determine from the passage if the author also believes that colorblindness can be tested at birth. Answer choice (E) infers details that are not supported by the passage.

QUESTION 24

Overview: Question 24 presents information about the historical location of Jamaica Inn, which was also the setting for a book of the same name by Daphne du Maurier. According to the author, the

real Jamaica Inn is set on Bodmin Moor, in Cornwall, and in du Maurier's book, the owners of the inn are participating in the criminal act of wrecking (luring ships to the coastline for the purpose of destroying and plundering them). The author of the passage notes that ghost stories are believed to be the source for du Maurier's book but that the story of wrecking does match actual events that occurred along the Cornish coast during the time setting of the book *Jamaica Inn*. The question asks the student to identify which of the answer choices best summarizes the main point of the passage. The student should first identify the main point of the passage: Although not completely historical in its plot, du Maurier's *Jamaica Inn* discusses real historical events that occurred in Cornwall. The answer choice that reflects this most clearly will be correct.

THE CORRECT ANSWER:

B   **Answer choice (B)** best restates the information above: that du Maurier took some creative license with plot but used historical events for her story about Jamaica Inn.

THE INCORRECT ANSWERS:

A   The author makes no mention of literary historians, mentioning only that Daphne du Maurier's story of *Jamaica Inn* is "hardly a historical textbook" but contains accurate historical information about events on the Cornish coast. Answer choice (A), therefore, infers details that are not supported by the passage and do not reflect the main point.

C   The passage does indicate that the information in answer choice (C) is correct: Lights *were* lit along the coastline to lure ships in. This information, however, is *not the main point* of the passage and reflects only a supporting detail.

D   The author does not discuss Daphne du Maurier's other books, nor is there any information in the passage to imply anything about the setting for other du Maurier books. Nor does this detail express the main point of the passage. (The fact that this piece of information is true is irrelevant; the question is asking for the main point of the statements in the passage.)

E   Answer choice (E) directly contradicts a statement made in the passage: "This being said, wrecking was a real activity in Cornwall during the 18th and 19th centuries." Therefore, answer choice (E) can be eliminated immediately for ignoring key information in the passage.

QUESTION 25

Overview: The final question in the second Logical Reasoning section of the test discusses discoveries made by psychologists about the differences between the way adults and children learn to play the piano. The author states that the learning differences are due largely to differences in mind development: Children's minds develop in such a way that they learn "certain skills more quickly and more effectively than adults." At the same time, the motor skills of children develop differently, so they do not learn to play as quickly as adults might; however, their minds allow them to *recall* the pieces better than adults can. Finally, the author notes that adults retain muscle memory and can reproduce the pieces merely by remembering the fingering of the pieces, implying that children actually retain a better memory of the piece itself and the notes and do not have to rely only on muscle memory. The question then asks which of the answer choices *cannot* be concluded from the passage. This means that four of the answer choices are implied in the passage, so the student needs to consider each answer choice carefully.

THE CORRECT ANSWER:

C   The author states early in the passage, "the piano is an instrument that knows no one age for learning and presents multiple opportunities for the successful attainment of musical skills." This suggests that the piano is *one* instrument that both adults and children can learn to play. This does not imply, however, that the piano is the *only* instrument that adults and children can learn to play. **Answer choice (C)** cannot be concluded from the passage.

THE INCORRECT ANSWERS:

A   The author states the information in answer choice (A) directly in the passage: "It does, however, offer a variety of challenges both to children and to adults—due to the differences in mind development." So, answer choice (A) can be inferred from the passage.

B   At the end of the passage, the author notes, "At the same time, adults are more likely to retain the muscle memory of the pieces that they learn and reproduce them blindly, just by allowing their fingers to recall the correct notes." Therefore, answer choice (B) is a conclusion that can be drawn from the passage.

D   In the second sentence of the passage, the author states, "In particular, the piano is an instrument that knows no one age for learning and presents multiple opportunities for the successful attainment of musical skills." This means that answer choice (D) is a conclusion that can be drawn from the passage.

E   The author notes in the passage, "How quickly children learn is often limited by their motor skills." This suggests that the fully developed motor skills of adults allow them to learn the hand and finger movements more quickly than children, so answer choice (E) is a conclusion that can be drawn from the passage.

Argumentative Writing

HOW TO APPROACH THE ARGUMENTATIVE ESSAY

There is no right or wrong answer for the writing sample, and LSAC does not actually give the essay a score. But the law schools to which the students apply will receive a copy of the essay, so students need to shape a response that indicates their writing skills to these schools. There are several important considerations to keep in mind when developing the essay:

1. Schools want to know that students have strong communication skills, so the essay should be clear and concise and provide a solid response to the topic, with a strong development of each paragraph.
2. The essay should stay entirely on topic: Students should not veer off the point by including unnecessary examples or by failing to address the primary focus of the topic. The key is to remain relevant and answer the topic question with clear exposition.
3. Essay writing establishes that a student is able to develop persuasive ideas and organize them effectively. Schools look for these skills, so the essay provides students with the opportunity to indicate an ability to make a credible and well-developed argument in written form.

Answers and Explanations for Test #1

LSAT Practice Tests #2 and #3

To take these additional LSAT practice tests, visit our bonus page:
mometrix.com/bonus948/lsat

How to Overcome Test Anxiety

Just the thought of taking a test is enough to make most people a little nervous. A test is an important event that can have a long-term impact on your future, so it's important to take it seriously and it's natural to feel anxious about performing well. But just because anxiety is normal, that doesn't mean that it's helpful in test taking, or that you should simply accept it as part of your life. Anxiety can have a variety of effects. These effects can be mild, like making you feel slightly nervous, or severe, like blocking your ability to focus or remember even a simple detail.

If you experience test anxiety—whether severe or mild—it's important to know how to beat it. To discover this, first you need to understand what causes test anxiety.

Causes of Test Anxiety

While we often think of anxiety as an uncontrollable emotional state, it can actually be caused by simple, practical things. One of the most common causes of test anxiety is that a person does not feel adequately prepared for their test. This feeling can be the result of many different issues such as poor study habits or lack of organization, but the most common culprit is time management. Starting to study too late, failing to organize your study time to cover all of the material, or being distracted while you study will mean that you're not well prepared for the test. This may lead to cramming the night before, which will cause you to be physically and mentally exhausted for the test. Poor time management also contributes to feelings of stress, fear, and hopelessness as you realize you are not well prepared but don't know what to do about it.

Other times, test anxiety is not related to your preparation for the test but comes from unresolved fear. This may be a past failure on a test, or poor performance on tests in general. It may come from comparing yourself to others who seem to be performing better or from the stress of living up to expectations. Anxiety may be driven by fears of the future—how failure on this test would affect your educational and career goals. These fears are often completely irrational, but they can still negatively impact your test performance.

Elements of Test Anxiety

As mentioned earlier, test anxiety is considered to be an emotional state, but it has physical and mental components as well. Sometimes you may not even realize that you are suffering from test anxiety until you notice the physical symptoms. These can include trembling hands, rapid heartbeat, sweating, nausea, and tense muscles. Extreme anxiety may lead to fainting or vomiting. Obviously, any of these symptoms can have a negative impact on testing. It is important to recognize them as soon as they begin to occur so that you can address the problem before it damages your performance.

The mental components of test anxiety include trouble focusing and inability to remember learned information. During a test, your mind is on high alert, which can help you recall information and stay focused for an extended period of time. However, anxiety interferes with your mind's natural processes, causing you to blank out, even on the questions you know well. The strain of testing during anxiety makes it difficult to stay focused, especially on a test that may take several hours. Extreme anxiety can take a huge mental toll, making it difficult not only to recall test information but even to understand the test questions or pull your thoughts together.

Effects of Test Anxiety

Test anxiety is like a disease—if left untreated, it will get progressively worse. Anxiety leads to poor performance, and this reinforces the feelings of fear and failure, which in turn lead to poor performances on subsequent tests. It can grow from a mild nervousness to a crippling condition. If allowed to progress, test anxiety can have a big impact on your schooling, and consequently on your future.

Test anxiety can spread to other parts of your life. Anxiety on tests can become anxiety in any stressful situation, and blanking on a test can turn into panicking in a job situation. But fortunately, you don't have to let anxiety rule your testing and determine your grades. There are a number of relatively simple steps you can take to move past anxiety and function normally on a test and in the rest of life.

Physical Steps for Beating Test Anxiety

While test anxiety is a serious problem, the good news is that it can be overcome. It doesn't have to control your ability to think and remember information. While it may take time, you can begin taking steps today to beat anxiety.

Just as your first hint that you may be struggling with anxiety comes from the physical symptoms, the first step to treating it is also physical. Rest is crucial for having a clear, strong mind. If you are tired, it is much easier to give in to anxiety. But if you establish good sleep habits, your body and mind will be ready to perform optimally, without the strain of exhaustion. Additionally, sleeping well helps you to retain information better, so you're more likely to recall the answers when you see the test questions.

Getting good sleep means more than going to bed on time. It's important to allow your brain time to relax. Take study breaks from time to time so it doesn't get overworked, and don't study right before bed. Take time to rest your mind before trying to rest your body, or you may find it difficult to fall asleep.

Along with sleep, other aspects of physical health are important in preparing for a test. Good nutrition is vital for good brain function. Sugary foods and drinks may give a burst of energy but this burst is followed by a crash, both physically and emotionally. Instead, fuel your body with protein and vitamin-rich foods.

Also, drink plenty of water. Dehydration can lead to headaches and exhaustion, especially if your brain is already under stress from the rigors of the test. Particularly if your test is a long one, drink water during the breaks. And if possible, take an energy-boosting snack to eat between sections.

Along with sleep and diet, a third important part of physical health is exercise. Maintaining a steady workout schedule is helpful, but even taking 5-minute study breaks to walk can help get your blood pumping faster and clear your head. Exercise also releases endorphins, which contribute to a positive feeling and can help combat test anxiety.

When you nurture your physical health, you are also contributing to your mental health. If your body is healthy, your mind is much more likely to be healthy as well. So take time to rest, nourish your body with healthy food and water, and get moving as much as possible. Taking these physical steps will make you stronger and more able to take the mental steps necessary to overcome test anxiety.

Mental Steps for Beating Test Anxiety

Working on the mental side of test anxiety can be more challenging, but as with the physical side, there are clear steps you can take to overcome it. As mentioned earlier, test anxiety often stems from lack of preparation, so the obvious solution is to prepare for the test. Effective studying may be the most important weapon you have for beating test anxiety, but you can and should employ several other mental tools to combat fear.

First, boost your confidence by reminding yourself of past success—tests or projects that you aced. If you're putting as much effort into preparing for this test as you did for those, there's no reason you should expect to fail here. Work hard to prepare; then trust your preparation.

Second, surround yourself with encouraging people. It can be helpful to find a study group, but be sure that the people you're around will encourage a positive attitude. If you spend time with others who are anxious or cynical, this will only contribute to your own anxiety. Look for others who are motivated to study hard from a desire to succeed, not from a fear of failure.

Third, reward yourself. A test is physically and mentally tiring, even without anxiety, and it can be helpful to have something to look forward to. Plan an activity following the test, regardless of the outcome, such as going to a movie or getting ice cream.

When you are taking the test, if you find yourself beginning to feel anxious, remind yourself that you know the material. Visualize successfully completing the test. Then take a few deep, relaxing breaths and return to it. Work through the questions carefully but with confidence, knowing that you are capable of succeeding.

Developing a healthy mental approach to test taking will also aid in other areas of life. Test anxiety affects more than just the actual test—it can be damaging to your mental health and even contribute to depression. It's important to beat test anxiety before it becomes a problem for more than testing.

Study Strategy

Being prepared for the test is necessary to combat anxiety, but what does being prepared look like? You may study for hours on end and still not feel prepared. What you need is a strategy for test prep. The next few pages outline our recommended steps to help you plan out and conquer the challenge of preparation.

STEP 1: SCOPE OUT THE TEST

Learn everything you can about the format (multiple choice, essay, etc.) and what will be on the test. Gather any study materials, course outlines, or sample exams that may be available. Not only will this help you to prepare, but knowing what to expect can help to alleviate test anxiety.

STEP 2: MAP OUT THE MATERIAL

Look through the textbook or study guide and make note of how many chapters or sections it has. Then divide these over the time you have. For example, if a book has 15 chapters and you have five days to study, you need to cover three chapters each day. Even better, if you have the time, leave an extra day at the end for overall review after you have gone through the material in depth.

If time is limited, you may need to prioritize the material. Look through it and make note of which sections you think you already have a good grasp on, and which need review. While you are studying, skim quickly through the familiar sections and take more time on the challenging parts.

Write out your plan so you don't get lost as you go. Having a written plan also helps you feel more in control of the study, so anxiety is less likely to arise from feeling overwhelmed at the amount to cover.

STEP 3: GATHER YOUR TOOLS

Decide what study method works best for you. Do you prefer to highlight in the book as you study and then go back over the highlighted portions? Or do you type out notes of the important information? Or is it helpful to make flashcards that you can carry with you? Assemble the pens, index cards, highlighters, post-it notes, and any other materials you may need so you won't be distracted by getting up to find things while you study.

If you're having a hard time retaining the information or organizing your notes, experiment with different methods. For example, try color-coding by subject with colored pens, highlighters, or post-it notes. If you learn better by hearing, try recording yourself reading your notes so you can listen while in the car, working out, or simply sitting at your desk. Ask a friend to quiz you from your flashcards, or try teaching someone the material to solidify it in your mind.

STEP 4: CREATE YOUR ENVIRONMENT

It's important to avoid distractions while you study. This includes both the obvious distractions like visitors and the subtle distractions like an uncomfortable chair (or a too-comfortable couch that makes you want to fall asleep). Set up the best study environment possible: good lighting and a comfortable work area. If background music helps you focus, you may want to turn it on, but otherwise keep the room quiet. If you are using a computer to take notes, be sure you don't have any other windows open, especially applications like social media, games, or anything else that could distract you. Silence your phone and turn off notifications. Be sure to keep water close by so you stay hydrated while you study (but avoid unhealthy drinks and snacks).

Also, take into account the best time of day to study. Are you freshest first thing in the morning? Try to set aside some time then to work through the material. Is your mind clearer in the afternoon or evening? Schedule your study session then. Another method is to study at the same time of day that you will take the test, so that your brain gets used to working on the material at that time and will be ready to focus at test time.

STEP 5: STUDY!

Once you have done all the study preparation, it's time to settle into the actual studying. Sit down, take a few moments to settle your mind so you can focus, and begin to follow your study plan. Don't give in to distractions or let yourself procrastinate. This is your time to prepare so you'll be ready to fearlessly approach the test. Make the most of the time and stay focused.

Of course, you don't want to burn out. If you study too long you may find that you're not retaining the information very well. Take regular study breaks. For example, taking five minutes out of every hour to walk briskly, breathing deeply and swinging your arms, can help your mind stay fresh.

As you get to the end of each chapter or section, it's a good idea to do a quick review. Remind yourself of what you learned and work on any difficult parts. When you feel that you've mastered the material, move on to the next part. At the end of your study session, briefly skim through your notes again.

But while review is helpful, cramming last minute is NOT. If at all possible, work ahead so that you won't need to fit all your study into the last day. Cramming overloads your brain with more information than it can process and retain, and your tired mind may struggle to recall even previously learned information when it is overwhelmed with last-minute study. Also, the urgent nature of cramming and the stress placed on your brain contribute to anxiety. You'll be more likely to go to the test feeling unprepared and having trouble thinking clearly.

So don't cram, and don't stay up late before the test, even just to review your notes at a leisurely pace. Your brain needs rest more than it needs to go over the information again. In fact, plan to finish your studies by noon or early afternoon the day before the test. Give your brain the rest of the day to relax or focus on other things, and get a good night's sleep. Then you will be fresh for the test and better able to recall what you've studied.

STEP 6: TAKE A PRACTICE TEST

Many courses offer sample tests, either online or in the study materials. This is an excellent resource to check whether you have mastered the material, as well as to prepare for the test format and environment.

Check the test format ahead of time: the number of questions, the type (multiple choice, free response, etc.), and the time limit. Then create a plan for working through them. For example, if you have 30 minutes to take a 60-question test, your limit is 30 seconds per question. Spend less time on the questions you know well so that you can take more time on the difficult ones.

If you have time to take several practice tests, take the first one open book, with no time limit. Work through the questions at your own pace and make sure you fully understand them. Gradually work up to taking a test under test conditions: sit at a desk with all study materials put away and set a timer. Pace yourself to make sure you finish the test with time to spare and go back to check your answers if you have time.

After each test, check your answers. On the questions you missed, be sure you understand why you missed them. Did you misread the question (tests can use tricky wording)? Did you forget the information? Or was it something you hadn't learned? Go back and study any shaky areas that the practice tests reveal.

Taking these tests not only helps with your grade, but also aids in combating test anxiety. If you're already used to the test conditions, you're less likely to worry about it, and working through tests until you're scoring well gives you a confidence boost. Go through the practice tests until you feel comfortable, and then you can go into the test knowing that you're ready for it.

Test Tips

On test day, you should be confident, knowing that you've prepared well and are ready to answer the questions. But aside from preparation, there are several test day strategies you can employ to maximize your performance.

First, as stated before, get a good night's sleep the night before the test (and for several nights before that, if possible). Go into the test with a fresh, alert mind rather than staying up late to study.

Try not to change too much about your normal routine on the day of the test. It's important to eat a nutritious breakfast, but if you normally don't eat breakfast at all, consider eating just a protein bar. If you're a coffee drinker, go ahead and have your normal coffee. Just make sure you time it so that the caffeine doesn't wear off right in the middle of your test. Avoid sugary beverages, and drink enough water to stay hydrated but not so much that you need a restroom break 10 minutes into the test. If your test isn't first thing in the morning, consider going for a walk or doing a light workout before the test to get your blood flowing.

Allow yourself enough time to get ready, and leave for the test with plenty of time to spare so you won't have the anxiety of scrambling to arrive in time. Another reason to be early is to select a good seat. It's helpful to sit away from doors and windows, which can be distracting. Find a good seat, get out your supplies, and settle your mind before the test begins.

When the test begins, start by going over the instructions carefully, even if you already know what to expect. Make sure you avoid any careless mistakes by following the directions.

Then begin working through the questions, pacing yourself as you've practiced. If you're not sure on an answer, don't spend too much time on it, and don't let it shake your confidence. Either skip it and come back later, or eliminate as many wrong answers as possible and guess among the remaining ones. Don't dwell on these questions as you continue—put them out of your mind and focus on what lies ahead.

Be sure to read all of the answer choices, even if you're sure the first one is the right answer. Sometimes you'll find a better one if you keep reading. But don't second-guess yourself if you do immediately know the answer. Your gut instinct is usually right. Don't let test anxiety rob you of the information you know.

If you have time at the end of the test (and if the test format allows), go back and review your answers. Be cautious about changing any, since your first instinct tends to be correct, but make sure you didn't misread any of the questions or accidentally mark the wrong answer choice. Look over any you skipped and make an educated guess.

At the end, leave the test feeling confident. You've done your best, so don't waste time worrying about your performance or wishing you could change anything. Instead, celebrate the successful completion of this test. And finally, use this test to learn how to deal with anxiety even better next time.

Review Video: Test Anxiety
Visit mometrix.com/academy and enter code: 100340

Important Qualification

Not all anxiety is created equal. If your test anxiety is causing major issues in your life beyond the classroom or testing center, or if you are experiencing troubling physical symptoms related to your anxiety, it may be a sign of a serious physiological or psychological condition. If this sounds like your situation, we strongly encourage you to seek professional help.

Additional Bonus Material

Due to our efforts to try to keep this book to a manageable length, we've created a link that will give you access to all of your additional bonus material:

mometrix.com/bonus948/lsat

Made in the USA
Las Vegas, NV
01 April 2025

20375676R10125